Australia

Identity, Fear and Governance in the 21st Century

Australia

Identity, Fear and Governance in the 21st Century

Juliet Pietsch and Haydn Aarons

E PRESS

Published by ANU E Press
The Australian National University
Canberra ACT 0200, Australia
Email: anuepress@anu.edu.au
This title is also available online at http://epress.anu.edu.au

---

National Library of Australia Cataloguing-in-Publication entry

Title: Australia : identity, fear and governance in the 21st century / edited by Juliet Pietsch and Haydn Aarons.

ISBN: 9781922144065 (pbk.) 9781922144072 (ebook)

Notes: Includes bibliographical references.

Subjects: Public opinion--Australia.
Australia--Social conditions--Public opinion.
Australia--Politics and government--Public opinion.

Other Authors/Contributors:
Pietsch, Juliet.
Aarons, Haydn.

Number: 303.380994

All rights reserved. No part of this publication may be reproduced, stored in a retrieval system or transmitted in any form or by any means, electronic, mechanical, photocopying or otherwise, without the prior permission of the publisher.

Cover design and layout by ANU E Press

This edition © 2012 ANU E Press

Contents

List of Tables vii
List of Figures. ix
Contributors xi

1. Social Attitudes Towards Contemporary
   Challenges Facing Australia 1
   Haydn Aarons and Juliet Pietsch

2. Keeping Our Distance:
   Non-Indigenous/Aboriginal relations in Australian society 15
   Maggie Walter

3. Australian Engagement with Asia:
   Towards closer political, economic and cultural ties 33
   Juliet Pietsch and Haydn Aarons

4. Minority Religious Identity and Religious Social
   Distance in Australia 47
   Gary D. Bouma

5. Are Neighbourhood Incivilities Associated with Fear of Crime? . . . 61
   Lynne D. Roberts and David Indermaur

6. Terrorism and Public Opinion in Australia 79
   Juliet Pietsch and Ian McAllister

7. Are We Keeping the Bastards Honest?
   Perceptions of corruption, integrity and influence on politics . . 95
   Clive Bean

8. A New Role for Government?
   Trends in social policy preferences since the mid-1980s. . . . 107
   Shaun Wilson, Gabrielle Meagher and Kerstin Hermes

9. WorkChoices: An electoral issue and its social,
   political and attitudinal cleavages 133
   Murray Goot and Ian Watson

10. How Do Australians Search for Jobs? 171
    Xianbi Huang and Mark Western

List of Tables

Table 2.1	Attitudes Towards Aboriginal Issues	20
Table 2.2	OLS Regression Variable Description and Coefficients Predicting 'Attitudes to Aboriginal Issues' Scores	21
Table 2.3	Social Distance Scenario Attitudes	23
Table 2.4	OLS Regression Variable Description and Coefficients Predicting 'Attitudes to Aboriginal Issues' Scores	26
Table 3.1	Australian Engagement with Asian Cultures, AuSSA 2007	41
Table 3.2	Factor Analysis of Australian Engagement with Asian Cultures	42
Table 3.3	Effects of Background Experiences on Engagement with Asia (OLS estimates), AuSSA 2007	43
Table 4.1	Social Distance Preferences for Selected Religious Groups: Anglicans, Catholics, United, Presbyterians	51
Table 4.2	Anglicans, Catholics, United, Presbyterians: Mean social distances for religious groups	53
Table 4.3	Catholics, Anglicans, Uniting and Presbyterians: One-way ANOVA—respondents' religions by social distance from select religions	55
Table 5.1	Ratings of Size of Problem of a Range of Incivilities in Local Area	67
Table 5.2	Percentage of Population Worried about Being the Victim of a Range of Crimes	69
Table 5.3	Correlations between Perceptions of Incivilities and Fear of Crime by Gender	71
Table 5.4	Unstandardised (B) and Standardised (β) Regression Coefficients, and Squared Semi-Partial Correlations (sr^2) for Each Predictor Variable on Each Step of a Hierarchical Multiple Regression Predicting Fear of Physical Crime	72
Table 5.5	Unstandardised (B) and Standardised (β) Regression Coefficients, and Squared Semi-Partial Correlations (sr^2) for Each Predictor Variable on Each Step of a Hierarchical Multiple Regression Predicting Fear of Identity-Related Crime	72
Table 6.1	Likelihood of a Terrorist Attack	82
Table 6.2	Concern about Terrorism and Socioeconomic Status	84
Table 6.3	Support for Measures to Counter Terrorism	86
Table 6.4	Support for Extending Legal Measures to Counter Terrorism	86
Table 6.5	Concern about Terrorism and Methods to Reduce the Threat	87

Table 7.1	Perceptions of Corruption in Australian Politics, 2007	97
Table 7.2	Perceptions of Fair Dealing and Influence in Australian Politics, 2007	98
Table 7.3	Perceptions of Efficacy and Trust in Australian Politics, 2007	99
Table 7.4	Perceptions of Corruption by Socio-Demographic Characteristics	101
Table 7.5	Perceptions of Treatment from Public Officials by Socio-Demographic Characteristics	102
Table 7.6	Perceptions of Political Efficacy by Socio-Demographic Characteristics	103
Table 8.1	Social Spending and Taxation Trends in Australia, 1985–2005	110
Table 8.2	Fiscal Mood, 1987–2007	112
Table 8.3	Australian Spending Preferences by Policy Area, 1985–2007	117
Table 8.4	Australian Beliefs about the Role of Government, 1985–2007	120
Table A8.1	Country Groups	130
Table A8.2	Ratios for Figure 8.1	131
Table 9.1	Approval Scale for WorkChoices, Combined Results for Models	148
Table 9.2	Predicted Probabilities, Union and Age	152
Table 9.3	Predicted Probabilities, Union and Occupation	152
Table 9.4	Predicted Probabilities, Class and Union	153
Table 9.5	Predicted Probabilities, Class and Union	153
Table 9.6	Predicated Probabilities, Left–Right Scale and Union	154
Table 9.7	Predicted Probabilities, Voting and Union	155
Table 9.8	Predicted Probabilities, Voting and Left–Right Scale	156
Table A9.1	Results for Multinomial Logit Model: Structural model	163
Table A9.2	Results for Multinomial Logit Model: Political model	165
Table A9.3	Results for Multinomial Logit Model: Attitudinal model	167
Table 10.1	Methods Used in Job-Search Processes, AuSSA 2007	173
Table 10.2	Associations between Job-Search Methods and Demographic and Socioeconomic Characteristics, AuSSA 2007	176
Table 10.3	Network Resources Accessed by Job Searchers, AuSSA 2007	180
Table 10.4	Types of Social Ties Mobilised by Job Searchers, AuSSA 2007	181
Table 10.5	Association between Network Resources and Social Ties, AuSSA 2007	181
Table 10.6	Association between Job-Matching Status and Job-Search Methods, AuSSA 2007	184
Table 10.7	Binary Logistic Regression in Predicting Effects of Job-Search Methods on Job Match, AuSSA 2007	184

List of Figures

Figure 2.1	Indigenous Population Across Geographic Regions, 2006, by State/Territory	16
Figure 2.2	Gender, Age and Education and Social Distance Items	24
Figure 2.3	Gender, Education, Age and Locality and Aboriginal Social Proximity	26
Figure 5.1	Types of Incivilities Rated as a Big Problem by Location	68
Figure 5.2	Worry about Being a Victim of Various Crimes by Location	70
Figure 5.3	Gender Differences in Worry about Being a Victim of Crime	70
Figure 6.1	Ideological Position and Attitudes Towards Terrorism	90
Figure 8.1	Pro-Spending Preferences: Part of a more liberal mood, 1987–2007	114
Figure 8.2	Beliefs about Government Responsibility, Australia and Other Welfare Regimes/Country Groups, 2006	122
Figure 8.3	Beliefs about Government Responsibility and Perceptions of Government Success, Mean Scores by Regime Type, 2006	124
Figure 8.4	Perceptions of Government Responsibility, Difference from Mean Scores Overall by Political Party Orientation, All Respondents, 2006	126
Figure 10.1	Job Matching between Job-Seekers and Positions, AuSSA 2007	183

Contributors

Dr Haydn Aarons is a Senior Lecturer in Public Health at La Trobe University.

Professor Clive Bean is a Professor of Political Science at the Queensland University of Technology.

Professor Gary Bouma is a Professor of Sociology (Emeritus) at Monash University.

Professor Murray Goot is an ARC Australian Professorial Fellow in the Department of Modern History, Politics and International Relations at Macquarie University.

Kerstin Hermes is a PhD candidate at the Department of Environment and Geography at Macquarie University in Sydney. Kerstin's PhD thesis focuses on residential segregation, health and social capital.

Dr Xianbi Huang is a Lecturer in Sociology at La Trobe University.

Associate Professor David Indermaur is a Research Associate Professor in the Crime Research Centre at the University of Western Australia.

Professor Ian McAllister is a Distinguished Professor of Political Science at The Australian National University.

Professor Gabrielle Meagher is a Professor of Social Policy at the University of Sydney.

Dr Juliet Pietsch is a Senior Lecturer in Political Science at The Australian National University.

Dr Lynne Roberts is a Senior Lecturer in Psychology at Curtin University.

Associate Professor Maggie Walter is Associate Professor in Sociology at the University of Tasmania.

Dr Ian Watson is a Visiting Senior Research Fellow at Macquarie University and the Social Policy Research Centre, University of New South Wales.

Professor Mark Western is Director of the Institute for Social Science Research at the University of Queensland.

Dr Shaun Wilson is a Senior Lecturer in the School of Social Science at the University of New South Wales.

1. Social Attitudes Towards Contemporary Challenges Facing Australia

Haydn Aarons and Juliet Pietsch

The latter years of the first decade of the twenty-first century were characterised by an enormous amount of challenge and change to Australia and Australians. Australia's part in these challenges and changes is borne of our domestic and global ties, our orientation towards ourselves and others, and an ever increasing awareness of the interdependency of our world. Challenges and changes such as terrorism, climate change, human rights, community breakdown, work and livelihood, and crime are not new but they take on new variations and impact on us in different ways in times such as these.

In this volume we consider these recent challenges and changes and how Australians themselves feel about them under three themes: identity, fear and governance. These themes suitably capture the concerns of Australians in times of such change. Identity is our sense of ourselves and how others see us. How is this affected by the increased presence of religious diversity, especially Islamic communities, and increased awareness of moral and political obligations towards Indigenous Australians? How is it affected by our curious but changing relationship with Asia? Fear is an emotional reaction to particular changes and challenges and produces particular responses from individuals, politicians, communities and nations alike; fear of crime, fear of terrorism and fear of change are all considered in this volume.

Governance is about leadership and management—crucial themes in times of change. What are the impacts on people's livelihoods of a changing economy and changes to our industrial relations system? What is the role of politicians and of political integrity in times of complex change? What do Australians think about the role of government spending and the very role of government in such times? This work attempts to unravel some of this complexity and provide the reader with insight into Australia as a changing nation at the start of the twenty-first century.

Empirical research takes many forms and survey research such as that presented in this volume has its drawbacks and disadvantages; however, a key advantage of survey research is that we have enough data, with the aid of an accurate and representative sample, to ascertain opinion for the whole nation. Another key advantage of this approach is that data such as those produced in the

Australian Survey of Social Attitudes (AuSSA) are longitudinal and to some extent transnational, giving researchers the means to compare measures and patterns over time and across countries.

Like *Australian Social Attitudes: The first report* and *Australian Social Attitudes 2*, this report provides interpretations of issues and events using survey data. In doing so it makes a claim for an empirically informed addition to the national debate around a set of important topics. Topics of national importance covered by this report include Indigenous issues, engagement with Asia, religion, crime, terrorism and the roles of government. Indeed, *Australia: Identity, Fear and Governance in the 21st century* presents a collage of themes, foci and evidence from Australian opinion and attitude about key contemporary dimensions of social, political and economic life. What characterises this report is the timely research into some of the more important questions that faced Australians in the last few years of the first decade of the twenty-first century. In doing so this third report provides readers with a unique, empirically informed, national snapshot of what Australians think and how they feel about these key issues. The ultimate rationale for this collection of writing is to provide the public with the benefits of empirical evidence in the hope of aiding public policy through rigorous and professional social scientific investigation, leading to insight and increased understanding of how these topics were crucial to how the nation has changed.

Identity, fear and governance: A changing Australia

The year 2007 was in many ways a watershed year for the nation. The key event signalling such change was the federal election. Kevin Rudd brought federal Labor back into office after 11 years in opposition. John Howard's defeat represented not only a disaffected electorate but also more broadly a reorientation of national priorities and concerns. Rudd's overwhelming victory in the November election of 2007 signalled a nation ready to change and more willing to properly consider Australia's responsibilities towards the environment, a greater willingness for and a different means of facilitating Aboriginal reconciliation, to re-evaluate profound change in industrial relations, and a reassessment of Australia's commitment to the 'war on terror' through revised thinking and policy about our engagement in the Iraq and Afghanistan theatres of war. Rudd's Labor campaigned on all of these issues and won the 2007 federal election convincingly, securing 83 seats in the House of Representatives with a swing of 5.4 per cent. Among the Rudd Government's first decisions of national significance was the signing of the Kyoto Protocol, the 2020 summit and the parliamentary apology to the Stolen Generations. For many commentators, Rudd's victory would bring a new maturity to a nation that in the Howard years had become more insular, conservative, fearful and obstinate. Rudd's government had enjoyed overwhelming support from the electorate, which largely endorsed his stand on the various issues that he considered important to how the nation should perceive itself and how it should be perceived by others. Irrespective of the subsequent successes and the ultimate failure of his prime ministership, Rudd and Labor's ascendency in 2007 signalled a forceful shift in the nation.

Elections are important and useful indicators of change but they do not provide us with a complete inventory of how a nation thinks and why. The government is voted in by the people, so it stands to reason that when there is a change of government such as there was in 2007, there is something stirring in the electorate and wider community. Of great interest and importance then was how the nation felt about various issues and how these attitudes impacted on our relationships with our institutions, with our national identity, our connections with a global network of 'friends' and 'enemies', and work and everyday life. The 2007 iteration of the AuSSA gives us another means of assessing national change through a ranging and unique view of a changing Australia with the benefit of professional analysis that can link data to themes and theories.

Reflecting a changing Australia in this regard, the report identifies and holds as seminal the themes of *identity, fear and governance*. While the 2007 AuSSA sought opinions and attitudes from Australians about a range of issues, these themes represent a coherent set of concerns of national importance for a changing Australia. These themes suitably contextualise and address some of the key substantive social, cultural and political challenges that Australia faces into the twenty-first century pertaining to its internal historical and social logics and external referents via relationships with other countries through trade, migration and cultural traffic. Identity, fear and governance provide a conceptual context and thematic backdrop for the empirical investigations contained in this volume. This third report, derived principally from the AuSSA 2007, brings together a collection of writing and analysis from leading social scientists around Australia. While ostensibly disparate, these themes are, for the time, interrelated and impact upon one another in a variety of ways. The writing here provides insight, analysis and empirical illustration of identity, fear and governance in Australia. These themes have a number of dimensions, be they internal or external to the nation, locally based or national, and correlate with similar change and concern internationally.

Public attitudes and opinions concerning such themes are arguably important to a nation and its people at any time in its history. These themes in a nation's history, however, are characterised by the differentiated social, economic, political and cultural contexts that produce change through time. There is value in examining these themes in times of particular change so as to gauge how people relate to the various impacts of change, revealing in kind a lot about a nation like Australia. The later years of the first decade of the twenty-first century represent for Australia a time of accelerated change associated with questions about what it means to be Australian, how we relate to the rest of the world, the role of terrorism, the changing nature of communities, the role and behaviour of government, the nature of work and the role of religion. These questions are not new but they are important for the time they were asked, and representative answers from the public are often difficult to ascertain without instruments such as the AuSSA.

Identity, among other things, is an ongoing reflection of who we are as individuals and as a nation. Identity, through processes of socialisation and acculturation, prescribes and proscribes belonging, relationships with specific groups and larger conceptual 'we' communities, and is a much debated source of self and community. Identity also shapes our views about groups with whom we may or may not be familiar but hear a lot about. Opinions are an excellent insight into what influences how people relate to those they have little experience with, with change and with difference, and also how they see themselves. This point is clearly evident in Walter's (Chapter 2) analysis of non-Indigenous opinions towards Aboriginal Australians and Bouma's (Chapter 4) examination of Australian feeling towards religious groups. Indigenous, religious and migrant groups have been a feature of the national conversation about identity and belonging of late and have drawn strong responses about how they relate to the nation.

Surveys such as the AuSSA consistently report a very large proportion of Australians as feeling 'close' or 'very close' to Australia or being Australian. In the 2007 AuSSA, 91 per cent of the sample reported this emotional connection to the nation, strongly affirming a key aspect of identity. This level of feeling is commensurate with a nationalism that some theorists such as Benedict Anderson report as being connected to a 'self sacrificing love' (2006, 141), propelling some people to even die for the nation. This form of nationalism carries the attendant cultural expression found in poetry, music and other art forms. What is often crucial in how we imagine a nation and how we feel about it is who imagines and what is imagined. The construction of a national consciousness often reveals the social fault lines and divisions of how the nation is thought of, who belongs to it and who does not.

For Indigenous Australians the battle for national recognition, belonging and acceptance has been protracted and difficult. The Federal Government's apology to the Stolen Generations in February 2008 was a powerful public act of recognition and contrition. Despite the widespread support for the apology, the question of how Indigenous Australians belong and connect with the wider Australian community remains, to some extent, unresolved. Walter finds that the reality of the social attitudes of a significant proportion of non-Indigenous Australians to Aboriginal equality, cultural viability and restorative justice is at odds with self-conceptions of the nation as a tolerant and egalitarian society. This has significant implications for Australian society and the way Australia projects its national identity. Walter reports that despite signs of significant momentum and support for particular Indigenous issues there still exist levels of intolerance towards some aspects of Aboriginal equality associated with particular social factors such as gender, age, location and education levels. These factors help us relate the various social and cultural dimensions of how we imagine the nation with regards to the importance of race, and reveal a level of complexity that exists in defining national identity.

Alongside Indigenous Australians, migrants have battled a historical peripheral status in the struggle for recognition and belonging to the nation. While there has been significant official support overall for migrants and immigration with policy shifts such as multiculturalism, the Howard years were seen to compromise the increasing openness that Australia had demonstrated since the 1970s. A key aspect of identity for many migrants, and indeed for many non-migrant communities in Australia, is religion. Religious identity has had an increased impact on politics and national identity in recent years. Certainly it has become a feature of federal politics to the extent that Kevin Rudd was emphasising his Christian values and background before the 2007 election and espousing its role in Western traditions of social justice. Religion has re-emerged also as a factor in debates about the decline in values in Australia, the lingering problems of social and economic development (Hitchens 2007) and knowledge and being (Dawkins 2006). Despite Australia's relatively exemplary record of religious harmony that has accompanied the waves of migration and religious settlement, the new century has seen some emergent divisions and challenges to this good record, reflected also in other countries. In particular, being Muslim in Western countries has aroused suspicion and challenged the notion of tolerance and adherence to cultural diversity. The 2007 AuSSA reports that feelings of closeness for Islamic countries are opposite those of how Australians feel for Australia, with about 95 per cent of the sample registering sentiments of 'not very close' or 'not close at all'. European leaders such as German Chancellor, Angela Merkel, have recently questioned the merits and highlighted the perceived failings of multiculturalism in Germany (Weaver 2010); others have supported this sentiment in Europe with particular reference to Muslims. The recent focus on Muslims and Islam in Australia from many quarters of course largely owes its being to the events of 11 September 2001 and links global political tensions and fear with one of the nation's marginal religious communities.

Chapter 4 substantively re-examines the place of religion in Australian society and identity after a long absence of general social scientific commentary by examining public opinion and attitudes about the relationships between various religious groups with the aid of social distance measures. Gary Bouma explores the extent of religious plurality and its implications for social cohesion in Australia. Given the discussion about the place and role of religion in society and particular religious groups, the chapter is timely in assessing how Australians feel about the faith dimension of multiculturalism, diversity and identity. Using specific indicators from the AuSSA, Bouma examines how Australians identify with religious groups in general and how religious Australians identify with other religious Australians whose religious identity is different from their own. Through Bouma's analysis, we can see that Australia faces cultural and identity challenges through emergent religious change as new waves of immigrants arrive with different cultural and religious backgrounds. Of particular note is how Muslims are received by the wider community in Australia and what this means for Australian tolerance.

Beyond the more internal dimensions of identity and belonging, Australians are intimately bound up with the globalised processes of economic, political and cultural change and therefore attuned to identity questions with the accent on externality and internationality. Pietsch and Aarons (Chapter 3) consider this dimension of identity in relation to Asia and Asian Australians. Asia was once feared as a threat and its perceived threat loomed large in the Australian imagination, reinforcing a singular notion of 'Australian-ness' through racial, cultural, political and social action that served to solidify identity; however, has the variety of change commensurate with late modernity that has been wrought upon Australia made us more open, cosmopolitan and tolerant? Or has it served to reinforce a guarded, reserved and closed identity mind-set still? Here again, federal politics may be instructive of change since 2007. John Howard was seen as promoting a lesser emphasis on Asian engagement compared with his predecessor, Paul Keating, who considered Australia's future lay in greater engagement with our regional neighbours. The Mandarin-speaking, Asian studies graduate Kevin Rudd was keen to re-establish Australia's commitment with Asia. Asia in particular—geographically near but in other ways very distant—has been a key relational feature of Australian identity historically, so our contemporary attitudes towards it will reveal a great deal about our cosmopolitanism and openness and how Asia has perhaps influenced being Australian through our relations with the region.

While questions of engagement with other countries and cultures are usually answered with reference to the fields of international relations, foreign policy and trade, the analysis of Asian engagement in this volume seeks a more holistic rendering by assessing individual behaviours concerning travel, food, business, friendship networks and involvement in Asian religions. This type of analysis of identity that emphasises less the governmental and considers more the everyday follows various forms of inquiry in the style of Campbell's (2007) *The Easternization of the West*. In doing so it presents another way of linking identity with a changing nation and a changing world through the seemingly irrepressible network of cultural traffic facilitated by migration, changing cities, extensive communications, education and travel. While much theoretical work has identified the potential for large shifts and changes in relations with societies such as Asia's, the empirical work on individual attitude and behaviour qualifies theorised changes with a closer look at how they are distributed through a population. Pietsch and Aarons claim that engagement with Asia is differentiated across a variety of social factors, most notably education. Recent studies of cosmopolitanism suggest that education is a key factor in being open to various influences and experiences (Woodward, Skrbis and Bean 2008).

Chapter 10 develops another aspect of identity through an analysis of how Australians attain jobs through various means. Work for most Australians is a major component of personal identity, conferring a range of related economic, social and cultural statuses. Work is also an avenue to personal dignity, a means of avoiding or climbing out of poverty, and, as Huang and Western inform us here, is strongly associated with a process of social connection. The lack of work, or the potential lack of work, creates of course a searing anxiety that translates into a fear that begins to impact beyond the individual and onto the broader society. How Australians attain work is, then, a crucial question associated with one of the most important aspects of the self. Notwithstanding the importance of how well an economy or a government is performing necessary for the provision of creating employment, getting a job has a pronounced non-structural and non-economic dimension. Huang and Western report that Australians rely on a variety of methods to secure a job. Prominent amongst them is the use of social networks. Social networks locate individuals within a greater universe of specific connection and identity links that actors use to derive particular benefits, employment being one of them. Beyond the formal market for employment, Huang and Western reveal the social network process that Australians use to get a job.

What it means to be Australian, how Australians relate to one another and how Australians relate to the broader international community are ongoing questions related to the vicissitudes of social and economic life. Australian identity is brought into sharp focus in late modernity wherein migration, the threat of terrorism, global trade and cultural traffic impact strongly on our sense of ourselves. These changes bring substantial political, social and ontological challenges with a variety of responses. Fear is a key response to change and challenge that threatens key aspects of Australian democracy and community. Fear is, in certain contexts, closely related to identity in times of change. If identity is about specific feelings and ways of belonging, emotional engagement to an 'imagined community' and settled patterns associated with everyday life then fear is a negative response to change that is perceived to threaten such assurances. Since 2007 an increasing fear of, among other things, Muslims, asylum-seekers, terrorism, the financial and geographic elements of restorative justice for Aboriginal Australians, the future of multiculturalism and environmental challenges such as climate change can be detected in the popular mood through various media and the tenor of public debate. These are key areas of change linked to the ongoing debate over our identity and the nation.

Aside from the connections between fear, identity and change that challenge a nation, fear has strong correlations to authority, governance and social order. This kind of fear is related to direct threats of various kinds, but particularly threats of violence manifested in terrorism, crimes against the person or property and incivility. Again there are both local and global dimensions of this variation of fear for which public opinion was sought in the AuSSA 2007 and which are considered empirically in this volume at both a transnational level (Pietsch and McAllister in Chapter 6) and a communal level (Roberts and Indemaur Chapter 5).

Fear of terrorism had promoted security, liberty and identity issues in many Western nations to prominence before 9/11 and most assuredly after it. Fear with its specific genesis in terrorism has impacted significantly on Australian tolerance, governance and political philosophy to the extent that Australia's commitments to immigration, asylum-seeking, multiculturalism, openness to differentiated religious identity and personal liberties have come under heavy scrutiny and review. In Chapter 6 Pietsch and McAllister take a closer look at perceptions of threat in the community by looking at whether Australians are fearful of a terrorist attack. Terrorism is still a major concern for a significant proportion of Australians. Pietsch and McAllister show widespread public concern about terrorism, with relatively little distinction being made between terrorist events occurring within Australia and within the Asian region. They argue that this may reflect the global reach of modern terrorism, but it is also a consequence of the Bali bombings, which occurred overseas but had major implications for public perceptions of terrorism and for national security policy. The reach of global or transnational terror operations impacts upon Australia through places like Bali that are popular holiday spots.

Besides the more global and transnational networks of threat that produce fear, fear is a theme for local communities and is associated with the everyday life worlds of individuals. Fear, considered more locally and communally, is usually associated with crime and the perception of crime. Fear is also associated with what many assume to be declining standards of everyday life, interaction and communal connections such as social capital. The consequences of communal fear are not only individualist but also collective and have serious social and economic consequences for development and future growth. Antisocial behaviour, public incivility and law and order issues have attracted a lot of attention from all levels of government, policy experts and community groups. Smith, Phillips and King (2010) attest to the heightened interest in incivility and increased urgency associated with its consequences with their recent work. Chapter 5 considers communally based fear in the form of the relationship between perceived incivility and perceptions of crime. Roberts and Indermaur inform us that a number of studies point to the vast range of impacts that fear of crime has on individuals inclusive of mental and physical health, and economic consequences such as mobility costs. Their perspective here, however, explores how perceptions of decline in social order are key to how people feel about crime and threat. The core of their argument is that perceptions of incivilities produce fear of both place-based physical violence and identity-based crime that is non-spatial. This is an emergent direction for criminological research so establishing the empirical ground goes a long way to gaining insight into the nature of communities and crime. The chapter also makes a number of important methodological claims about the validity of measures and considers alternative ways of tapping key concepts of use to readers with an interest in this field.

For many, the management of fear, be it through threats of violence, incivility, identity change or other, is often seen as ultimately an issue of governance. Governance is a prominent issue for Australians and attitudes and opinions are a crucial ingredient in the relationship between the governors and the governed. Governance in this book covers the very role of governments, the relationship between the government and the people, and how governments impose or relax various restraints. One important aspect of the reality and the perception of terrorism in Western countries is the extent to which people in democracies are willing to have civil liberties compromised to control the threat of terrorism. How far a government should and can go in the restraint of individual and group rights to combat terrorism is an issue for governance associated with the level of trust a populace has in its government and a core concern for a functioning democracy such as Australia. How accepting a citizenry is of the demands of government can be determined by how well it is trusted and thought to be acting in the interests of the people, its level of corruption and its level of transparency. Many of these issues relate directly to the behaviour of politicians themselves and the political systems in which they serve and act. The actual role of government, commensurate with the nature of change in recent years, has also come under question in various quarters presently, in particular government expenditure. What areas of public life are important and are deemed worthy of funding? Are funding levels right? Are they in need of increase or decrease in various sectors of public life? Of course these questions are related to policy, electoral promises and the will and wishes of citizens. This volume offers three chapters dealing with governance.

Clive Bean addresses trust and reliability issues in Chapter 7, exploring public opinion on issues of integrity, corruption, influence and trust in politics and politicians in Australia. While Australia is not known for the widespread institutional corruption prevalent in some nations, there has been no shortage of corrupt practices, which tend to occur more in the form of individual or personal corruption rather than in a systematic, institutionalised form. Research into citizen perceptions of honesty and integrity in Australian politics has found that, among other things, the public expects higher ethical standards from politicians than politicians expect from themselves. Bean finds that there is a good deal of concern about how fairly ordinary people are treated by public officials and about a perceived lack of external political efficacy.

In Chapter 8 Wilson, Meagher and Hermes examine public perceptions of the role of government and spending preferences more generally. Using a variety of survey data, their analyses of the role of government and spending preferences suggest that Australians do not seek a drastically reduced role for government, in terms of their willingness to pay more taxes and their desire to see more spending in some key policy areas. Wilson, Meagher and Hermes consider some key elements of the changing nation and its relation to governance up to the time of Rudd's prime ministership. Specifically they consider social policy preferences in the context of the recent economic crisis, failing infrastructure and adverse climate change. Their findings indicate that Australians tend to want more spending on education, health care and the environment and suggest that perceptions of rundown education and health systems are major factors driving the strong spending preferences that have become a longer-term trend. The consequences of social policy choices through government spending have implications for the liberal model of governance.

As we began with the 2007 election so we shall conclude this introduction to the chapters in this volume with reference to it. Here we have another dimension to work and livelihood pertinent to governance, in contrast with Chapter 10 where work is related to identity. In Chapter 9, Goot and Watson examine governance through the state of industrial relations in Australia, which registered as an important concern for many voters in the 2007 election after a long campaign around changes to industrial relations called WorkChoices. In looking at WorkChoices, Goot and Watson also look at the nature of electoral cleavages in contemporary Australian politics and society. They note the significance of union membership and Labor partisanship as the most important determinants in structuring views about WorkChoices. The issue of the power of employees' vis-a-vis employers will continue to be an important issue for many Australians in the future. In essence this chapter is about perceptions of power and the importance of attitudes to unions and management in explaining the strong views about governance of such an important area of national life. The chapter also highlights the increasing importance voters placed on the issue leading up to the 2007 election, and its evolution from an issue of little consideration to a key battleground. The election of Labor saw the legislation repealed.

The thematic backdrop here is a reflection on some of the key themes and issues facing Australians as measured by the 2007 AuSSA and as thought valuable and informative by the researchers and editors. Importantly the chapters in this book empirically assess and interpret the public response to the themes, allowing the provision of analysis and interpretation, and can therefore be adjudged alongside the topical claims related to identity, fear and governance made by various media sources. As the media is an overwhelmingly powerful informational device of varying quality, it is important to complement media-generated public perception and opinion with systematic social scientific analysis of public attitudes to offer public debate additional resources and varied interpretation. In addition to the reporting of public opinion and attitudes, and as a work of empirical social science, the report also seeks to reveal what social, cultural, economic and political influences are at the heart of the opinions and attitudes of Australians. In doing so we are able to ascertain the key lines of division and unity, difference and similarity, conservation and change demonstrated by Australians.

About the 2007 Australian Survey of Social Attitudes

The research in this book draws primarily from the third AuSSA completed in late 2007 and early 2008. The AuSSA is a product of the ACSPRI Centre for Social Research at The Australian National University in collaboration with researchers from other Australian and overseas universities. The AuSSA is also the official Australian contribution to the world's two major social survey consortiums: the International Social Survey Program (ISSP), covering 41 countries, and the World Values Survey, covering more than 80 countries. Version A contains the ISSP 2006 Role of Government module and Version B contains the ISSP 2007 Leisure Time and Sports module.

The AuSSA takes the form of a mail questionnaire sent to more than 10 000 Australian citizens every two years. The survey itself was prepared by five Principal Investigators—Timothy Phillips, Bruce Tranter, Deborah Mitchell, Juliet Pietsch and Ken Reed—in cooperation with the AuSSA Advisory Panel, which met to draft the survey at The Australian National University at the end of 2006. Core survey questions are reviewed every two years and new items—from a variety of national and international sources—are proposed by members of the team. Our aim is to ensure the AuSSA has comparability over time and with other national and international surveys, but also to ensure new topics relevant to Australia are surveyed, and that we contribute to developing survey methodology. Accordingly, AuSSA 2007 was distributed to a stratified systematic random sample of 10 000 Australians aged eighteen or over who were selected from an up-to-date version of the Australian Electoral Commission's Electoral Roll. The sample reflects the State-by-State distribution of the Australian population. To view the AuSSA 2007 questionnaires, see the AuSSA web site at: <http://aussa.anu.edu.au/questionnaires.html>

Along with a wealth of other opinion data, AuSSA 2007 results are available publicly through the Australian Data Archive's online data analysis system, NESSTAR, at: <http://www.ada.edu.au> Access online is free (but you will need to register with a password). The data are also available through the ASSDA direct at: <assda@anu.edu.au>; they can also supply the data set in machine-readable formats as well as provide the AuSSA 2007 User's Guide (Study No. 01088).

Acknowledgments

The Australian Survey of Social Attitudes has consistently provided the scholarly community and the broader public with high quality data from which informed commentary and original scholarship has issued. This volume is the latest production to utilize this valuable resource with the aim of contributing to an increasingly informed and intelligent public debate around a number of key issues facing Australia. With this larger aim, and all the various smaller components involved in an edited work in mind, the editors would like to acknowledge the assistance and advice of a number people in the preparations of this volume. In particular we sincerely thank Ann Evans, Deborah Mitchell, and Marian Sawer for their various efforts and guidance throughout the course of assembling this work. Thanks and acknowledgments also need to go to those involved in the design, construction, and administration of the 2007 wave of the Australian Survey of Social Attitudes; Timothy Phillips especially, and the AuSSA 2007 advisory committee including Gabrielle Meagher, Shaun Wilson, David Denemark, Mark Western, and Bruce Tranter. We also than Beth Battrick from ANU E Press and Jan Borrie for their editorial support. Finally, our recognition and thanks go to the team at the Australian Data Archive at The Australian National University.

References

Anderson, Benedict. 2006. *Imagined Communities: Reflections on the origin and spread of nationalism*. Second edition. London: Verso.

Campbell, Colin. 2007. *The Eastenization of the West: A thematic account of cultural change in the modern era*. Boulder, Colo.: Paradigm Publishers.

Dawkins, Richard. 2006. *The God Delusion*. London: Bantam.

Hitchens, Christopher. 2007. *God is not Great: How religion poisons everything*. New York: Twelve.

Smith, Philip, Phillips, Timothy and King, Ryan. 2010. *Incivility: The rude stranger in everyday life*. Melbourne: Cambridge University Press.

Weaver, Matthew. 2010. 'Angela Merkel: German multiculturalism has "utterly failed"'. *Guardian*, 17 October, <http://www.guardian.co.uk/world/2010/oct/17/angela-merkel-german-multiculturalism-failed> accessed 27 February 2012.

Woodward Ian, Zlatko, Skrbis and Clive, Bean. 2008. 'Attitudes towards globalization and cosmopolitanism: cultural diversity, personal consumption and the national economy'. *British Journal of Sociology*: 207–26.

2. Keeping Our Distance: Non-Indigenous/Aboriginal relations in Australian society

Maggie Walter

In February 2008, then Prime Minister Kevin Rudd made a national apology to members of the Stolen Generations. For Indigenous[1] and non-Indigenous Australians alike this was a significant political and social moment. The intense media and public interest in, and scrutiny of, the apology demonstrate that the relationship between the original Australians and those who have arrived since colonisation remains salient, if not central, to who Australians are what Australians and Australia is in the twenty-first century. The terrain of this relationship is key to Australia's self-concept, its identity as a nation and that of its peoples, old and new.

Yet these relations are also highly contested. The image of Australia reflected here is a two-sided visage. One face—as manifested in the apology, the elevating of Professor Mick Dodson to 2009 Australian of the Year and the groundswell of public action in the March for Reconciliation in 2000—is openly encouraging of reconciliation and acknowledging of a historical legacy of entrenched marginalisation and poverty. The other face forestalls the prospect of formal rapprochement, casting as undeserved and unearned attempts at social, economic or political equity—a position manifested by the now long-stalled reconciliation process and the commonness of publicly expressed negative sentiment towards Indigenous peoples and culture (see, for example, Andrew Bolt's 2008 blog in relation to the new Indigenous representative body). This distinctively Australian, but contradictory, picture suggests a country and a national identity ill at ease with the place of Indigeneity in its consciousness, one in which Indigeneity remains unreconciled with everyday concepts of Australian society and Australian identity. This uniquely Australian unease is reflected in the often confused and conflicting direction of public attitudes towards Indigenous people, Indigenous culture issues and Indigenous political topics. As with public conversation, supportive and reconciliatory attitudes and substantial levels of anti-Aboriginal sentiment appear to incongruously coexist as the Australian norm.

---

1 The term 'Aboriginal' is used in the AuSSA questions rather than the group term 'Indigenous'. This terminology is selected because the large majority of Indigenous people are Aboriginal (more than 90 per cent) and because this is the term commonly used in public discourse on Indigenous-related topics. Torres Strait Islanders are also a distinct people culturally and geographically.

Explaining attitudinal and public conversation incongruence is complicated by a dearth of information on the interaction between non-Indigenous and Aboriginal Australians in everyday life. Indigenous Australians form only 2.5 per cent of the total population, but this equates to more than 500 000 people and, in contrast with popular perceptions, three-quarters of these people live alongside non-Indigenous residents in regional or urban locations. Population trends also indicate that, just like the non-Indigenous population, Indigenous people are increasingly resident in larger urban areas. In 2006 nearly one-third of Indigenous Australians lived in our major cities, with many families resident in urban areas for generations (ABS 2007; Fredericks, Leitch and Barty 2008). By State, New South Wales is home to the largest proportion of the Indigenous population (28 per cent), with the largest Indigenous population resident in Sydney. Nearly the same proportion (27 per cent) resides in Queensland (27 per cent) followed by Western Australia (15 per cent) and the Northern Territory (13 per cent). As shown in Figure 2.1, in all regions except Western Australia and the Northern Territory at least 80 per cent of the Indigenous population lives in urban areas.

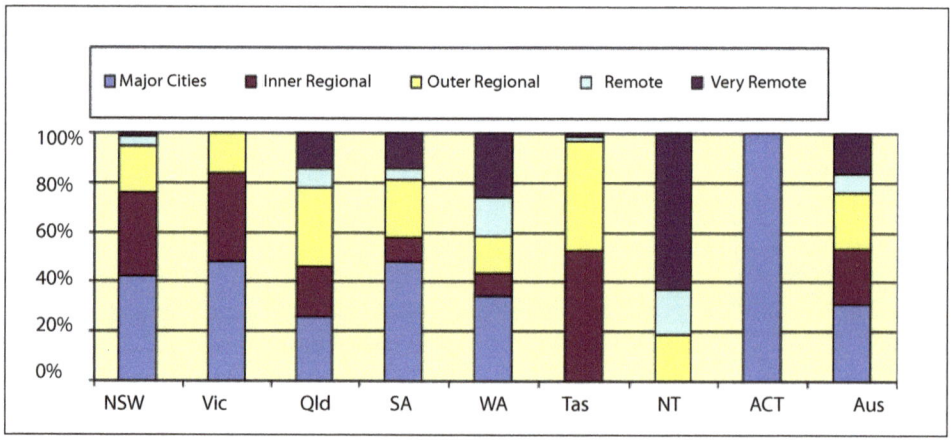

Figure 2.1 Indigenous Population Across Geographic Regions, 2006, by State/Territory

Source: ABS (2007).

This chapter's topic of an uneasy Australian identity takes two dimensions of the relations between non-Indigenous and Indigenous Australians as its empirical focus. These are: public attitudes towards Aboriginal issues, and social interaction by non-Indigenous people. The empirical analysis is guided by two questions based on these dimensions. The first queries the shape of contemporary social attitudes and whether these reflect wider socioeconomic and demographic patterns—that is: *what are the patterns of non-Indigenous Australians' attitudes towards Aboriginal people, culture and issues and are these associated with demographic, social and/or economic characteristics?* The second queries the level of individual interaction between non-Indigenous and Aboriginal Australians—that is: *how socially distant from or proximate to Aboriginal people are non-Indigenous Australians?* The analysis is based on data from the 2007 Australian Survey of Social Attitudes (AuSSA) in which a series of questions canvassed respondents' attitudes on a range of topical Aboriginal-related issues (H1a to H1f) and sought indicators on the level of respondents' social distance (H3a to H3d) and social proximity (H2) with Aboriginal people. Bringing these two dimensions together, the overall aim of this chapter is to throw an empirical light onto the conflicting elements of the Australian landscape of race relations. In doing so it illustrates a largely unexplored, but deeply resonating, aspect of contemporary Australian life, and Australian identity, for its Indigenous and non-Indigenous peoples.

Australian public attitudes

Australian public attitudes towards Aboriginal people and issues have been variously canvassed since at least the late 1960s (see Beswick and Hills 1969; Western 1969) with the range of data collections and results summarised in a recent book by Goot and Rowse (2007). The Australian Election Studies (Bean, Gow and McAllister 2001), for instance, have asked a short series of attitudinal questions on Aboriginal topics in every collection since the 1980s. Collection of data on attitudes towards Aboriginal people, however, has remained relatively sporadic and limited and their analysis has generally been aimed at addressing wider social and public issues. For example, political science explorations of the reasons for the rise of Pauline Hanson and the One Nation in the mid-1990s found that underlying attitudes towards Aborigines were a factor (Charnock 1999; Goot and Watson 2001). The psychological underpinnings of race-related attitudes have also featured in research. For example, a small-scale study by Ray (1981) found negative attitudes towards Aboriginal people and culture associated with conservatism. More recently, WA studies (Pedersen et al. 2004; Walker 1994) find low empathetic concern correlated with negative attitudes towards Aboriginal people.

Existing research has also found that socioeconomic and demographic variables tend to be linked with attitudinal direction. For example, a recent survey study on racism (Dunn et al. 2004) found a persistence of intolerance towards Asian, Jewish and Indigenous people. Those with higher levels of intolerant attitudes were more likely to be male, older and non–tertiary educated. A cross-wave (1993–2004) analysis of Australian election studies data (Walter and Mooney 2007) on respondents' agreement with the statement 'Government help for Aborigines has gone too far' also found older, male, less educated respondents were statistically more likely to agree with the statement. This analysis, however, also found that public attitudes on the topic both varied and remained consistent. Respondent statement agreement levels were 46 per cent in 1993, rose to more than 50 per cent agreement in 1996 and 1998, but by 2004 had returned to their 1993 levels of just less than a majority. The period of higher agreement, 1996–98, coincides with the political influence of Pauline Hanson's One Nation party. This link suggests attitudes can be affected by dominant public discourses, but also tend to reflect an underlying population norm.

Social distance and social proximity

Even less literature directly relates to the second question: *what is the level of social distance and social proximity between non-Indigenous and Aboriginal Australians?* The primary research tool used to measure social distance between ethnic groups is the Bogardus social distance scale, developed in the United States in the 1920s. The scale assesses respondents' degree of warmth, indifference or hostility to levels of social relationships, which are then taken as a measure of ethnic relations and prejudice (Marshall 1998). Such studies, however, tend to analyse relations between the dominant cultural or racial group and ethnic (usually) migrant minorities, not between a non-indigenous and indigenous population—for example, an Australian representative study by McAllister and Moore (1991), examining the social distance of respondents from the majority migrant groups, finding a social distance closest to furthest continuum from European groups to Vietnamese people. Indigenous people were not included as a target group. A smaller-scale study did explore social distance from Aboriginal people, Asian people, the aged and homosexual people, finding social distance highest for homosexual people and smallest towards Aborigines (Matsuda and Harsel 1997). The low sample size and mixing of ethnic and social groups, however, reduce this study's usefulness to the inquiries in this chapter. More critically, social proximity—the level and regularity of social interaction between non-Indigenous and Aboriginal people—has not been a significant research topic, although a recent study by Reconciliation Australia (ABC 2009a) does find significant levels of distrust between the two groups. Given the spatial proximity, with the majority of non-Indigenous and Aboriginal people living alongside, the questions of social proximity and social distance have direct relevance to social attitudes.

AuSSA 2007 data and attitudes to Aboriginal people, culture and place

To examine the first question—the shape of contemporary attitudes and whether these are patterned by socioeconomic and demographic factors—a series of six 'Aboriginal' statements was posed. Respondents were asked to indicate their level of agreement with each statement. This series was developed to reflect the essence of Aboriginal topics current in national public conversations—that is, what is being said by non-Indigenous people about Aboriginal issues in blogs and the letters pages of newspapers and on talkback radio. Two statements (H1a, H1f) sought perceptions of the current positioning of Aboriginal people within Australian society; two statements (H1c, H1e) canvassed attitudes to Aboriginal cultural topics, and two statements (H1b, H1d) explored attitudes towards government policy and/or legislation that ameliorate Aboriginal disadvantage or loss. The tenor of the statements was varied from negative to positive, as was the dimensional order, to avoid response sets. In this and subsequent analyses, the four cases in the AuSSA sample who identified as having an Aboriginal or Torres Strait Islander ancestry[2] are excluded.

As shown in Table 2.1, there is a patterned but varied level of agreement/disagreement across the statements. The two statements that look at equality are majority positively supported, as are both of the statements that deal with issues of culture. Nearly 60 per cent disagree (14 per cent strongly disagree and 40 per cent disagree) that Aboriginal people are now treated equally and just more than half disagree that injustices are now all in the past. Similar proportions strongly disagree (14 per cent) or disagree (43 per cent) that a traditional lifestyle defines Aboriginality and strongly agree (12 per cent) or agree (41 per cent) that cultural change should not be necessary to fit into Australian society. The two statements relating to the restorative actions of land rights and extra government assistance, however, do not receive majority support. Only 9 per cent strongly agree and 36 per cent agree (45 per cent in total) that Aboriginal disadvantage justifies extra government assistance. The level of disagreement with the statement that granting land rights to Aboriginal people is unfair is even lower, with only 8 per cent strongly disagreeing and 25 per cent disagreeing (33 per cent in total). These findings suggest a cognitive dissonance between egalitarian belief systems and willingness to endorse social actions to address inequality. While there is majority agreement among non-Indigenous Australians that Indigenous people remain unfairly and disadvantageously positioned, should not have to change their culture and do not have to follow a traditional lifestyle to retain their identity, the statements on land rights and extra government assistance were not equally accepted.

---

2 Twenty-seven respondents answered 'yes' to the question 'Do you identify as Aboriginal or Torres Strait Islander?'; however, only four respondents gave their ancestry as Australian Aboriginal on the ancestry questions and no respondents gave their ancestry as Torres Strait Islander. Cross-checking the 27 'yes' responses with ancestry responses indicates that ancestry responses are likely to be the more accurate measure of Australian Indigeneity and this has been used in this chapter.

Table 2.1 Attitudes Towards Aboriginal Issues (per cent)

	How strongly do you agree or disagree with the following statements?	SA %	A %	N %	D %	SD %
a.	Aboriginal people are now treated equally to other Australians N = 2624	6	17	19	44	14
f.	Injustices towards Aboriginal people are now all in the past N = 2612	8	18	22	37	14
c.	Aboriginal people should not have to change their culture to fit into Australian society N = 2619	12	41	23	20	5
e.	Aboriginal people who no longer follow traditional lifestyles are not really Aboriginal N = 2617	7	16	20	43	14
b.	Aboriginal people's levels of disadvantage justify extra government assistance N = 2614	9	36	20	26	9
d.	Granting land rights to Aboriginal people is unfair to other Australians N = 2618	14	29	25	25	8

Note: SA = strongly agree; A = agree; N = neither agree nor disagree; D = disagree; SD = strongly disagree.

Source: Australian Survey of Social Attitudes 2007.

Social and demographic patterns in attitudinal alignment

Previous research suggests that age, gender, educational level and location are likely to be significantly associated with non-Indigenous Australians' attitudes towards Aboriginal issues (Dunn et al. 2004; Goot and Watson 2001; Walter and Mooney 2007). To ascertain the pattern of attitudes to Aboriginal issues across these and other relevant socioeconomic and demographic variables, a principal component analysis was conducted using the six attitudinal question variables H1a, b, c, d, e, f. A single component explaining 45 per cent of the variance (Eigenvalue 2.70) was identified with reliability analyses indicating that all six variables could be used in a single scale (Cronbach's Alpha 0.75). This variable was labelled 'Attitudes towards Aboriginal issues'. Scores calculated for the 'Attitudes towards Aboriginal issues' scale were then used as the dependent variable in an ordinary least squares (OLS) regression. Independent variables were age group, gender, educational level, geographic location, ancestry, respondent income and occupation (see social proximity section for details of second OLS analysis).

Table 2.2 OLS Regression Variable Description and Coefficients Predicting 'Attitudes to Aboriginal issues' Scores

Variable	B	N	%
Constant	0.255		
Age			
18–34 years	0.087	493	18.8
35–49 years	0.033	768	29.3
50–64 years#		813	31.0
50–64 years	0.115	545	20.8
Gender			
Male**	−0.155		52.6
Female		1248	47.4
Education##			
< Year 12***	−0.622	527	20.2
Year 12***	−0.481	281	10.8
Trade/technical***	−0.673	437	16.7
Certificate/diploma***	−0.480	730	28.0
Bachelor degree or above		634	24.3
Occupation##			
Manager	−0.111	373	14.9
Professional		553	22.1
Technical/trade	−0.139	346	13.8
Community/personal Service worker*	−0.212	240	9.6
Clerical/administration*	−0.175	441	17.6
Sales*	−0.199	208	8.3
Machinery operator/driver	−0.145	126	5.0
Labourer**	−0.249	216	8.6
Location			
Capital city***	0.242	1560	59.4
Other urban*	0.155	215	8.2
Rural		863	32.5
Respondent individual income			
$0 – $15 599	0.088	635	26.0
$15 600 – $36 399	0.031	665	27.2
$36 400 – $77 900	−0.083	804	32.9
$78 000+		342	14.0
Ancestry			
Euro-Australian*	0.180	2466	93.7
Non–Euro Australian		166	6.3
Adj R²			0.111

\# p = 0.05

* p < 0.05

** p < 0.01

*** p < 0.000

\#\# Collinearity diagnostics do not indicate multi-collinearity between Education and Occupation variables.

Source: Australian Survey of Social Attitudes 2007.

The OLS results confirm previous research with the exception of age. Holding all other variables constant, for non-Indigenous Australians, gender, education, geographic location, occupation and ancestry are associated with 'Attitudes towards Aboriginal issues' scores. As shown in Table 2.2, Australian non-Indigenous women were significantly more likely to record higher attitude scores than Australian non-Indigenous men; those living in capital cities and other urban areas had significantly higher attitude scores than those living in rural areas; non-Indigenous people working as community and personal service workers, clerical and administration workers and sales workers and labourers are significantly more likely to record lower Aboriginal issues attitudes scores than non-Indigenous Australian professionals. Education is the most influential variable, with all non-Indigenous Australians with education levels below that of bachelor degree significantly more likely to have lower attitude scores than those with a bachelor degree or above. Interestingly, ancestry also makes a difference, with non-Indigenous Australians of Euro-Australian background having significantly higher attitude scores than Australians from other than European backgrounds. The influence of age is less marked than expected, with attitudinal scores for those aged forty-six to sixty-four (but not those aged eighteen–thirty-four years or thirty-five to forty-five years) compared with those aged sixty-five years marginally significant, falling just on the 0.05 significance level. Only non-Indigenous respondents' income was not significantly associated with attitudes towards Aboriginal issues.

Social distance and social proximity

This section addresses this chapter's second question: *how socially distant from or proximate to Aboriginal people are non-Indigenous Australians?* The social distance and social proximity aspects of the question are assessed separately as each reflects a different dimension of social interaction.

Social distance

The AuSSA items developed to assess the level of social distance between non-Indigenous and Aboriginal people in Australian society are based on the social distance measurement aims, but do not directly replicate the Bogardus social distance scale. The variation is because the Bogardus scale presumes that the socially distant group is migrant—that is, three of the seven Bogardus items ask about the acceptability of a group as visitors to the country or as a fellow citizen (Wark and Galliher 2007). The AuSSA questions ask respondents to nominate how happy or unhappy they would be in four hypothetical situations involving an Aboriginal person: marriage to an immediate family member; as an immediate neighbour; as a supervisor; and as a co-worker at the same level. The results shown in Table 2.3 indicate only limited social distance between non-Indigenous and Aboriginal Australians. Although unhappiness tends to increase as the hypothetical situation becomes socially closer—that is, the proportion of non-Indigenous Australians who would be very unhappy or unhappy about an Aboriginal person marrying into their family is higher than the proportion who would be very unhappy or unhappy working at the same level as an Aboriginal person—the general level of unhappiness is low across the four scenario items. And slightly against the general pattern of social distance scale responses, non-Indigenous respondents would be unhappier with an Aboriginal neighbour than with an Aboriginal person marrying an immediate member of their family.

Table 2.3 Social Distance Scenario Attitudes

	How would you feel if…:	VH %	H %	N %	U %	VU %
H3a.	Aboriginal person married an immediate member of your family? N = 2609	11	25	53	8	3
H3d.	Aboriginal person moved into the house next-door to you? N = 2612	14	26	46	9	4
H3b.	Aboriginal person was employed in the same area as you at a similar job level as you? N = 2632	22	43	35	0.4	0.5
H3c.	Aboriginal person was made your supervisor at work? N = 2604	19	37	40	2	1

Note: VH = very happy; H = happy; N = neither happy nor unhappy; U = unhappy; VU = very unhappy.

Source: Australian Survey of Social Attitudes 2007.

As in the general attitudinal data, the next question is whether social distance varies by age, gender, educational level or location. A cross-tabulation of these data with these socio-demographic variables finds statistically significant differences for each social distance scenario by gender ($p < 0.000$ for all scenarios), age ($p < 0.000$ for all scenarios) and education ($p < 0.000$ for all scenarios), but not by locality (not shown here). The abbreviated results summarised in Figure 2.2 present the amalgamated proportion of those who would be 'unhappy' or 'very unhappy' if the scenarios were to occur by gender, education level and age group. As can be seen, non-Indigenous women indicate an observable lower social distance than non-Indigenous men on the marriage and neighbour scenarios while those with a higher level of education, defined here as a bachelor degree or above, report lower social distance on the marriage, neighbour and work supervisor scenarios than those with a middle level of education (post-school qualifications below degree level). Younger non-Indigenous people are more likely to be 'very happy' and less likely to be 'unhappy' or 'very unhappy' than older people, with the level of social distance across scenarios rising with age.

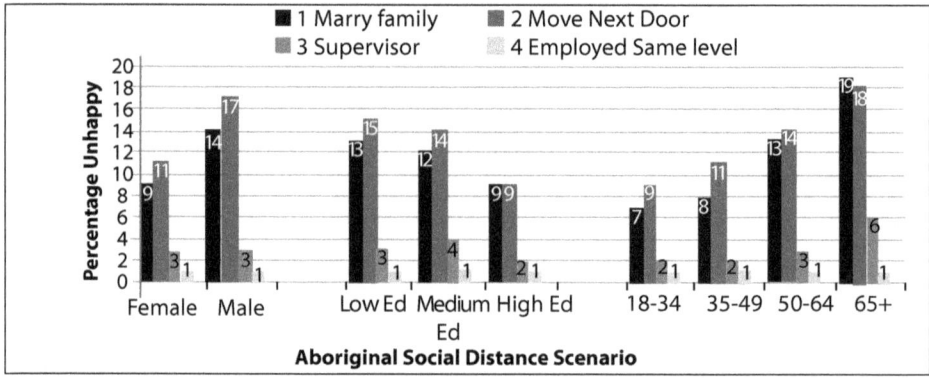

Figure 2.2 Gender, Age and Education and Social Distance Items

Note: Percentages refer to the proportion of respondents who would be 'unhappy' or 'very unhappy' with each scenario item.

Source: Australian Survey of Social Attitudes 2007.

As shown, the closer the social scenario, the higher is the proportion of all groups who would be unhappy, although again the second-closest scenario—having an Aboriginal neighbour—has higher levels of social distance than having an Aboriginal in-law for most groups. Nearly one-fifth of those aged over sixty-five years would be unhappy or very unhappy if an Aboriginal person were to marry a member of their immediate family and a similar proportion would be unhappy should an Aboriginal person move next-door. The comparison respective 'unhappy' proportions for those aged eighteen to thirty-four years are less than half these at 7 and 9 per cent. The ratios of male to female unhappiness with these two socially closer scenarios are also higher, with the same pattern repeated between those with higher education levels and those with secondary-only schooling.

Levels of unhappiness with the more socially remote employment scenarios were less differentiated, with the significant differences explained by the higher proportions of women, the higher educated and younger people who report they would be 'very happy' with this scenario (not shown here). Across categories and variables, the number of those who would be unhappy if an Aboriginal person were employed in the same area and level is minimal at 1 per cent or lower and the only group with more than 5 per cent of respondents unhappy with an Aboriginal supervisor is of those aged sixty-five years and over.

Social proximity

The Bogardus distance scale presumes, in testing the relationship between ethnically different populations, a likelihood that the scenarios outlined might actually occur. This presumption is untested in Australia; the question of how much interaction there is between non-Indigenous and Aboriginal people has, to date, not been asked or answered. The very limited relevant data suggest non-Indigenous and Indigenous people occupy different spatial realms. For example, Atkinson, Taylor and Walter (2010), analysing capital-city 2006 census data, find Indigenous and non-Indigenous populations concentrated in different suburbs and areas.

To assess the dimension of social proximity, AuSSA 2007 respondents were asked to select from three descriptive statements that which most closely reflected their own level of interaction with Aboriginal people. These are

1. I mix regularly with Aboriginal people on a day-to-day basis *(selected by 9 per cent)*

2. I know Aboriginal people but do not mix regularly with them *(selected by 45 per cent)*

3. I do not know any Aboriginal people personally *(selected by 46 per cent)*.

The second category data need to be interpreted with caution. The mailout/mailback form of the AuSSA restricted capacity to clarify for respondents that 'knowing Aboriginal people' meant personally knowing on a one-to-one basis rather than knowing 'of' an Aboriginal person such as Cathy Freeman. Given the small number of non-Indigenous people who interact regularly it may be that a significant portion of this mid-category 'know of' rather than 'personally know' an Aboriginal person. This inadequacy will be addressed in further research on this topic. Nevertheless, these initial analyses reveal that less than one in 10 non-Indigenous Australians knows and mixes regularly with Aboriginal people and about half of all non-Indigenous Australians (at least) do not know any Aboriginal person personally.

How do these results spread across the socio-demographic variables used in the previous analyses? For this question, Category 1 data—those who report knowing personally and mixing on a day-to-day basis with Aboriginal people—are used as the indicator of social proximity. Within the results (Figure 2.3), statistically significant differences are found within education ($p < 0.05$), age ($p < 0.000$) and locality ($p < 0.000$).

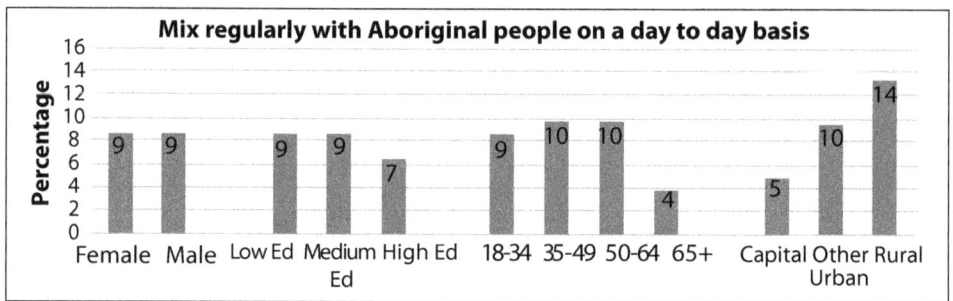

Figure 2.3 Gender, Education, Age and Locality and Aboriginal Social Proximity

Note: Percentages refer to the proportion of respondents who report they mix regularly with Aboriginal people on a day-to-day basis.

Source: Australian Survey of Social Attitudes 2007.

Non-Indigenous Australians over sixty-five years are less than half as likely to mix regularly with Aboriginal people as those in the other age groups. Nearly two-thirds of this group also report they do not know any Aboriginal people compared with about 42–45 per cent of other age groups (not shown here). By locality, non-Indigenous people living in rural areas are more than twice as likely to mix regularly with Aboriginal people than those from capital cities, suggesting that interaction is more likely in smaller communities. Although not directly assessable, the higher levels of interaction among younger age groups suggest that sporting environments, rather than social networks, might be the key environments for this interaction.

Finally, to test whether social proximity to Aboriginal people had an effect on attitudes towards Aboriginal issues, the social proximity categorical variable was added to the OLS analysis described in the first section. The results show no significant difference in attitude scores between non-Indigenous Australians who 'mix regularly with Aboriginal people on a day-to-day basis' compared with those who 'know Aboriginal people but do not mix regularly with them' and those who 'do not know any Aboriginal people personally'. This finding is interpreted to indicate that interaction with Aboriginal people is not a significant factor in its own right in predicting non-Indigenous Australians' Aboriginal issues attitudes.

Table 2.4 OLS Regression Variable Description and Coefficients Predicting 'Attitudes to Aboriginal Issues' Scores

Variable	B	N	%
Constant	0.345		
Social proximity			
Mix regularly with Aboriginal people on a day-to-day basis		236	9.1
Know Aboriginal people but do not mix regularly with them	0.012	1161	44.6
Do not know any Aboriginal people personally	030	1207	45.9

Note: Table should be read as an addition to Table 2.3. The addition of the social proximity variable did not change the significance or the level of significance of any other variable reported in Table 2.3.

Source: Australian Survey of Social Attitudes 2007.

Discussion

This chapter used AuSSA data to empirically investigate conflicting elements of the Australian national identity landscape as reflected in non-Indigenous/Indigenous race relations. In doing so it posed two questions. The answer to the first—*What are the patterns of non-Indigenous Australians' attitudes towards Aboriginal people, culture and issues and are these associated with demographic, social and/or economic characteristics?*—is that: a small majority of non-Indigenous Australians tends to hold egalitarian belief systems about Aboriginal people's position in society, but, incongruously, these do not extend to the restorative actions of land rights or extra government assistance. Moreover, the overall pattern of attitudes varies across the non-Indigenous population with this variation related to socioeconomic and demographic factors. In line with previous studies, for non-Indigenous Australians, being female, residing in an urban location, being a professional and being of Euro-Australian background and especially holding a bachelor degree or higher level of education are statistically associated with more positive attitudes towards Aboriginal issues in general. In contrast with previous research, however, age does not have an independent effect. The second question asks: *how socially distant or socially proximate are non-Indigenous Australians with Aboriginal people?* The initial answer to this question is that while the overall social distance between non-Indigenous people and Aboriginal people is low, social distance increases with interactive closeness. On this measure, being female, younger and having a higher level of education are associated with lower levels of social distance.

The straightforward interpretation of these results is that they fit, with the notable exception of an age effect, with previous Australian attitudinal research (Dunn et al. 2004; Goot and Watson 2001; Walter and Mooney 2007) and also make theoretical sense. Older non-Indigenous Australians who show greater social distance grew up in the era before Aboriginal rights activism and this is likely to effect their reaction to the social distance items even if they have changed attitudes alongside the changing times. Similarly with gender, it might be theorised that non-Indigenous women will be more egalitarian in their attitudes given the time line similarities of calls for equality for women and Aboriginal people in Australian society. The results around education and occupation, taken here as proxies for social class position, are more definitive. Tertiary-educated non-Indigenous professionals stand apart from non-Indigenous Australians with lower education and lower occupational status in having more positive Aboriginal issues attitudes. Moreover, education and occupation had independent effects on predicting attitude scores. The explanation may be that not only do the more educated and those in professional occupations have higher exposure to an ongoing range of opinions, perspectives and debates around Aboriginal Australia and so are more open in their attitudes, but also, more pragmatically, with their higher status they may be less likely to feel potential for a loss of social privilege through Aboriginal restorative action. Rural non-Indigenous Australians also tend towards conservative values (Goot and Watson 2001) and these values, it seems, are reflected in their attitudes towards Aboriginal issues. Finally, an explanation of why attitude scores are lower among non-Indigenous Australians of a non-European ancestry is immediately apparent. This group has not been included in previous analyses and the results suggest more research is needed.

The social proximity results, however, complicate this interpretation. While the attitudinal and social distance results show clear patterns, the finding that more than 90 per cent of non-Indigenous Australians do not interact regularly with Aboriginal people suggests that non-Indigenous Australians, in the main, do not occupy the same social realms as Aboriginal people. That at least half of non-Indigenous Australians do not know any Aboriginal people at all further suggests that a substantial proportion, if not a majority, of the non-Indigenous population lives their lives in a largely Aboriginal-free social zone. This finding raises the contentious issue of how and why non-Indigenous Australians hold the attitudes towards Aboriginal Australians and Aboriginal issues that they do. If non-Indigenous lives are largely separated from those of Aboriginal people, even when residing in the same geographic location, then attitudes are also predominantly formed and held without direct interaction with Aboriginal people. This interpretation is supported by the finding from the multivariate analysis that the level of social proximity did not have an independent effect on the pattern of attitudes to Aboriginal issues.

Taken together, these results suggest that most attitudes towards Aboriginal social issues are framed through interaction with other non-Indigenous people and the dominant discourse of the media and political realms. The obvious risk from being informed about Aboriginal people and issues from outside sources is that conceptions of Aboriginal people and life are more likely to be garnered through Indigenous stereotypes, which in Australia, to date, are usually pejorative. Such views are also likely to be static. The disconnect between interaction *with* Aboriginal people and attitudes *towards* Aboriginal people perhaps offers at least a partial explanation of the relative intractability of such attitudes (see Goot and Rowse 2007). It also might go some way to explaining the finding of why a belief that Aboriginal people are still disadvantaged and treated unfairly in Australian society does not seem to translate into a belief in legal, social or policy action to remedy this situation.

The upside of this analysis and interpretation, however, is that a change in the public, media and political presentation and focus on Aboriginal life from the negative (social dysfunction, alcoholism, welfare dependency) to the more positive (strong community, success against the odds, aspirations for children) might also result in changing attitudes. Just as the One Nation period through the mid-1990s engendered less tolerant attitudes (Walter and Mooney 2007), higher exposure to Aboriginal perspectives, perhaps, is also likely to positively influence public attitudes. Initiatives such as Reconciliation Australia's 2009 advertising campaign (ABC 2009b) to challenge negative stereotypical attitudes about Aboriginal people might just bring the ideal and reality closer together.

Conclusion

Australian social attitudes towards, and levels of interaction with, Aboriginal peoples are more than just interesting social phenomena. They form a central, if largely undiscussed, facet of contemporary Australian identity—one that this study has demonstrated remains conflicted and ill at ease. The reality of the social attitudes of a significant proportion of non-Indigenous Australians towards Aboriginal people and issues is at odds with self-conceptions of the nation as a tolerant and egalitarian society. Further, the juxtaposition of Australian egalitarian ideals with these attitudes indicates that the terrain of Indigenous/non-Indigenous relations in Australia is still socially and politically strained. The ambiguous, and perhaps ambivalent, territory of how non-Indigenous Australians perceive the national identity place of Aboriginal Australians along with the lack of interaction between non-Indigenous and Indigenous peoples are signifiers of the ambiguous and perhaps sometimes ambivalent notions that swirl unresolved around just what it is to be Australian. A notion and a feature of Australian identity, perhaps, that will need to be resolved before the nation and its citizenry can feel at ease within its own national belonging. As a nation, we need to move past 'us' and 'them' to 'we'.

References

Atkinson, Rowland, Taylor, Elizabeth and Walter, Maggie. 2010. 'Burying Indigeneity: the spatial construction of reality and Aboriginal Australia'. *Social and Legal Studies* 19(3): 311–30.

Australian Broadcasting Corporation (ABC). 2009a. 'Indigenous, non-Indigenous Australians don't trust each other: study'. *ABC News Online*, 9 February, <http://www.abc.net.au/news/stories/2009/02/09/2486027.htm> accessed 18 March 2009.

Australian Broadcasting Corporation (ABC). 2009b. 'Campaign tackles anti-Indigenous prejudice'. *ABC News Online*, 12 March, <http://www.abc.net.au/news/stories/2009/03/12/2514092.htm> accessed 18 March 2009.

Australian Bureau of Statistics (ABS). 2007. *Population Distribution, Aboriginal and Torres Strait Islander Australians 2006*, catalogue no. 4705.0. Canberra: Australian Bureau of Statistics.

Bean, Clive, Gow, David and McAllister, Ian. 2001. Australian Election Study: User's guide for the machine-readable data file: SSDA Study No 1048. Canberra: Social Science Data Archive, The Australian National University.

Beswick, David. G. and Hills, Michael D. 1969. 'An Australian ethnocentrism scale'. *Journal of Psychology* 21: 211–25.

Bolt, Andrew. 2008. 'No to this racism'. Andrew Bolt Blog, *The Herald Sun*, 13 July, <http://blogs.news.com.au/heraldsun/andrewbolt/index.php/heraldsun/comments/no_to_this_racism/asc/P20/> accessed 10 December 2008.

Charnock, David. 1999. 'Voting at the 1998 Australian federal election: studying major and minor parties simultaneously'. In *Proceedings of the 1999 Conference of the Australasian Political Studies Association*, University of Sydney, Sydney, 26–29 September.

Dunn, Kevin, Forrest, James, Burnley, Ian and McDonald, Amy. 2004. 'Constructing racism in Australia'. *Australian Journal of Social Issues* 394: 409–30.

Fredericks, Bronwyn, Leitch, Angela and Barty, Robert. 2008. '"Big mobs in the city now": the increasing number of Aboriginal and Torres Strait Islander people living in urban areas'. Presented at World Indigenous Peoples' Conference: Education (WIPC:E), Melbourne, 7–11 December.

Goot, Murray and Rowse, Tim. 2007. *Divided Nation: Indigenous affairs and the imagined public*. Melbourne: Melbourne University Press.

Goot, Murray and Watson, Ian. 2001. 'One Nation's electoral support: where does it come from, what makes it different and how does it fit?'. *Australian Journal of Politics and History* 47(2): 159–91.

McAllister, Ian and Moore, Rhona. 1991. 'Social distance among Australian ethnic groups'. *Sociology and Social Research* 75(2): 95–100.

Marshall, Gordon 1998. 'Bogardus social distance scale'. *A Dictionary of Sociology*. <http://www.encyclopedia.com/doc/1O88-Bogardussocialdistancescl.html> accessed 26 March 2009.

Matsuda, Yoshimi and Harsel, Sheldon. 1997. 'Factors influencing social distance from ethnic minorities, homosexuals, and the aged'. *Australian Journal of Social Research* 3(1): 37–56.

Pedersen, Anne, Beven, Jiaime, Walker, Iain and Griffiths, Brian. 2004. 'Attitudes towards Indigenous Australians: the role of empathy and guilt'. *Journal of Community & Applied Social Psychology* 14: 233–59.

Randall, Nancy Horak and Delbridge, Spencer. 2005. 'Perceptions of social distance in an ethnically fluid community'. *Sociological Spectrum* 21(2): 103–22.

Ray, John. J. 1981. 'Explaining Australian attitudes towards Aborigines'. *Ethnic and Racial Studies* 46(3): 348–52.

Walker, Iain. 1994. 'Attitudes to minorities: survey evidence of Western Australians' attitudes to Aborigines, Asians and women'. *Australian Journal of Psychology* 46(3): 137–43.

Walter, Maggie and Mooney, Gavin. 2007. 'Employment and welfare'. In *Social Determinants of Indigenous Health*, eds Bronwyn Carson, Terry Dunbar, Richard Chenhall and Ross Bailie, pp. 153–69. Sydney: Allen & Unwin.

Wark, Colin and Galliher, John F. 2007. 'Emory Bogardus and the origins of the social distance scale'. *The American Sociologist* 38(4): 383–95.

Western, John. 1969. 'What white Australians think'. *Race* 10: 411–34.

3. Australian Engagement with Asia: Towards closer political, economic and cultural ties

Juliet Pietsch and Haydn Aarons

This chapter reports on the results of a series of questions the survey asked Australians about engagement with Asia. Australia's relationship with Asia has commanded much interest from observers both within Australia and within Asia, given geographic nearness and cultural differences. Historically Australia has had an indifferent and uneasy relationship with Asia, yet since the postwar period Australia and Asia have embarked upon greater interaction and cooperation through increased trade, immigration, security concerns, travel, leisure and cultural exchange. Seminal in the evolution of this relationship have been the various Australian federal government policy agendas and contemporary movements and processes such as globalisation that have set the tone of the relationship between Australia and Asia. Recent federal governments have sought to connect Australia to Asia more meaningfully through a variety of measures, yet little is known about how ordinary Australians think and feel about Asia or how and to what extent they might have connected or not to Asia through lifestyle, work or cultural pursuits. Data of this kind enable us to assess the extent that Australia is cosmopolitan, open and embracing of aspects of multiculturalism.

While few systematic survey data exist to ascertain popular Australian perceptions of Asia as a whole over time, much has been written by historians and political scientists to reveal Australian attitudes towards Asia through foreign policy, trade unions and other organisations involved in nation-building and governance. Australia, through its policy outlook, has evolved in its relationship to Asia from an inward-looking, Anglocentric and culturally narrow society, to a more engaged, open and interactive entity within the Asia-Pacific region; however, has this change in policy and governance facilitated by trade, security, cultural and travel relationships with Asia translated to how ordinary Australians engage with Asia? Through a set of unique measures, this chapter offers a first glimpse of how close Australians feel to Asia and the level of engagement with Asia Australians currently practice. We prefigure the exploration of the engagement with Asia by individual Australians with a brief review of Australia's recent political engagement with Asia, with the aim of informing the reader about the broader systemic connections between Australia and Asia that might influence the level of engagement of individual Australians.

Political engagement since 1990

Since the 1990s successive governments have held different viewpoints on the extent to which Australia should develop closer economic, political and cultural ties with the Asian region. In the early 1990s, Labor Prime Minister Paul Keating focused Australia's foreign policies on Asia. The previous Prime Minister, Bob Hawke, had established the groundwork for closer economic ties through the founding of the Asia-Pacific Economic Cooperation (APEC) group, which apart from Australia included Brunei Darussalam, Canada, Indonesia, Japan, the Republic of Korea, Malaysia, New Zealand, the Philippines, Singapore, Thailand and the United States. While the original aims of APEC were focused on economic cooperation, Keating acknowledged that it was in Australia's security interests to foster a deeper engagement with Asia (see Milner 1997). Keating also promoted the importance of an Australian identity and Australian values as needing to shift closer to Asia. For example, Keating often talked about a new 'Asian vision' or strategies for an Asian Australia (Milner 1997).

The Keating Labor Government made a number of initiatives to raise awareness among Australia's youth of Australia's future economic, political and cultural engagement with Asia. One of the most important initiatives for deepening Australian cultural engagement in Asia included the National Asian Languages Study in Australian Schools (NALSAS) program. The focus of this program was to build a future generation of Australians with a level of expertise and awareness of the Asian region. The overall focus of this program included Asian literacy, with a priority in Japanese, bahasa Indonesia and Mandarin. Another part of this initiative included the foundation in 1990 of the Asia-Australia Institute, an independent policy think tank based at the University of New South Wales. The aim of the institute was to build on ideas for a future East Asian regional political grouping.

Not only was Australia establishing closer economic, political and cultural ties with the Asian region, but also accepting large numbers of immigrants from Asia, gradually shifting the demographic landscape in Australia. For example, the Labor government supported an immigration policy that accepted refugees and applicants from Asian countries under its family reunion, skilled labour and business programs. During this period the largest populations of Asian-born arrivals were from Vietnam, Malaysia, the Philippines, Hong Kong, India and Mainland China (Jupp 1995). By 1996, Asian migrants living in Australia exceeded one million, of whom the largest numbers were from Vietnam (169 600) and China, Hong Kong and Macao (204 700) (Jupp 2001, 74).

During this time, public opinion was not necessarily in tune with Keating's ideas of a national culture that was to be shaped by the surrounding Asian region (McAllister and Ravenhill 1998). Public opinion showed that there was some resistance to the notion of a closer engagement with Asia (McAllister and Ravenhill 1998). In fact, findings from public opinion research suggest that Keating was well ahead of his time. Furthermore, the large number of Asian migrants reactivated the appeal of new parties that formed during the 1990s: Australia First and One Nation (Jupp 2001).

In 1996, Pauline Hanson expressed the following concerns about Asian immigration in her maiden speech in Federal Parliament:

> I and most Australians want our immigration policy radically reviewed and that of multiculturalism abolished. I believe we are in danger of being swamped by Asians. Between 1984 and 1995, 40 percent of all migrants coming into this country were of Asian origin. They have their own culture and religion, form ghettos and do not assimilate. (Hanson 1996)

This view of Australia being 'swamped by Asians' was, according to Stokes, an account of the people and their vulnerabilities and a call for a return of power to the people and away from the elites (Stokes 2000, 23–4). For Hanson, a unified, stable and homogenous nation was undermined by multiculturalism (Leach 2000, 42). The view that Australia was becoming too multicultural and losing its core national identity was also supported by a number of academics and public opinion leaders. For example, historian John Hirst criticised the term 'multiculturalism' because of the way it conveyed diversity but not the unity of commitment to core values and institutions (Hirst 1996, 15). Former Ambassador to Indonesia and Japan Rawdon Dalrymple also observed that in terms of Asian social and cultural attitudes and values, 'the average Australian is less "Asian" than almost anyone on earth' (quoted in Milner 1997, 40).

Not only was public opinion resistant to Australia being part of Asia but leaders in Asia also argued that Australia could not become an integral member of Asia because of its long association with Britain and close military ties with the United States. For example, former Malaysian Prime Minister Dr Mahathir was most outspoken on Australia's position in Asia, stating that Australia should not be part of any future East Asia Economic Caucus (EAEC) grouping. As further evidence of Australia's exclusion from the region, in 1996, Australia was excluded from the Asia–Europe summit meeting including the Association of South-East Asian Nations (ASEAN) members as well as China, Korea and Japan (see Milner 1997). Non-acceptance of Australia in regional groupings was partly due to the fact that Australia had different views on human rights and democracy that were more closely aligned with the values of the United States.

It was against this backdrop of public resistance to Australian attempts to more fully integrate with Asia that John Howard was elected Prime Minister of Australia. In line with Australian popular opinion and criticisms from Asia, the Howard Government unravelled many of the Hawke and Keating Labor Government initiatives of closer political and cultural engagement with Asia. It wasn't long, however, before the Howard Government was faced with the need to confront the realities of instability in the region with the 1999 crisis in East Timor. According to Cotton (2004), East Timor functioned as a test for Australia's engagement with the Asian region.

Following the vote for independence from Indonesia in a UN-supervised referendum, the Indonesian military and militias instigated a campaign of fear, intimidation and violence aimed at those who contested Indonesian sovereignty (Cotton 2004, 5). In contrast with the previous, Labor government's policy of engagement with Indonesian elites, the Howard Government lobbied for a 'coalition of the willing' prepared to support an intervention force in East Timor. The first parts of the International Force for East Timor (INTERFET) operation landed in East Timor on 20 September 1999. While Australia had the largest group in INTERFET, there were also smaller detachments from South Korea, Thailand, New Zealand and the United Kingdom. The presence of INTERFET generated resentment in Indonesia about Australia's motives and posed a major challenge for future engagement within the region (Cotton 2004).

The terrorist attacks in New York (2001), Bali (2002) and Jakarta (2004) and the following chaos in Iraq led to a closer alignment of the government's foreign and security policies with the Bush Administration. Australia's support of a pre-emptive strike in Iraq, preoccupation with terrorism in the region and our support for the American missile defence system further distanced Australia from the Asian region (see Woolcott 2005). The collective policies towards Asia based on fear and policies towards the United States based on compliance have filtered into other aspects of Australian life. For example, Australia's close alignment with the United States and the West more generally was reflected in a shift in domestic education policies, which began to focus less on Asia and more on establishing an education curriculum firmly rooted in Western values, civic belonging and Australian history.

In 2002 the Howard Government abandoned the NALSAS program, which was largely viewed among Asian studies academics as a backward step. The loss of Asian languages in the curriculum also had an indirect affect on the teaching of Asian studies and languages in the higher education sector. Student enrolments in Asian languages and cultures declined significantly, resulting in a loss of cultural and political expertise in Asian studies. Other factors that contributed to this loss of expertise in the higher education sector included the 2002 terrorist bombings in Bali, which had an enormous impact on the numbers of students wanting to enrol in Indonesian and Malay studies. On the flipside, the rise of China as a growing presence in the region has encouraged a growth in numbers in Chinese studies (see Rudd 2009b).

In 2004, results from the Australian Election Study survey showed that more than 70 per cent of the Australian public believed that it was either 'fairly likely' or 'very likely' that Indonesia posed a threat to Australia's security (see McAllister and Clark 2008). The increased fear of Asia and in particular Indonesia reflected a broader trend of attempts to strengthen the US relationship and the importance of bilateral relationships over multilateral forums in the region; however, between 2004 and 2007, the Australian public started to become more in tune with non-traditional security issues such as the environment, world poverty and Indigenous affairs. The Iraq war was also losing domestic support in Australia and the United States due to its protracted nature and large numbers of casualties. There was an increased awareness of global environmental problems and in particular support for the ratification of the Kyoto Protocol. Domestic concerns such as WorkChoices legislation and the increased awareness of global and interconnected security problems contributed to a change in public attitudes and a change in government in 2007.

In a more conservative manner than the previous Labor governments of Hawke and Keating, the newly elected 2007 Rudd Labor Government began a mission to develop closer regional integration and cooperation with the Asian region. In 1980, Kevin Rudd graduated with a Bachelor of Arts (Asian studies) degree with First Class Honours. The title of Rudd's honours thesis was 'Human rights in China: the case of Wei Jingsheng' (see Rudd 2009a). Rudd's studies prepared him for a career as a diplomat in China and later domestic politics, shaping his outlook and support for multilateralism in the Asia-Pacific region. In 2004, Rudd said that

> Australians should…develop an appropriate form of national modesty, which enables us in our dealings with people in East Asian Societies to avoid being over the top or grossly humble. Only by doing so can we hope to undo the damage that has recently been done to perceptions of Australia in the region. (Quoted in Broinowski 2003, 13)

At the sixteenth APEC meeting in Peru (in 2008), political leaders discussed a new commitment to Asia-Pacific development, which focused on the importance of reducing the gap between developed and developing member countries. A significant part of APEC's new agenda involved working on new strategies that helped member countries tackle the current economic, food, energy and counter-terrorism security challenges affecting the region (Economic Leaders of the APEC Forum 2008). These new human security challenges, which transcend national borders, are what provide a significant motivation for closer cooperation and integration among member countries and in particular between Australia and Asia.

On 4 December 2008, Prime Minister Rudd announced new national security policies that would incorporate transnational issues affecting the Asia-Pacific region such as climate change, pandemic diseases and people smuggling (see Coorey 2008). A response to the new security challenges would involve strengthening regional security cooperation with Japan, South Korea, Singapore, Indonesia and Malaysia and strengthening diplomatic ties with India and China (Dodd 2008). While the Rudd Government was moving forward with a new vision of Australia involving closer cooperation with Asia, we knew relatively little about the Australian public and whether they felt more closely connected with Asia compared with the 1990s, when Australia witnessed a public backlash against the idea of Asia in Australia.

The next section examines the extent to which Australian political engagement with Asia has a broader influence on Australia's cultural relationship with Asia. The findings to this section may provide answers as to whether the Labor Government will achieve widespread support for closer engagement with Asia. Australia's political engagement with Asia has an important influence on Australia's level of cultural and economic engagement with the region. This is reflected in a number of different ways. First, Australia's political interests in the region are often followed through in the education system. For example, during the early 1990s, Australian interest in Japanese language and culture studies at Australian schools and universities boomed because of our closer political and economic ties with Japan. More recently, as previously mentioned, student numbers for Indonesian studies have declined because of the increased fear of terrorism in Indonesia; however, student numbers have dramatically increased for students interested in China at universities because of the rising economic and political presence of China in the region.

A second reason explaining the influence of Australia's political engagement with Asia on levels of cultural and economic engagement can be found in Australia's immigration patterns. As new groups of immigrants arrive in Australia, they bring their cultural heritage with them. Some of this cultural heritage is shared with the Australian-born population through business, entertainment and sporting opportunities. Over time, a growing proportion of the Australian-born population and migrant communities absorbs hybrid Asian–Australian cultural practices as part of their own identity and lifestyle. A third and final reason that demonstrates the influence of politics on cultural and economic engagement is the growth of business relationships. As the government encourages international trade through a number of policy instruments, this opens the way for new business opportunities and industry partnerships between Australia and Asia.

Cultural and economic engagement with Asia

Culture and economics are key dimensions of the concept of globalisation, which social scientists use to explain the links, connections and processes of engagement and interaction between societies and cultures across the world (Giddens 1990). Though a near neighbour, Asia of course has not figured prominently in Australian cultural history given the nature of Australia's cultural, ethnic and political ties with Britain and Europe; however, the transfer of ideas, people and objects between Australia and Asia as a result of globalisation and social and political change has intensified since the 1970s. Signs of Australian connections, influences and engagement with Asia are quite visible in Australian cities and in Australian homes. The increasing ease and decreased cost of travel, the increased volume of trade with Asia and the settling of Asians in Australia have brought greater familiarity of Asian cultures and possibly an increased Australian engagement compared with previous eras of Australian history.

Before turning to the data the present section introduces a broad collection of conceptual material that might typify Australian engagement with Asia, with the main focus on engagement with Asian culture, and a lesser focus on economic engagement with Asia. Australian engagement with Asia is possible on at least two fronts: the first is engagement *in* Australia with Asian cultural, economic and social phenomena, people and institutions. The second is *outside* Australia and in Asia,[1] and pertains to place, however experienced but usually through travel.

In Australia, then, Asia, through people, culture and institutions, is a visible presence. In 2007, the Australian Bureau of Statistics calculated that of the estimated resident population of Australia (21 million people), one-quarter (5.3 million people) was born overseas (ABS 2007). In 2007 just more than 41 per cent of immigrants who arrived in Australia for permanent settlement were born in South-East Asia, North-East Asia or Central Asia (ABS 2007). These changing demographic trends indicate a marked Asian presence in Australian cities and towns. Like many other migrant groups, Asian Australian communities have brought a range of cultural and economic accoutrements such as businesses, cuisine, religion and community organisations that have produced a visible geographic and architectural change to Australian urban settings.

---

1   Indeed, a third is easily considered: engagement through the Internet.

Education has also made its mark in Asian–Australian relations. An increasing number of foreign students studying at Australian universities are from Asia. Australian schools have to some extent in recent times refocused foreign language education to emphasise offerings of Asian languages in place of the traditional European language curricula in recognition of the deeper links Australia has developed with Asia. Australian cities have also hosted Asian or, more specifically, Chinese quarters such as the various 'Chinatowns' that have housed Asian food, film, art and literature through a variety of businesses and cultural organisations. Other forms of Asian cultural engagement by Australians include involvement in Asian religions, spiritualities and agents to wellbeing such as Buddhism, yoga, Tai Chi and Chinese medicine (Phillips and Aarons 2005, 2007). Australians are also quite familiar with and keen consumers of selections of Asian popular culture including film, literature and music. Manga comics and anime films from Japan have a devoted following in Australia as they do in other non-Asian countries (Sugimoto 2003). Martial arts such as karate and Tae Kwon Do are also more familiar forms of Asian cultural engagement that Australians have embraced.

Perhaps the most visible and tangible Australian engagement with Asia, however, is through food, and while some Asian cultures (for example, Nepal and Sri Lanka) have only recently enabled Australians to taste their culinary offerings, Chinese restaurants of all sorts have been a feature of Australian cities and country towns for many decades. Asian food, cuisine and restaurants of a broad variety are a key feature of the contemporary 'foodscape' of Australian cities and some larger towns.

Turning to the data, the Australian Survey of Social Attitudes 2007 carried a succinct but important set of measures tapping Australian engagement in Asian culture within a broader set of measures seeking to ascertain general Australian engagement with Asia. Respondents were asked how often they spent time with Asian friends; participated in an Asian cultural event; visited Asian restaurants; studied an Asian language or culture; engaged in Eastern spiritualities; volunteered services or finances to developing Asian countries; travelled to an Asian country; travelled with an Asian airline; and conducted business negotiations with Asia.

Table 3.1 reports that Australians are quite connected personally with Asians through personal friendship, with well more than half the sample (62 per cent) spending at least some time with friends with an Asian heritage. Travelling to Asia, travelling via an Asian airline and participation in Asian cultural festivals are activities that Australians do less frequently but are by their nature predictably infrequent activities. Notwithstanding the practical barriers to this form of engagement, about one in four Australians engages in these activities at least once a year. There is a significant minority of Australians who participate in religions and spiritualities that are widely practised in Asia with variable frequency (23 per cent). Considered against the percentage of Australians who participate regularly in the more traditional religious faiths of Australia, such as Christianity (20 per cent who frequently attend religious services; AuSSA 2007), this level of engagement is comparatively high and suggests that the Australian engagement with Asian religions and spiritualities apart from, or even in addition to, Christianity, offers Australians a meaningful form of religious and spiritual identity.

Financial and other aid is crucial to ensuring the continued economic and social progress of countries in the Asian region. Some developing Asian countries have also experienced natural disasters and other catastrophes that have devastated these societies and economies in recent years. Giving in response to these situations represents a meaningful measure of how attuned Australians are to the difficulties experienced by some of their Asian neighbours. Australians do contribute to the redevelopment and recovery of some Asian countries through financial or other aid, although not in great numbers (17 per cent) or very frequently, yet appeals for aid from the public are usually reserved for severe natural disasters that are fortunately less frequent in occurrence, such as the tsunami that wreaked havoc in many developing Asian nations in 2004.

Table 3.1 Australian Engagement with Asian Cultures, AuSSA 2007 (per cent)

	At least once a week	At least once a month	Several times a year	At least once a year	Never
Spend time with Asian friends	16.8	12.5	19.4	13.6	37.7
Visit Asian restaurants	11.1	30.3	36.1	11.4	11.0
Study an Asian language or culture	2.0	1.5	3.4	9.5	83.5
Travel to an Asian country	0.3	0.2	1.4	23.8	74.3
Travel with an Asian airline	0.2	0.0	1.4	22.1	76.3
Participate in an Asian cultural event	0.4	0.8	3.7	19.4	75.8
Engage in Eastern spiritualities	4.3	3.3	5.3	10.3	76.8
Volunteer services or finances to developing Asian countries	0.5	3.0	2.7	10.3	83.4
Conduct business negotiations in Asia	0.7	0.3	1.5	2.6	94.9

Note: Total number = 2583.

Source: Australian Survey of Social Attitudes 2007.

A significant minority of Australians have showed an interest in learning an Asian language or culture. Table 3.1 confirms this by revealing that 16 per cent of Australians have participated in learning an Asian language or studied an Asian culture. By far the most frequent means of Australian engagement with Asia is, however, through food. A minority of only 11 per cent of Australians claim to never eat at an Asian restaurant. Conversely nearly four in five Australians claim to eat at Asian restaurants at least 'several times a year'. Food is a key indicator of cultural traffic; the impact that Asian food has made on Australian culinary tastes is substantial.

The distinct ways in which Australians engaged with Asia are recorded in Table 3.2. The data in Table 3.2 suggest that Australian engagement with Asia is essentially dichotomous with a focus on participation in Asian culture combined with an association with Asian people, and engagement with the Asian economy, reflective of the two dimensions of globalisation posited earlier. The measures of Asian cultural and economic engagement formed a coherent and robust scale of indicators against which Australian engagement can be further investigated and assessed. Factor 1 in Table 3.2 indicates that Australians engaged with Asia through a set of cultural means that has become more familiar to Australians since the 1970s due to Asian immigration and cultural traffic. Table 3.2 reports that education, religious and spiritual traditions, culinary traditions, voluntary services and Asian friendships combine to reveal the contours of Australia's cultural engagement with Asia. Factor 2 in Table 3.2 indicates a more direct economic involvement with Asia involving travel and business in Asia or in-Asia experience.

Table 3.2 Factor Analysis of Australian Engagement with Asian Cultures

	Factor matrix (Varimax rotation)	
	Factor 1	**Factor 2**
Spend time with Asian friends	0.70	0.14
Participate in an Asian cultural event	0.69	0.29
Visit Asian restaurants	0.62	0.20
Study an Asian language or culture	0.62	0.34
Engage in Eastern spiritualities	0.61	−0.09
Volunteer services or finances to developing Asian countries	0.46	0.12
Travel to an Asian country	0.25	0.85
Travel with an Asian airline	0.21	0.85
Conduct business negotiations in Asia	0.05	0.59
Eigenvale	2.44	2.09
Percentage of variance	27.07	23.22
Alpha	0.68	0.72

Note: Total number = 2583.

Source: Australian Survey of Social Attitudes 2007.

Social background can have a considerable influence on the likelihood of cultural and economic engagement with Asia. The findings in Table 3.3 show a number of significant predictors of engagement with Asia both within Australia and within Asia. For example, the university educated are more likely than those without a university education to be involved in cultural engagement with Asia within Australia. The younger age groups are also more likely to be involved with Asia within Australia than older age groups. This is partly because they have had greater exposure to Asian cultures and languages throughout their education. Professionals, those who live in urban areas and those with a left political orientation are also more likely to be culturally engaged with Asia within Australia compared with non-professionals, those living in rural and regional areas and those with a political orientation leaning towards the right. Those who are born overseas, live in urban areas, earn a relatively high income and work in professional occupations are also more likely to have lived, travelled or worked in Asia compared with those born in Australia, those living in rural areas, on lower incomes and working in non-professional occupations. Interestingly, gender, age and political orientation are not associated with in-country experience in Asia.

Table 3.3 Effects of Background Experiences on Engagement with Asia (OLS estimates), AuSSA 2007

	Cultural engagement		In-country engagement	
	(b)	(beta)	(b)	(beta)
(Constant)	145.83		18.23	
Gender (male)	−0.70	−0.93	0.00	0.00
Education (university educated)	1.32	0.17***	0.19	0.07*
Location (urban)	1.32	0.16***	0.24	0.09***
Age (in single years)	0.6	0.25***	0.00	0.03
Income (over $36 400 per year)	0.28	0.04	0.36	0.14***
Occupation (professional)	0.52	0.07**	0.19	0.08*
Birthplace (Australia)	−0.99	−0.11***	−0.46	−0.16***
Political orientation (left orientation)	0.17	0.10***	0.02	0.03
Adjusted R²		0.22		0.11

* $p < 0.05$

** $p < 0.01$

*** $p < 0.001$

Note: Total number = 2583.

Source: Australian Survey of Social Attitudes 2007.

Conclusion

The results from this study suggest that Australia's political engagement with Asia is followed by closer cultural and economic ties with Asia among particular groups in Australian society. In general, the university educated, professional, young people and urban dwellers are the ones who tend to engage with Asia through both cultural practices and economic relations within Australia and throughout Asia. A key finding from our data on these points is that despite particular negative reactions to government policy concerning Asian immigration in the 1990s, today there is a significant population of Australians who are very much engaged with Asia within both Australia and Asia more broadly. Overall, the findings suggest that Australians are generally embracing of a selection of Asian culture within Australia and have personal connections with Australians of Asian ancestry, as well as economic links to Asia.

While the results can and do stand alone to be considered as a benchmark of Asian cultural engagement, of further interest here are the links between the broader or macro-level of engagement that is pursued by recent federal government policy agendas and ideologies and how they translate to the everyday lives of Australians more generally. These links, properly studied, provide a systematic framework for the analysis and evaluation of such processes and can assist in further policy design. Cultural engagement can be seen as an indicator of how open and perhaps how cosmopolitan Australians are in conditions of late modernity and globalisation, which are characterised by change through the mass movement of peoples, capital, labour and culture. Cultural engagement also stands as one important test of how the policies of multiculturalism and diversity operate at the level of individual Australians through habits associated with everyday living and the association of people normally differentiated through culture, ethnicity and experience.

In conclusion, our findings also have a number of specific policy implications for the Australian Government. First, it would seem that the promotion of Asian languages in schools may receive widespread support in urban, middle-class areas but more resistance in rural and regional areas where there is less openness towards engaging with the Asian region. Second, at the regional level, these findings show a possible glance into the future of a new generation of young people interested in closer engagement with Asia and the rest of the world more generally. This will become increasingly important given that the current Gillard Government is seeking to strengthen multilateralism throughout Asia and will need the support of a significant proportion of the nation on a range of transnational policy issues involving both Australia and Asia. A greater level of cross-cultural understanding between Australia and Asia can only be advantageous for future dialogue on important international policy issues such as the environment and the economic crisis.

References

Australian Bureau of Statistics (ABS). 2007. *Migration Australia, Permanent Arrivals*, catalogue no. 3412.0. Canberra: Australian Government Publishing Service.

Broinowski, Alison. 2003. *About Face: Asian accounts of Australia*. Melbourne: Scribe Publications.

Coorey, Phillip. 2008. 'Rudd reinforces fight against terrorism'. *Sydney Morning Herald*, 3 December, <http://www.smh.com.au/news/national/rudd-reinforces-fight-against-terrorism/2008/12/03/1228257139106.html> accessed 5 March 2009.

Cotton, James. 2004. *East Timor, Australia and Regional Order: Intervention and its aftermath in Southeast Asia*. London: Routledge Curzon.

Dodd, Mark. 2008. 'Kevin Rudd wants to redraw security priorities'. *The Australian*, 5 December.

Economic Leaders of the Asia-Pacific Economic Cooperation (APEC) Forum. 2008. *Sixteenth APEC Economic Leaders' Meeting: A new commitment to Asia-Pacific development*. Lima: Asia-Pacific Economic Cooperation. <http://www.apec.org/etc/medialib/apec_media_library/downloads/news_uploads/2008/aelm/aelm.Par.0002.File.tmp/08_aelm_LeadersStatement.pdf> accessed 13 January 2009.

Giddens, Anthony. 1990. *The Consequences of Modernity*. Cambridge: Polity Press.

Hanson, Pauline. 1996. *Pauline Hanson's Maiden Speech in Federal Parliament*. Canberra: Parliament of Australia.

Hirst, John. 1996. 'Unity in a tolerant diversity'. *The Australian*, 18 October.

Jupp, James. 1995. 'From "White Australia" to "Part of Asia": recent shifts in Australian immigration policy towards the region'. *The International Migration Review* 29(1): 207–28.

Jupp, James (ed.). 2001. *The Australian People: An encyclopaedia of the nation, its people and their origins*. Cambridge: Cambridge University Press.

Leach, Michael. 2000. 'Hansonism, political and Australian identity'. In *The Rise and Fall of One Nation*, eds Michael Leach, Geoffrey Stokes and Ian Ward. Brisbane: University of Queensland Press.

McAllister, Ian and Clark, Juliet. 2008. *Trends in Australian Political Opinion: Results from the Australian Election Study: 1987–2007*. Canberra: Australian Social Science Data Archives.

McAllister, Ian and Ravenhill, John. 1998. 'Australian attitudes towards closer engagement with Asia'. *The Pacific Review* 11(1): 198–205.

Milner, Anthony. 1997. 'The rhetoric of Asia'. In *Seeking Asian Engagement: Australia in world affairs, 1991–95*, eds James Cotton and John Ravenhill. Melbourne: Oxford University Press.

Phillips, Timothy and Aarons, Haydn. 2005. 'Choosing Buddhism in Australia: towards a traditional style of reflexive spiritual engagement'. *British Journal of Sociology* 56(2): 215–32.

Phillips, Timothy and Aarons, Haydn. 2007. 'Looking "East": an exploratory analysis of Western disenchantment'. *International Sociology* 22(3): 325–41.

Rudd, Kevin. 2009a. Human rights in China: the case of Wei Jingsheng. ANU Honours Theses Topics. Faculty of Asian Studies, The Australian National University, Canberra. <http://asianstudies.anu.edu.au/Honours> accessed 13 January 2009.

Rudd, Kevin. 2009b. 'Rudd sparks surge in Chinese studies'. *The Australian*, 9 January, <http://www.theaustralian.news.com.au/higher-education/rudd-sparks-surge-in-chinese-studies/story-e6frgcjx-1111118521962> accessed 9 January 2009.

Stokes, Geoffrey. 2000. 'One Nation and Australian populism'. In *The Rise and Fall of One Nation*, eds Michael Leach, Geoffrey Stokes and Ian Ward. Brisbane: University of Queensland Press.

Sugimoto, Yoshio. 2003. *An Introduction to Japanese Society*. Second edition. Cambridge: Cambridge University Press.

Woolcott, Richard. 2005. 'Foreign policy priorities for the Howard Government's fourth term: Australia, Asia and America in the post-11th September world'. *Australian Journal of International Affairs* 59(2): 141–52.

4. Minority Religious Identity and Religious Social Distance in Australia[1]

Gary D. Bouma

Australia's early colonial history was one of religious freedom and an absence of religious discrimination. Anglicans enjoyed a comfortable dominance due to their state church position in England, but in Australia Anglican establishment was never enacted in law. From about 1830 local officials and governments made room for other religious groups and provided them state support (Carey 1996; Fletcher 2002). From first European settlement in 1788 through to the late twentieth century, Anglicans, Presbyterians, Methodists, other Protestants, Catholics, Jews—and, later, Orthodox and some Muslims—mostly cooperated in the development of a new nation. These settlers and their families were distanced both socially and geographically from the religious powers, conflicts and prejudices of Britain and Europe. Most Australians mixed with people of other religions in school, work and leisure and religious identity was de-emphasised (Carey 1996; Levi 2006; Levi and Bergman 2002). This basic pattern has continued to the present as religious diversity in Australia has increased substantially since 1947 due primarily to migration (Bouma 2006).

To be sure, religious identity was never insignificant in Australian inter-group relations. Religious groups' differences were expressed in differences in family lifestyles, education, politics, ethics and even sporting loyalties (Bouma and Dixon 1986). Recognition of religious identity differences patterned forms of religious exclusiveness and inter-religious suspicions and sectarian rivalries (Hogan 1987). Social cohesion, though, was never threatened. Australians have developed an overriding identity in their nationalism, which has been associated with the norms of fairness for people of differing backgrounds, and general 'mateship'.

This context has been challenged since the late 1960s, when Australia began accepting significant numbers of migrants from outside Europe. Religious diversity has become broader and more complex, with significant and growing minorities of Buddhists, Muslims and Hindus. Australia also has a broader range of Christian denominations, new religious movements and 'nature' religions (Bouma 2006; Cahill et al. 2004). Indigenous religions, while small in number, are also recognised now (Bell 2009).

---

1 An earlier version of this chapter was presented to the annual meetings of the Society for the Scientific Study of Religion, Louisville, Kentucky. The author wishes to acknowledge his indebtedness to Dr Rodney Ling who provided much needed assistance in analysing the data.

Australia's social cohesion continues to allow much equality and non-discrimination. Muslims, Buddhists, Hindus and other religious groups—particularly those expanding significantly—are integrating into everyday Australian society and achieving in education, the arts, business, public service and politics (Jupp, Niewenhuysen and Dawson 2007; Markus 2008, 2009, 2010). Integration has not, however, always been smooth as certain groups, particularly Muslims, have been singled out in public as 'others' whose difference is too great or as a religious group to be feared (Bouma et al. 2011; Deen 2009). While in the mid-1990s concern was expressed about coping with Asian migration, following the events of 11 September 2001, Muslims have been the focus of concern (Bouma et al. 2006). In recent years there have been notable incidents of religious-based tension, exclusion and, in some reported cases, violence (HREOC 2004). It is timely to consider how particular religious groups are regarded among Australians, and the implications for Australia's social cohesion.

Using data from the Australian Survey of Social Attitudes (AuSSA), a large biannual public survey, this chapter examines differences in attitudes among Australia's largest and most consolidated religious groups—Catholics, Anglicans, Uniting, Presbyterians—towards a set of minority religious groups: Greek Orthodox, Buddhists, Born Again Christians, Hindus, Jews, Jehovah's Witnesses and Muslims. The degree of welcome or feelings of distance towards particular minority religious groups is interesting in itself; however, since some challenges to religious inter-group relations have historically been generated by religious differences (Appleby 2000) and appear to be today as well in Australia (Bouma et al. 2011), the sentiments of several religious groups towards other religious groups are compared.

Those declaring that they had 'no religion' have been excluded from the analysis as the group lacks sufficient internal defining consistency beyond this denial. Moreover, its range of attitudes towards religious groups was understandably negative towards both major and minority groups. They were over-represented among those least welcoming to the majority groups, in the mid-range among those not welcoming Muslims, Hindus and Jews, and least welcoming of the 'born again'.

The data

The data were taken from a 'module' or stage of the 2007 AuSSA. Total respondents for the module numbered 2769. Respondents were randomly selected from the electoral roll and the survey was administered by mail. This particular module included a set of Bogardus social distance scales (Bogardus 1925, 1933, 1947), measuring respondents' preferred degrees of social distance from people from a range of religious groups. The Bogardus social distance scales continue to be used in studies of inter-group relations (Dietrich et al. 2004; Parrillo and Donoghue 2005).

This chapter will use a sub-sample from the 2007 survey—those respondents who identified with one of Australia's major religious groups: Anglican, Catholic, Uniting Church and Presbyterian. Other religious groups lacked sufficient numbers for meaningful statistical analysis and were not able to be grouped into meaningful subgroups. This sub-sample totalled 1500, with Catholics the largest group at 657 or 43.8 per cent, Anglicans at 556 or 37.1 per cent, Uniting 204 or 13.6 per cent and Presbyterian and Reformed at 83 or 6.5 per cent. On most characteristics the distribution of the sub-sample closely mirrors the 2006 Australian Census percentage portions, when persons aged under eighteen are omitted.

Social distance scale responses: Description and basic results

Respondents were asked to specify the level of social distance they would prefer to members of the following religious groups: Anglican, Born Again Christian, Buddhist, Catholic, Greek Orthodox, Hindu, Jehovah's Witness, Jew and Muslim. Responses to Anglicans and Catholics were omitted from analysis as these groups are not minority groups and enjoyed very high levels of acceptability in comparison with the minority religious groups.

The following Bogardus social distance scale (BSDS) responses were offered for each group: 'How close are you prepared to be with Muslims, etc?'

1. family member
2. close friend
3. next-door neighbour
4. workmate
5. fellow Australian citizen
6. foreign visitor only
7. should keep out of Australia altogether
8. don't know.

Bogardus (1947) argued on the basis of extensive research using more than 60 scale items that these items represented equidistant points on the social distance scale.

Reliability

As stated above, this analysis uses data from BSDS responses relating to Greek Orthodox, Buddhists, Born Again Christians, Hindus, Jews, Jehovah's Witnesses and Muslims. Since analysis of the responses to the BSDS will include comparisons of the BSDS responses with each of the religious groups, a calculation of scale reliability is appropriate. Cronbach's alpha provides an assessment of the internal consistency of a scale through an average correlation of the items in a survey comprising the scale. Cronbach's alpha across all the above BSDSs, for respondents who answered all BSDSs (n = 1297), was 0.950, which would be lowered by the deletion of any item.

Analysis

As stated above, the respondents are those from the 'most established' religious institutions in Australia: Anglican Church, Catholic Church, Uniting Church and Presbyterian Church. These groups also are sufficiently numerous to generate meaningfully and useably large samples for statistical analysis. Analysis will examine each of these groups' responses to BSDSs for a set of 'religious minorities': Greek Orthodox, Buddhists, Born Again Christians, Jews, Hindus, Jehovah's Witnesses and Muslims.

In Australian society today, these 'religious minorities' carry varied qualities of social meaning. Hindus, Buddhists and Muslims have grown very significantly since the 1960s and 1970s and would generally be labelled as 'significant' minority religious communities. Their growth reflects major cultural changes in Australia away from the old hegemony of Catholicism and British Protestantism. This is reflected in the fact that as of 2006 there were more Buddhists than Baptists, more Muslims than Lutherans and twice as many Hindus as Jews in Australia (Bouma 2006). Jews have been publicly practising in Australia since early European settlement, and until the 1960s and 1970s were the country's only significant and socially accepted 'religious minority' (Levi 2006). In the religiously diverse society of the present though, Jews represent an established 'old minority' in contrast with the growing 'new minorities' of Hindus, Buddhists and Muslims.

4. Minority Religious Identity and Religious Social Distance in Australia

Table 4.1 Social Distance Preferences for Selected Religious Groups: Anglicans, Catholics, United, Presbyterians

	Greek Orthodox		Buddhist		Born Again Christian		Jew		Hindu		Muslim		Jehovah's Witness	
SDS responses for:	N	%	N	%	N	%	N	%	N	%	N	%	N	%
1. Welcome as family member	415	31.0	348	26.1	344	25.8	329	24.5	296	22.2	236	17.5	192	14.4
2. Welcome as close friend	354	26.4	308	23.1	259	19.5	324	24.1	301	22.5	227	16.8	199	14.9
3. Have as next-door neighbour	214	16.0	201	15.1	212	15.9	209	15.6	196	14.7	151	11.2	199	14.9
4. Welcome as workmates	56	4.2	60	4.5	90	6.8	73	5.4	79	5.9	66	4.9	122	9.1
5. Allow as Australian citizen	124	9.3	159	11.9	123	9.2	154	11.5	155	11.6	97	7.2	175	13.1
6. Have as visitor only	21	1.6	53	4.0	77	5.8	54	4.0	74	5.5	104	7.7	130	9.7
7. Keep out of Australia altogether	10	0.7	30	2.3	36	2.7	33	2.5	29	2.2	266	19.7	103	7.7
Don't know	146	10.9	173	13.0	190	14.3	167	12.4	206	15.4	201	14.9	216	16.2
Total	1340	100.0	1332	100.0	1331	100.0	1343	100.0	1336	100.0	1348	100.0	1336	100.0
Missing	160		168		169		157		164		152		164	
Total	**1500**		**1500**		**1500**		**1500**		**1500**		**1500**		**1500**	

Source: Australian Survey of Social Attitudes 2007.

The term 'Born Again Christians' does not apply to a specific denomination. Rather, it refers to Christians with vigorous re-found faith. Born Again Christians may identify with any Protestant denomination, but they are probably associated most with evangelical and growing Pentecostal groups outside the main denominations (Hutchinson 2009; Piggin 2009). In Australia, Jehovah's Witnesses are a small but viable Christian denomination, considered 'marginal' due to special beliefs and practices that offend Australian norms on respect for personal space, religious belief and military service (Jupp 2009a, 342–5). In contrast with Jews, Jehovah's Witnesses have not come to be viewed as an established or accepted religious minority.

Table 4.1 presents the absolute responses for each religious group. The Greek Orthodox attracts the greatest percentage BSDS scores in the category of closest social distance, 'Welcome as a family member'. This is not surprising as Greek Orthodox churches have operated in Australia for about a century and Greeks are a significant and integrated ethnic group, highly associated with post–World War II migration (Jupp 2001; Tamis 2009). When response categories one ('Welcome as a family member') and two ('Welcome as close personal friend')—the categories of closest social distance—are combined, 57.4 per cent of the respondents 'welcomed' Greek Orthodox in this way.

For response category one, scores were close on scales for Buddhists, Born Again Christians, Jews and Hindus respectively at 26.1 per cent, 25.8 per cent, 24.5 per cent and 22.2 per cent. Also, each of these religious groups had more than 40 per cent of BSDS responses in categories one and two. Given the closeness of scores on BSDS responses for these groups, they will be considered as together occupying the second-highest level of social closeness. Combined percentages for the two most distant response categories—'Have as visitors only' and 'Keep out of Australia'—were also similar across the BSDS responses for these groups: Buddhists, 6.3 per cent; Born Again Christians, 8.5 per cent; Jews, 6.5 per cent; and Hindus, 7.7 per cent.

Respondents wanted greatest social distance from Muslims and Jehovah's Witnesses. These groups had the lowest percentage BSDS category one responses at 17.5 and 14.4 per cent, respectively. Combined, scores in categories one and two were 34.4 per cent for Muslims and 29.3 per cent for Jehovah's Witnesses. Moreover, almost one-fifth or 19.7 per cent of respondents considered that Muslims should 'keep out of Australia altogether', compared with the comparatively high but lower 7.7 per cent for Jehovah's Witnesses. Muslims may be identified by significant numbers of respondents primarily as undesirable migrants while Jehovah's Witnesses are seen as Australians with an undesirable religion.

According to the BSDS responses to the questions, the religious groups fell into three levels of social acceptance from most accepted to least. Australians who identified as Anglican, Catholic, Uniting or Presbyterian found: 1) Greek Orthodox most acceptable; 2) Buddhists, Born Again Christians, Jews and Jehovah's Witnesses in the next level of acceptance; and 3) Jehovah's Witnesses and Muslims least acceptable.

Assessing religious differences in religious social distance

In order to compare the responses of respondents from different religious groups BSDS scores were calculated for each religious group using the ordinal codes of response categories (see Table 4.2). This follows the usual practice for the analysis of BSDS data (see Bogardus 1947; Thyne and Lawson 2001). For this analysis, respondents who chose the category '8–Don't Know' are omitted. This response category lies outside the incremental plane of social distance described by the other response values. Inclusion of respondents who chose '8–Don't know' would inflate mean values without a clear meaning to the shift, which could be mistakenly interpreted as preference for a greater level of social distance. Unfortunately this lowered the valid response rate across scales. Chronbach's alpha still showed high reliability at 0.935, which would have been lowered with the exclusion of any BSDS item.

Table 4.2 Anglicans, Catholics, United, Presbyterians: Mean social distances for religious groups

	Scale: 1 (closest) to 7 (most distant)				
				95 % confidence interval	
SDS from:	Valid n	Sample mean	Std error of mean	Lower	Upper
Greek Orthodox	1194	2.35	0.041	2.27	2.43
Buddhists	1159	2.70	0.049	2.60	2.80
Jews	1176	2.74	0.049	2.64	2.83
Born Again Christians	1141	2.79	0.051	2.69	2.89
Hindus	1130	2.85	0.051	2.75	2.95
Jehovah's Witnesses	1120	3.62	0.058	3.50	3.73
Muslims	1147	3.82	0.068	3.68	3.95

Source: Australian Survey of Social Attitudes 2007.

Table 4.2 presents the mean BSDS response to each of the 'target groups' for this sample of those who identified as Catholic, Anglican or Presbyterian/Reformed. The numbers in the column 'Valid n' can be verified by subtracting the 'Don't know' responses for each scale in Table 4.2. This descriptive analysis is sensibly consistent with Table 4.1. The higher the mean BSDS score, the greater is the level of social distance preferred, or the lower is the degree of acceptance. There are basically three levels for which the sample preferred progressively greater social distance: 1) Greek Orthodox—least; 2) Buddhists, Jews, Born Again Christians, Hindus—moderate; 3) Jehovah's Witnesses and Muslims—most. The 95 per cent confidence intervals for the SDSs with the lowest and second-lowest means, Greek Orthodox and Buddhists, do not intersect, indicating that there is a clear difference between the mean BSDS responses for these groups, with the Greek Orthodox being lower—that is, more acceptable. The confidence intervals of scores for Buddhists, Jews, Hindus and Born Again Christians, however, intersect and thus these groups can be classified as a range of religions with the second-lowest set of means, or a group which received the second level of acceptance receiving the second-closest set of social distance preferences. Jehovah's Witnesses and Muslims have means with confidence intervals that are clearly higher as their confidence intervals do not overlap with those groups with lower scores and are hence the least accepted of the groups considered.

The analysis is guided by a single research question: to what extent do major religious groups in Australia—Anglican, Catholic, Uniting and Presbyterian/Reformed—differ in their social distance preferences for Greek Orthodox, Buddhists, Born Again Christians, Hindus, Jehovah's Witnesses and Muslims. To assess whether associations exist between religious identification and the BSDS responses for each of the religious groups considered, two basic statistical tests were used. First, independent sample t-tests were administered to compare mean scores of categories for independent variables with only two response categories. Second, one-way ANOVA tests were applied where independent variables had three or more categories. The post-hoc test used with the ANOVA was the Scheffe test, chosen because it is appropriate for unequal sample sizes (Jones 2008). The Scheffe test indicates whether there are significant differences between the means of response categories of the independent variable, using a formula similar to an F-test.

Table 4.3 Catholics, Anglicans, Uniting and Presbyterians: One-way ANOVA—respondents' religions by social distance from select religions

	Mean scores: 1 (closest) to 7 (most distant)							
	Respondent religious groups							
	1	2	3	4				
SDS	Catholic	Anglican	Uniting Church	Presbyterian	Total	F	Sig.	Scheffe sig. diffs
Greek Orthodox	2.16	2.52	2.44	2.54	2.35	5.907	**	2 > 1
Buddhists	2.48	2.88	2.88	2.86	2.70	5.409	**	2 > 1
Jews	2.58	2.87	2.89	2.77	2.74	2.973	*	None
Born Again Christians	2.75	2.86	2.76	2.81	2.79	0.333		None
Hindus	2.64	2.98	3.10	3.05	2.85	4.649	*	(2 > 1) and (3 > 1)
Jehovah's Witnesses	3.41	3.78	3.76	3.83	3.62	3.384	*	2 > 1
Muslims	3.47	4.12	4.05	4.01	3.82	6.990	**	2 > 1

Source: Australian Survey of Social Attitudes 2007.

Religious identity and religious social distance

The one-way ANOVA analysis presented in Table 4.3 reveals that differences in respondents' religious identity across BSDS responses were statistically significant with the exception of responses to Born Again Christians. Scheffe tests revealed the following patterns: 1) except for the BSDS responses to Jews and Born Again Christians, the means of Catholic respondents are significantly lower (more accepting) than those from Anglicans; 2) Uniting Church respondents' mean BSDS responses for Hindus were significantly higher (less accepting) than Catholics.[2] The greatest difference was the statistically significant higher BSDS response from Anglicans in comparison with the more accepting Catholics. From this result the conclusion is drawn with substantial confidence that Catholics are more tolerant of inter-religious difference than Anglicans.

Discussion

This analysis of religious social distance preferences used nationally representative data provided by respondents from Australia's largest and most consolidated religious identities: Anglicans, Catholics, Uniting and Presbyterians. Responses to Bogardus social distance scales indicated that people who identify with these religious groups were prepared to be socially closest to Greek Orthodox; second-closest to Buddhists, Jews, Born Again Christians and Hindus; and that they preferred to be most distant from Jehovah's Witnesses and Muslims.

Respondents were most likely to prefer greater social distance from Jehovah's Witnesses and Muslims. As a larger percentage of respondents wanted Muslims to 'keep out of the country altogether', the negative response to Muslims is possibly a reaction to both their religion and the fact that they are a migrant group. This, however, is equally true of Buddhists and even more so of Hindus, both of whom are religiously different and most of whom are migrants. Thus, it would appear that the significantly greater negative reaction is to Muslims as a religious group rather than as a migrant group. This is made all the more likely by the fact that there are groups in Australia who actively campaign to limit, reduce or eliminate Muslim migration (Bouma et al. 2011 70–2, 81).

---

2   Post-hoc tests, including the Scheffe, have anomalies. For example, when comparing the mean responses to the Greek Orthodox, the mean social distance scale response of those identifying with the Uniting Church is not significantly different from Anglican or Catholic, but the mean social distance scale response of Anglicans is significantly greater than that for Catholic respondents. The anomalies can be understood as a consequence of comparing categories with populations of significantly different sizes. Categories with lower populations have larger standard errors of the mean, and so the 95 per cent confidence intervals of their means are likely to be wider, and have greater chance of overlapping with other categories. The standard errors of the means of larger population give narrower 95 per cent confidence intervals, increasing the chance that when compared with other categories, they will be different.

Comparisons with earlier attempts to assess religious social distance in Australia indicate a softening of negative attitudes towards Muslims over the past two decades. In a 1988 national survey conducted by the Office of Multicultural Affairs (OMA 1989) 32 per cent of Australians responded 'Visitor only' or 'Keep out' to Muslims compared with 24 per cent in this sample taken in 2007. This softening is also seen for responses to other groups. In 1988, 26 per cent responded in these two most negative response categories to Buddhists, while in this 2007 survey it was 5.4 per cent. Similarly, in 1988, 12 per cent responded in this way to Jews compared with 6.2 per cent in 2007.

Thus, in a context of increasing acceptance of religious diversity and seen by the greater acceptance of particular religious groups into Australian society and into the domestic lives of Australians, Muslims have progressed towards full acceptance more slowly than Buddhists and Jews. An outstanding finding from this analysis is that Anglicans are the most negative towards other religious groups in comparison with Catholics in five out of seven cases. This result has subsequently been confirmed in the social cohesion research conducted by Markus (2011). Catholics who have a well-articulated official policy of inter-religious respect were found to be the most accepting while the Uniting and Presbyterians were closer to Anglicans. Uniting respondents were the most negative in their responses to Hindus.

Religious identity is clearly a factor in Australian life. Australians are more accepting of some groups than of others, while overall levels of acceptance of religious diversity are increasing, negative attitudes towards Muslims are expressed by nearly one-quarter of Australians. Religious identity is also a predictor variable shaping who is more likely to be accepting and who is not. Catholics were shown to be more accepting than Presbyterians and Uniting, but Anglicans the least welcoming of all.

References

Appleby, R. Scott. 2000. *The Ambivalence of the Sacred: Religion, violence and reconciliation*. New York: Rowman & Littlefield.

Bell, Diane. 2009. 'Aboriginal and Torres Strait Islander religions'. In *The Encyclopedia of Religion in Australia*, ed. James Jupp. Melbourne: Cambridge University Press.

Bogardus, Emory. 1925. 'Social distance and its origins'. *Journal of Applied Sociology* 9: 216–26, <http://www.brocku.ca/MeadProject/Bogardus/Bogardus_1925b.html> accessed 20 September 2008.

Bogardus, Emory. 1933. 'A social distance scale'. *Sociology & Social Research* 17: 265–71.

Bogardus, E. S. 1947. "Measurement of Personal-Group Relations," *Sociometry*, 10: 4: 306–311

Bouma, Gary. 2006. *Australian Soul: Religion and spirituality in the 21st century*. Cambridge: Cambridge University Press.

Bouma, Gary and Dixon, Beverly. 1986. *The Religious Factor in Australian Life*. Melbourne: MARC.

Bouma, Gary, Cahill, Desmond, Delall, Hass and Zwartz, Athalia. 2011. *Freedom of Religion and Belief in 21st Century Australia*. Sydney: Human Rights and Equal Opportunity Commission.

Bouma, Gary, Pickering, Sharon, Dellal, Hass and Halafoff, Anna. 2006. *Managing the Impact of Global Crisis Events on Community Relations in Multicultural Australia: Models and processes*. Report to Multicultural Affairs Queensland and Victorian Office of Multicultural Affairs. <http://mp3.news.com.au/bcm/Multicultural/MAQ_Global_Crisis_bkgrnd_report.pdf>

Cahill, Desmond, Bouma, Gary, Dellal, Hass and Leahey, Michael. 2004. *Religion, Cultural Diversity and Safeguarding Australia*. Canberra: Department of Immigration and Multicultural and Indigenous Affairs.

Carey, Hilary. 1996. *Believing in Australia*. Sydney: Allen & Unwin.

Cimino, Richard. 2005. '"No God in common": American evangelical discourse on Islam after 9/11'. *Review of Religious Research* 47: 162–74.

Deen, Hanifa. 2009. *The Jihad Seminar: A true story of religious vilification and the law*. Perth: University of Western Australia Press.

Dietrich, Sandra, Beck, Michael, Bujantugs, Bujana, Kenzine, Dennis, Matschinger, Herbert and Angermeyer, Matthias. 2004. 'The relationship between public causal beliefs and social distance toward mentally ill people'. *Australian and New Zealand Journal of Psychiatry* 38: 348–54.

Fletcher, Brian. 2002. 'The Anglican ascendancy: 1788–1835'. In *Anglicanism in Australia: A history*, ed. B. Kaye. Melbourne: Melbourne University Press.

Hogan, Michael. 1987. *The Sectarian Strand: Religion in Australian History*. Ringwood VIC: Penguin.

Human Rights and Equal Opportunity Commission (HREOC). 2004. *Ismaū—listen: national consultations on eliminating prejudice against Arab and Muslim Australians*. Report. Sydney: Human Rights and Equal Opportunity Commission.

Hutchinson, Mark. 2009. 'Pentecostals'. In *The Encyclopedia of Religion in Australia*, ed. James Jupp. Melbourne: Cambridge University Press.

Jones, James. 2008. *Scheffe and Tukey Tests*. <http://people.richland.edu/james/lecture/m113/post_anova>, accessed 26 September 2008.

Jupp, James (ed.). 2001. *The Australian People*. Second edition. Melbourne: Cambridge University Press.

Jupp, James. 2009a. 'Jehovah's Witnesses'. In *The Encyclopedia of Religion in Australia*, ed. James Jupp. Melbourne: Cambridge University Press.

Jupp, James (ed.). 2009b. *The Encyclopedia of Religion in Australia*. Melbourne: Cambridge University Press.

Jupp, James, Nieuwenhuysen, John and Dawson, Emma (eds). 2007. *Social Cohesion in Australia*. Melbourne: Cambridge University Press.

Levi, John. 2006. *These are the Names: Jewish lives in Australia 1788–1850*. Melbourne: Miegunyah.

Levi, John and Bergman, George. 2002. *Australian Genesis: Jewish convicts and settlers 1788–1860*. Melbourne: Melbourne University Press.

Markus, Andrew. 2008, 2009, 2010, 2011. *Mapping Social Cohesion—The Scanlon Foundation surveys—Summary report*. Melbourne: Monash Institute for the Study of Global Movements.

Office of Multicultural Affairs (OMA). 1989. *Issues in Multicultural Australia*. Canberra: Office of Multicultural Affairs.

Parrillo, Vincent and Donoghue, Christopher. 2005. 'Updating the Bogardus social distance studies: a new national survey'. *The Social Science Journal* 42: 257–71.

Piggin, Stuart. 2009. 'Evangelical Christianity in Australia'. In *The Encyclopedia of Religion in Australia*, ed. James Jupp. Melbourne: Cambridge University Press.

SPSS Help. 2008. *GLM Post Hoc Comparisons*.

Tamis, Anastasios. 2009. 'Greek Orthodoxy in Australia'. In *The Encyclopedia of Religion in Australia*, ed. James Jupp. Melbourne: Cambridge University Press.

Thyne, Maree and Lawson, Rob. 2001. 'The design of a social distance scale to be used in the context of tourism'. *Asia Pacific Advances in Consumer Research* 4: 102–7.

5. Are Neighbourhood Incivilities Associated with Fear of Crime?

Lynne D. Roberts and David Indermaur

Beyond the direct harm that crime has on individuals and their communities, crime also has destructive effects indirectly through fear of crime. Whether or not such fear is based on a realistic assessment of the likelihood of crime victimisation, it can have debilitating effects on an individual's physical and mental wellbeing and social functioning. Based on a longitudinal study of persons aged fifty to seventy-five, Stafford, Chandola and Marmot (2007) reported that fear of crime was associated with reduced quality of life, higher rates of depression and poorer mental health. In addition, fear of crime was associated with reduced physical functioning. The authors hypothesised that the poorer mental and physical health outcomes are the result of the curtailment of physical and social activities resulting from the fear of crime. While attempts to estimate the economic and social costs of fear of crime have been limited by the difficulty of measuring intangible costs, Dolan and Peasgood (2007) highlight the need to consider the tangible costs of fear of crime (for example, costs resulting from changed behaviour to reduce the perceived risk of victimisation such as the cost of taking taxis rather than public transport) and associated health costs (in the United Kingdom estimated at £19.5 per year per person).

In addition to the effect on individuals, communities can also be affected where fear of crime is high. Skogan (1986) detailed how fear of crime in 'disintegrating' neighbourhoods can result in residents physically withdrawing from community life and focusing their concerns (and by extension their informal control through surveillance) within the household. This weakening of social organisation and informal social control within the community can provide the opportunity for increased delinquency and disorder, further contributing to physical and social incivilities and neighbourhood decline. This sequential interaction of community disorganisation and incivilities has been the subject of much criminological investigation dating back at least to the seminal work of Skogan and Maxfield (1981) and popularised through the 'broken windows' thesis of Wilson and Kelling (1982). Work in this area continues, including within Australia with key studies including the major National Campaign Against Violence and Crime fear-of-crime research project (Tulloch et al. 1998a, 1998b) and, more recently, McCrea et al.'s (2005) exploration of the relative contribution of the social disorganisation and incivilities of fear of crime within Brisbane.

Although the corrosive effects of fear of crime have been well documented and are widely accepted, the picture is not as simple as it is often depicted. Recent research has confirmed the doubts some criminologists have had for some time in regard to the construct of fear of crime, questioning the validity of the survey measures frequently used to measure fear of crime (Ditton and Farrall 2007). Further, trying to disentangle the effects of fear from other highly related and co-occurring social dynamics is complex. In this chapter we attempt to tease apart some of these dynamics and look at how fear of crime fits into the social life of Australians drawing on the results of the Australian Survey of Social Attitudes (AuSSA) 2007.[1]

Fear of crime

There are a number of factors that may contribute to fear of crime. Some research has focused on differences in levels of fear of crime by demographic groupings. The consistent finding in the literature that those who are least likely to be victimised (women and the elderly) experience the greatest fear of crime (see, for example, Brunton-Smith and Sturgis 2011; Ziersch et al. 2007) has been described as 'a central paradox' (Smith and Torstensson 1997, 608) of fear-of-crime research. Punitive attitudes among the elderly and women point to greater personal and social vulnerability experienced by these groups. Fear of crime is also reflected in greater levels of routine precautions taken by the elderly to protect themselves (Pinkerton James 1992). There may also be interactions between gender and age. One study reported that with increasing age, women increased in their likelihood of feeling safe in the home, but decreased in their likelihood of feeling safe in the neighbourhood (Quine and Morrell 2008b).

Location has also been explored as a source of variation in fear of crime. Quine and Morrell (2008a, 2008b) analysed data from a population survey of older adults (aged sixty-five or older) in New South Wales. The majority of both older men (68.5 per cent) and women (62.6 per cent) reported feeling safe in their home all the time, with a smaller proportion reporting feeling safe in their neighbourhood all the time (men 60.3 per cent, women 52.1 per cent). Older adults in non-metropolitan areas reported feeling safer in their neighbourhood than those living in metropolitan areas, but conversely felt less safe in their homes (Quine and Morrell 2008b). Specifically, older adults living in small rural communities were the most likely to report that they felt safe in their community all of the time (Quine and Morrell 2008a).

---

1 The Australian Institute of Criminology commissioned a range of crime and justice items for inclusion in AuSSA 2007. The analyses reported in this chapter are based on fear-of-crime and incivilities measures that formed part of the range of items commissioned. Please see Roberts and Indermaur (2009) for further details.

Previous criminal victimisation may also affect fear of crime, although data from the British Crime Survey suggest that it is only in areas of high physical and social disorder that previous victims experience higher rates of fear of crime (Box, Hale and Andrews 1988).

Research has also focused on whether fear of crime simply reflects actual crime rates (the 'instrumental hypothesis'). At an aggregate level, people within a neighbourhood largely agree on the degree of disorder within their neighbourhood (McCord et al. 2007), although there is considerable individual variation. Research from the United Kingdom and Canada suggests that somewhere between 8 and 12 per cent of the variance in fear of crime can be directly attributed to differences in neighbourhood context (Brunton-Smith and Sturgis 2011; Fitzgerald 2008). Taken together, these findings suggest that actual crime rates have a relatively modest effect on fear of crime.

Probably the biggest issue to affect the fear-of-crime research is the successful challenge of the underlying concept by a group of British researchers (for example, Ditton and Farrall 2007). What these researchers found was that much of the earlier research was likely to be flawed as it relied on an inadequate methodology of directly asking people about their *level* of fear of crime. Surveys using this methodology typically result in high levels of fear being reported; however, when respondents are asked *how often* they felt afraid or what they did as a result of their fear it appeared the 'fear' had only relatively marginal or negligible effects. It now appears likely that earlier methodologies typically employed to measure fear of crime could have produced elevated and artificial readings of the true extent of fear of crime in the population. Briefly, this occurs because when posing simple questions about fear of crime (Are you afraid? How much are you afraid?), there is a strong acquiescence effect: people are likely to respond positively to the suggestion contained in the question that they are, or should be or could be, afraid of crime. This is perhaps not surprising as 'fear' is an appropriate affective response or partner to the concept of 'crime'.

Thus it appears that the alarm over 'fear of crime' appears to have been, at least to some degree, an artefact of the measurement instruments. Although this is likely to be true it remains that the indirect effects of crime—concern about crime, fear of crime and anger about crime—are potent realities in the community and do affect important life choices made by individuals. There is, however, also sufficient doubt about the root causes of this fear, in particular the belief that fear is a simple reflection of overall crime rates (the instrumental hypothesis outlined earlier). There may even be doubt that fear is the result of intermediary variables such as the presence of threatening behaviours such as incivilities. For example, Tyler and Boeckmann (1997) found in their investigation of the deeper causes of punitive-ness that punitive-ness is better explained and understood as the outcome of an experience—a loss of social power and an expression of anger about crime. Support for measures such as the 'three strikes and you are out' sentencing legislation introduced in California in 1994 thus is seen as 'expressive' of social power needs rather than a rational response to perceived threats from crime. In this view, looking for a connection between incivilities and fear of crime is useful as incivilities also reflect a loss of certainty or order in the world and should be related to fear of crime, independent of actual crime rates.

Incivilities

In a nutshell, the incivilities thesis is that 'uncivil' (antisocial, careless and disrespectful) behaviour in the community will directly contribute to the experience of fear of crime. This thesis posits that physical and social disorder in the community, rather than crime itself, lead to increased fear of crime through an emotional response to a loss of social order or certainty (LaGrange, Ferraro and Supancic 1992; Perkins and Taylor 1996; Robinson et al. 2003; Taylor 1999). 'Incivilities' is a term used to describe a range of aspects of the physical environment (such as graffiti, litter, abandoned vehicles) as well as public order problems (such as drug sale and use, violence and drunkenness). Visible signs of neighbourhood disorder are predictive of fear of crime (Brunton-Smith and Sturgis 2011). It should be noted, however, that there are varying conceptions of the incivilities thesis (see Taylor 1999 for a description of five variations of the incivilities thesis). In tracing the development of the incivilities thesis since its inception, Taylor (1999) notes that over time the focus has shifted from the impact of incivilities on the individual to an increased emphasis on ecological processes (for example, Perkins and Taylor 1996) and community change. In this chapter we return the focus to the individual, examining perceptions of incivilities in Australian survey respondents' local area and their relationship to worry about being the victim of a range of crimes.

Previous research has supported the proposed relationship between perceptions of incivilities and fear of crime. Perceptions of incivilities significantly predict fear of crime (Borooah and Carcach 1997; Carcach et al. 1995; Kanan and Pruitt 2002; McCrea et al. 2005; Wyant 2008), perceived risk of victimisation (Kanan and Pruitt 2002; LaGrange, Ferraro and Supancic 1992) and decreased sense of safety (Kanan and Pruitt 2002). Feelings of personal safety are positively associated with perceptions of the neighbourhood as clean and quiet (Ziersch et al. 2007).

There may be significant differences in the proportion of people who feel unsafe in their neighbourhoods according to their perception of incivilities. For example, Fitzgerald (2008) examined fear of crime in Canada based on the results of the Canadian 2004 General Social Survey. Approximately one-third (33.8 per cent) of Canadians surveyed who viewed physical disorder as a problem in their neighbourhood felt somewhat or very unsafe from crime in their neighbourhoods compared with only one in seven (14.8 per cent) of those who did not view physical disorder as a problem. Similar results were obtained for perceptions of social disorder as a problem (23.2 per cent versus 13.1 per cent). The effect was even larger if we consider individuals' perceptions of crime in their own neighbourhood compared with other neighbourhoods. Where individuals perceived that their own neighbourhoods had a higher crime rate than other neighbourhoods, almost half (42.2 per cent) of residents experienced fear of crime; however, where respondents believed that their neighbourhood was safer than other neighbourhoods only 15 per cent experienced the same level of fear. Naturally, perceptions of safety and experiences of fear are closely related concepts and it is important not to assume that residents' perceptions are an accurate reflection of the actual level of safety.

Kanan and Pruitt (2002) suggested that perceptions of incivilities reflect social vulnerability and perceived lack of control. Similarly, Jackson (2005) found that perceptions of incivilities affect perceptions of community cohesion, perceived likelihood of crime and the frequency of worry about crime, suggesting the inability of the individual to manage the risk of criminal victimisation and its consequences is one of the reasons individuals worry. Based on qualitative research in neighbourhoods in Adelaide, Palmer et al. (2005) noted how in stigmatised neighbourhoods with high rates of incivilities, fear of crime may restrict social interaction and trust. This relationship may be 'self-reinforcing': perceptions of increasing incivilities increase fear of crime, which in turn reduces social interaction and organisation and further increases incivilities.

Gender may interact with perceived incivilities in influencing fear of crime. As noted earlier, on average, women experience higher levels of fear of crime than men. Females who perceive high incivility in their neighbourhood are almost twice as likely as other females to experience fear of crime. For males, the relationship is even stronger, with males who perceive high rates of incivility in their neighbourhood almost three times as likely to experience fear of crime. That is, while females experience higher overall levels of fear of crime, males' fear of crime is more strongly influenced by perceived incivilities (Carcach et al. 1995).

While there is ample evidence of an association between measures of fear of crime and measures of perceptions of incivilities, it is quite possible, perhaps even likely, that both of these phenomena are the manifestation of sensitivity, concern about crime and/or deeper social factors such as those discussed by Tyler and Boeckmann (1997), including feelings of a loss of social power.

Measures

Data for this analysis are drawn from the AuSSA 2007. The two main measures used in this analysis are a measure of incivilities and a measure of fear of crime.

Incivilities

Incivilities were measured using a five-item scale that asked: *'How would you rate the following problems in your local area?'* The content areas were rubbish and litter; graffiti on footpaths and walls; unsupervised groups of young people; people drunk; and people dealing illicit drugs. Each item was measured on a four-point response scale ranging from 'Not a problem at all' to 'A very big problem'. Factor analysis was used to examine the underlying structure of the five incivilities items. These five items form a uni-dimensional scale with good internal reliability (Cronbach's alpha = 0.84). Responses from each item were combined to provide a scale score. Data were recoded so that higher scores on the scale reflected greater problems. Possible scale scores ranged from 5 (the five types of incivilities not a problem at all) to 20 (all five types of incivilities a very big problem).

Fear of crime

While 'fear of crime' is a term in common public use, it has been conceptualised in a number of ways in the research literature: concern about crime; perceived risk of victimisation; perceived threat; and behavioural responses to fear (Skogan 1999). In this survey, fear of crime was measured using a seven-item scale that asked" 'How worried are you that the following will occur to you?' The content areas were: being physically attacked at home; being physically attacked on the street or other public space; being sexually assaulted; having your home/place of residence broken into; having your identity stolen via the Internet; having your credit card stolen; and having your credit card details used illegally via the Internet. Each item was measured on a four-point response scale ranging from 'Not worried at all' to 'Very worried'.

Factor analysis was used to examine the underlying structure of the fear-of-crime items. Two underlying components were identified. The first component includes the items on worry about physical attack within the home and on the street, sexual assault and having the home broken into. This component has been labelled *Fear of physical crime*. The four items were computed into a scale with good internal consistency (Cronbach's alpha = 0.86). The second component includes the remaining three items on worry about having personal identity stolen and credit cards stolen and illegally used on the Internet. This component has been labelled *Fear of identity theft-related crime*. The three items were computed into a scale with good internal consistency (Cronbach's alpha = 0.88). Data were recoded so that higher scores on the scales reflect higher levels of fear of crime. Possible scale scores range from 4 to 16 on the fear of physical crime scale and 3 to 12 on the fear of identity theft-related crime scale. The two fear-of-crime scales are moderately correlated (r = 0.47, p < 0.001). That is, people who scored highly on the fear of physical crime scale were also likely to score highly on the fear of identity theft-related crime scale, while those who scored low on one scale were likely to score low on the other scale.

Results

Incivilities

AuSSA 2007 respondents were asked how much of a problem a range of 'incivilities' was in their local area. The results (Table 5.1) indicate that the proportion of Australians nominating incivilities as a problem ranged from 24 per cent (for litter) to 37 per cent (for drug dealing).

Table 5.1 Ratings of Size of Problem of a Range of Incivilities in Local Area (per cent)

Size of problem	Rubbish/litter	Graffiti	Unsupervised groups of young people	Drunk people	Drug dealing
A very big problem	6.3	8.6	12.8	9.3	13.9
A fairly big problem	17.4	20.1	23.9	18.2	23.0
Not a very big problem	60.6	52.9	47.2	50.6	41.0
Not a problem at all	15.8	18.4	16.0	22.0	22.2
Total	100	100	100	100	100

Source: Australian Survey of Social Attitudes 2007.

Response options of 'A very big problem' and 'A fairly big problem' were collapsed into one category ('A big problem') to allow comparisons across types of locations. Approximately four out of 10 survey respondents (41.5 per cent) do not report a big problem with any of the five incivilities in their local area, while 7.1 per cent report a problem across all five types of incivilities.

There are differences in perceptions of incivilities across types of locations (Figure 5.1). With the exception of graffiti, remote-area respondents reported higher rates of incivilities than respondents from capital cities, other metropolitan areas and rural areas.

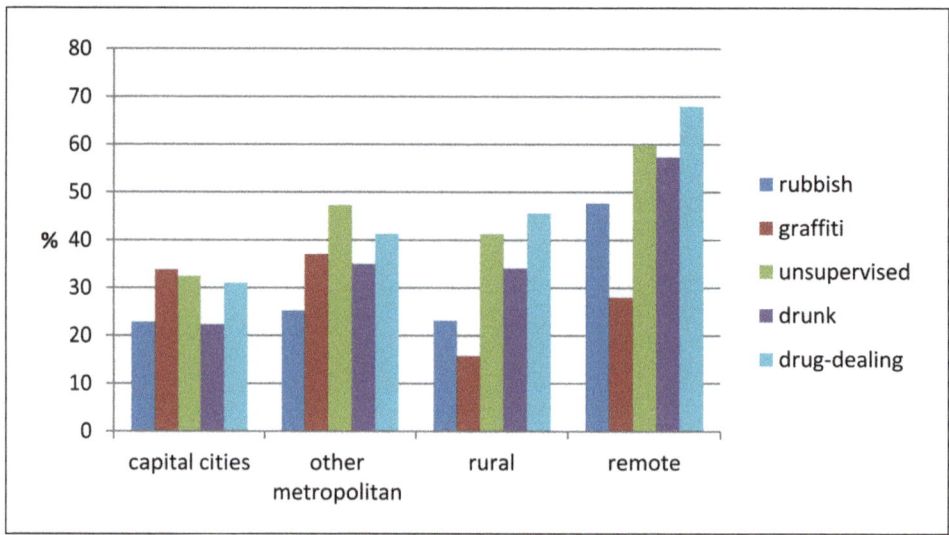

Figure 5.1 Types of Incivilities Rated as a Big Problem by Location (per cent)

Source: Australian Survey of Social Attitudes 2007.

There were no significant differences between males and females in perceptions of incivilities, and only a very weak negative association with age ($r = -0.06$, $p < 0.001$).

Fear of crime

The same AuSSA 2007 respondents who responded to questions about incivilities were asked how worried they were about being a victim of a range of crimes. The results are presented in Table 5.2 and indicate that the proportion of Australians fairly or very worried about crime varies widely according to the type of crime. While less than one in five (18.5 per cent) is worried about sexual assault, almost half (49.5 per cent) are worried about having their home broken into.

Response options of 'Very worried' and 'Fairly worried' were collapsed into one category to examine differences in worry about being the victim of crime by location. The results are presented in Figure 5.2. A smaller percentage of survey respondents in rural areas was worried about each of the crimes compared with survey respondents from other locations.

Table 5.2 Percentage of Population Worried about Being the Victim of a Range of Crimes

	Physical attack: home	Physical attack: street	Sexual assault	Home broken into	Identity stolen via Internet	Credit card stolen	Credit card used illegally via Internet
Very worried	6.0	8.3	6.0	14.9	15.9	17.5	23.0
Fairly worried	13.6	22.3	12.5	34.6	24.4	28.0	27.9
Not very worried	49.9	52.3	41.3	41.6	32.8	37.5	27.1
Not worried at all	30.5	17.1	40.2	8.9	26.9	17.0	22.0
Total	100	100	100	100	100	100	100

Source: Australian Survey of Social Attitudes 2007.

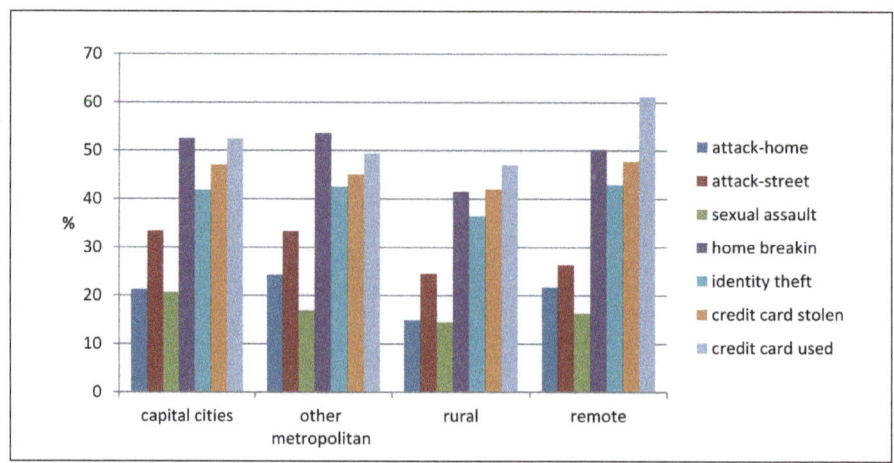

Figure 5.2 Worry about Being a Victim of Various Crimes by Location (per cent)

Source: Australian Survey of Social Attitudes 2007.

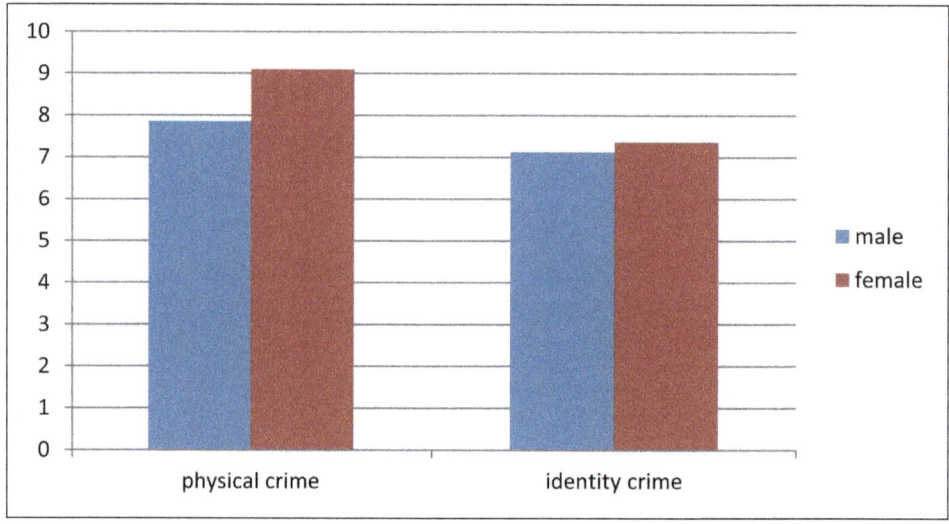

Figure 5.3 Gender Differences in Worry about Being a Victim of Crime

Source: Australian Survey of Social Attitudes 2007.

Total scores for physical crime and identity theft-related crimes were computed. Females scored significantly higher than males on the fear of physical crime (t [4983.9] = 16.04, p < 0.005) and the fear of identity theft-related crime (t [4983] = 2.82, p < 0.01) scales (see Figure 5.3). Differences in scores between males and females were, however, greater for traditional 'physical crimes' than for identity-related crimes, providing some support for the notion that higher levels of fear of physical crime are due to the perceived greater personal and social vulnerability of women to violent crime. Fear of physical crime was not significantly associated with age, with only a very weak significant decrease in fear of identity theft-related crime scores with age ($r = -0.03$, $p < 0.05$), accounting for less than 1 per cent of the variance in scores.

Testing the incivilities hypothesis

Consistent with the incivilities hypothesis, there was a moderate relationship between perceptions of incivilities and fear of physical crime ($r = 0.38$, $p < 0.001$) and a weaker relationship between incivilities and fear of identity theft-related crime ($r = 0.22$, $p < 0.001$). To test whether the impact of perceptions of incivilities on fear of crime was greater for males than females, separate correlations were run for males and females for both fear of physical crime and fear of identity-related theft. The results are presented in Table 5.3. Perceptions of incivilities account for 19 per cent of the variation in males' fear of physical crime, but only 12 per cent of the variation in females' fear of physical crime. Perceptions of incivilities account for 6 per cent of the variation in males' fear of identity theft-related crime, but only 4 per cent of the variation in females' fear of identity theft-related crime. In combination, these results indicate that incivilities have their strongest influence on fear of physical crime, and more so for males than females.

Table 5.3 Correlations between Perceptions of Incivilities and Fear of Crime by Gender

	Physical crime	Identity-related crime
Males	0.44	0.25
Females	0.35	0.21

Source: Australian Survey of Social Attitudes 2007.

Further analyses were conducted to examine the unique contribution of gender, age, education, location and perceptions of incivilities to fear of crime. Two multiple regression analyses were used to predict fear of physical crime and fear of identity crime. In the first step of each analysis, the demographic variables of age, gender and years of education were examined. In the second step of each analysis, location (metropolitan versus rural and remote) and perception of incivilities were added to see if they accounted for further variance in fear of crime beyond that of the demographic variables of age, gender and education. The results are presented in Tables 5.4 and 5.5.

Table 5.4 Unstandardised (B) and Standardised (β) Regression Coefficients, and Squared Semi-Partial Correlations (sr^2) for Each Predictor Variable on Each Step of a Hierarchical Multiple Regression Predicting Fear of Physical Crime

Variable		B	β	sr^2
Step 1				
	Age	−0.003	−0.018	< 0.001
	Education	−0.088**	−0.119	0.013
	Gender	−1209**	−0.214	0.045
Step 2				
	Age	0.003	0.015	< 0.001
	Education	−0.064**	−0.086	0.007
	Gender	−1.199**	−0.212	0.045
	Location	0.707**	0.097	0.009
	Incivilities	0.321**	0.382	0.143

** $p < 0.001$

Source: Australian Survey of Social Attitudes 2007.

In step one of predicting fear of physical crime, gender and years of education were both significant predictors but age was not. Fear of crime was lower for males than females and decreased with years of education. Together, these variables accounted for 6.2 per cent of the variation in fear of physical crime scores. In step two, location and perceptions of incivilities were both significant predictors and combined accounted for an additional 14.7 per cent of variance in fear of physical crime scores. In total, 20.9 per cent of variance in physical crime scores could be accounted for by the combination of gender, years of education, location and perceptions of incivilities, with perceptions of incivilities and gender being the strongest predictors, accounting for 14.3 per cent and 4.5 per cent unique variance respectively.

Table 5.5 Unstandardised (B) and Standardised (β) Regression Coefficients, and Squared Semi-Partial Correlations (sr^2) for Each Predictor Variable on Each Step of a Hierarchical Multiple Regression Predicting Fear of Identity-Related Crime

Variable		B	β	sr^2
Step 1				
	Age	−0.003	−0.018	< 0.001
	Education	−0.002	−0.003	< 0.001
	Gender	−0.225*	−0.04	0.002
Step 2				
	Age	0	0.002	< 0.001
	Education	0.017	0.023	< 0.001
	Gender	−0.218*	−0.039	0.002
	Location	0.426**	0.06	0.003
	Incivilities	0.19**	0.23	0.052

* $p < 0.05$

** $p < 0.001$

Source: Australian Survey of Social Attitudes 2007.

In step one of predicting fear of identity-related crime, gender was a significant predictor but age and years of education were not. Fear of crime was lower for males than females, but accounted for less than 1 per cent of the variation in fear of identity-related crime scores. In step two, location and perceptions of incivilities were both significant predictors and, combined, accounted for an additional 5.3 per cent of variance in fear of identity-related crime scores. In total, 5.5 per cent of variance in identity-related crime scores could be accounted for by the combination of gender, location and perceptions of incivilities, with perceptions of incivilities being the strongest predictor, accounting for 5.25 per cent of the unique variance.

Discussion

The AuSSA 2007 provided a vehicle for a national snapshot of fear of crime in Australia. The results indicate that although the majority of Australians are not worried about being the victim of crime there is a significant minority of Australians who report being 'fairly' or 'very' worried. Many more Australians are negatively impacted indirectly through the fear of crime than directly by being the victims of crime. This fear of crime can influence many critical aspects of the individual's functioning and wellbeing, from physical activities to social intercourse and the general erosion of trust (Stafford, Chandola and Marmot et al. 2007). The effect on individuals also ultimately aggregates to a negative effect on communities, which in turn amplifies the deleterious effect further (Skogan 1986).

This survey allows us to compare worry about traditional place-based crime with worry about emerging forms of criminal activity enabled by the rapid development of information and communication technologies, particularly the Internet. An interesting finding from this research is that worry about identity-related crime is now matching, and for some offences exceeding, worry about more traditional place-based crime. The illegal use of credit cards over the Internet was one of the crimes included in this survey that generated the highest levels of worry. Traditional predictors of fear of crime (gender, age, years of education, location) were found to be poor predictors of worry about this new type of crime, and suggest further work is required to develop an understanding of the issues at play here. Future work is required to disentangle worry about identity-related cyber-crime from the actual risk of cyber-crime. For example, Wall (2008a, 2008b) has argued that 'cyberfear' is largely driven by myth perpetuated by the media, and may not be in proportion to the objective reality of cyber-crime.

As predicted, perceptions of incivilities were significantly associated with fear of crime in this research, supporting the incivilities thesis and previous research findings (Borooah and Carcach 1997; Carcach et al. 1995; Kanan and Pruitt 2002; LaGrange et al. 1992; McCrea et al. 2005; Perkins and Taylor 1996; Robinson et al. 2003; Taylor 1999; Wyant 2008). Consistent with previous research, gender and perceptions of incivilities were found to interact in predicting fear of crime (Carcach et al. 1995). While females reported higher levels of crime, males' fear of crime was more strongly influenced by perceived incivilities. These findings suggest that reducing perceptions of incivilities may work to reduce fear of crime, particularly for men.

The results of this analysis point once again to the complex interaction between measures of fear of crime and concern about incivilities. Whether these two phenomena are separate manifestations of the same underlying sensitivity about social control or whether they tap qualitatively separate domains remains uncertain; however, the results presented here suggest that the perceptions of incivilities may contribute to, or at least exacerbate, the experience of fear. The most relevant finding of the present study which advances our understanding of the interaction of perception of incivilities and fear is that perceptions of incivilities are associated with both fear of place-based physical crime and non–place-based identity-related crime. This connection is at a global level, suggesting that general individual dispositional factors are more relevant in understanding fear of crime than reality-based or specific factors, thus further challenging the instrumental hypothesis that fear of crime simply reflects actual crime rates. Because the new Internet-based crimes are not connected with incivilities in the neighbourhood they suggest individual beliefs such as a general loss of trust in all aspects of society and/or the loss of social power are the most relevant factors to look at as contributing to the experience of fear of crime; however, while the perception of incivilities is an important predictor of fear of both place-based physical crime and identity-related crime, perceptions of incivilities have a stronger relationship with fear of physical crime. This suggests that while all three measures may partially tap into an underlying sensitivity about social control, each also measures specific concerns.

One of the methodological implications of the current research is the finding that the acquiescence effect discussed in the introduction as distorting measures of fear of crime may affect the responses of only some research participants. For each of the crimes listed, a proportion of survey respondents (ranging from 17 per cent in relation to having a credit card stolen to 40.2 per cent for sexual assault) answered that they were 'not worried at all'. Further, the varying percentages who were not worried about each of the crimes suggest that this measure is at least partially tapping into concerns about each specific crime rather than a more generalised fear (or absence of fear). This increases our confidence in the use of these types of measures; however, from the questions asked in this study it is not possible to assess whether some respondents overestimated their level of fear, and this is an area that requires further research comparing the effects of differently worded questions.

Conclusion

This chapter has examined the incivilities thesis—the proposition that disorder in the community, rather than crime itself, leads to increased fear of crime through an emotional response of perceived vulnerability—within the Australian context. Our analysis of the Australian Survey of Social Attitudes conducted in 2007 provides some support for the incivilities thesis. Fear of crime increased as perceptions of incivilities in the local area increased. The results have direct policy implications, suggesting that attending to sub-criminal incivilities within neighbourhoods may reduce fear of crime and increase perceptions of safety.

References

Borooah, Vani K. and Carcach, Carlos A. 1997. 'Crime and fear: evidence from Australia'. *British Journal of Criminology* 37: 635–57.

Box, Steven, Hale, Chris and Andrews, Glen. 1988. 'Explaining fear of crime'. *British Journal of Criminology* 28: 340–56.

Brunton-Smith, Ian and Sturgis, Patrick. 2011. 'Do neighbourhoods generate fear of crime? An empirical test using the British Crime Survey'. *Criminology* 49: 331–69.

Carcach, Carlos, Frampton, Peta, Thomas, Kaye and Cranich, Mathew. 1995. 'Explaining fear of crime in Queensland'. *Journal of Quantitative Criminology* 11: 271–87.

Ditton, Jason and Farrall, Stephen. 2007. 'The British Crime Survey and fear of crime'. In *Surveying Crime in the 21st Century*, eds Mike Hough and Max Maxfield. Monsey, NY: Criminal Justice Press.

Dolan, Paul and Peasgood, Tessa. 2007. 'Estimating the economic and social costs of the fear of crime'. *British Journal of Criminology* 47: 121–32.

Fitzgerald, Robin. 2008. *Fear of crime and the neighbourhood context in Canadian cities*. Crime and Justice Research Paper Series. Ottawa: Canadian Centre for Justice Statistics.

Jackson, Jonathan. 2005. 'Validating new measures of the fear of crime'. *International Journal of Social Research Methodology* 8: 297–315.

Jackson, Jonathan and Gray, Emily. 2010. 'Functional fear and public insecurities about crime'. *British Journal of Criminology* 50: 1–22.

Kanan, James W. and Pruitt, Matthew V. 2002. 'Modeling fear of crime and perceived victimization risk: the (in)significance of neighborhood integration'. *Sociological Inquiry* 72: 527–48.

Kelling, George L. and Coles, Catherine M. 1996. *Fixing Broken Windows: Restoring order and reducing crime in our communities*. New York: Free Press.

LaGrange, Randy L., Ferraro, Kenneth F. and Supancic, Michael F. 1992. 'Perceived risk and fear of crime: role of social and physical incivilities'. *Journal of Research in Crime and Delinquency* 29: 311–34.

McCord, Eric S., Ratcliffe, Jerry H., Garcia, R. Marie and Taylor, Ralph B. 2007. 'Nonresidential crime attractors and generators elevate perceived neighbourhood crime and incivilities'. *Journal of Research in Crime and Delinquency* 44: 295–318.

McCrea, Rod, Shyy, Tung-Kai, Western, John and Stimson, Robert J. 2005. 'Fear of crime in Brisbane: individual, social and neighbourhood factors in perspective'. *Journal of Sociology* 41: 7–27.

Palmer, Catherine, Ziersch, Anna, Arthurson, Kathy and Baum, Fran. 2005. '"Danger lurks around every corner": fear of crime and its impact on opportunities for social interaction in stigmatised Australian suburbs'. *Urban Policy and Research* 23: 393–411.

Perkins, Douglas D. and Taylor, Ralph B. 1996. 'Ecological assessments of community disorder: their relationship to fear of crime and theoretical implications'. *American Journal of Community Psychology* 24: 63–107.

Pinkerton James, Marianne. 1992. 'The elderly as victims of crime, abuse and neglect'. *Trends & Issues in Crime and Criminal Justice* no. 37. Canberra: Australian Institute of Criminology.

Quine, Susan and Morrell, Stephen. 2008a. 'Feeling safe in one's neighbourhood: variation by location among older Australians'. *Australian Journal of Rural Health* 16: 115–16.

Quine, Susan and Morrell, Stephen. 2008b. 'Perceptions of personal safety among older Australians'. *Australasian Journal on Ageing* 27: 72–77.

Roberts, Lynne and Indermaur, David. 2009. *What Australians think about crime and justice: results from the 2007 Survey of Social Attitudes*. Research and Public Policy Series no. 101. Canberra: Australian Institute of Criminology. <http://www.aic.gov.au/publications/current%20series/rpp/100-120/rpp101.aspx>

Robinson, Jennifer B., Lawton, Brian A., Taylor, Ralph B. and Perkins, Douglas D. 2003. 'Multilevel longitudinal impacts of incivilities: fear of crime, expected safety and block satisfaction'. *Journal of Quantitative Criminology* 19: 237–74.

Skogan, Wesley. 1986. 'Fear of crime and neighbourhood change in communities and crime'. *Crime and Justice: A Review of Research* 8: 203–29.

Skogan, Wesley. 1999. 'Measuring what matters: crime, disorder and fear'. In *Measuring What Matters*, ed. Robert H. Langworthy. Washington, DC: US Department of Justice, National Institute of Justice and Office of Community Oriented Policing Services.

Skogan, Wesley and Maxfield, Max. 1981. *Coping with Crime*. Beverley Hills, Calif.: Sage.

Smith, William R. and Torstensson, Marie. 1997. 'Gender differences in risk perception and neutralizing fear of crime: toward resolving the paradoxes'. *British Journal of Criminology* 37: 608–34.

Stafford, Mai, Chandola, Tarani and Marmot, Michael. 2007. 'Association between fear of crime and mental health and physical functioning'. *American Journal of Public Health* 97: 2076–81.

Taylor, Ralph B. 1999. 'The incivilities thesis: theory, measurement and policy'. In *Measuring What Matters*, ed. Robert H. Langworthy. Washington, DC: US Department of Justice, National Institute of Justice and Office of Community Oriented Policing Services.

Tulloch, John, Lupton, Deborah, Blood, Warwick, Tulloch, Marian, Jennett, Christine and Enders, Mike. 1998a. *Fear of Crime: Audit of the literature and community programs. Volume 1*. Sydney: National Campaign Against Violence and Crime.

Tulloch, John, Lupton, Deborah, Blood, Warwick, Tulloch, Marian, Jennett, Christine and Enders, Mike. 1998b. *Fear of Crime: The fieldwork research. Volume 2*. Sydney: National Campaign Against Violence and Crime.

Tyler, Tom R. and Boeckmann, Robert J. 1997. 'Three strikes and you are out, but why? The psychology of public support for punishing rule breakers'. *Law and Society Review* 31: 237–65.

Wall, David S. 2008a. 'Cybercrime and the culture of fear'. *Information, Communication and Society* 11: 861–84.

Wall, David S. 2008b. 'Cybercrime, media and insecurity: the shaping of public perceptions of cybercrime'. *International Review of Law, Computers and Technology* 22: 45–63.

Wilson, James Q. and Kelling, George L. 1982. 'The police and neighbourhood safety: broken windows'. *The Atlantic Monthly* 127: 29–38.

Wyant, Brian R. 2008. 'Multilevel impacts of perceived incivilities and perceptions of crime risk on fear of crime'. *Journal of Research in Crime and Delinquency* 45: 39–64.

Ziersch, Anna Marie, Putland, Christine, Palmer, Catherine, MacDougall, Colin J. and Baum, Frances E. 2007. 'Neighbourhood life, social capital and perceptions of safety in the western suburbs of Adelaide'. *Australian Journal of Social Issues* 42: 549–62.

6. Terrorism and Public Opinion in Australia

Juliet Pietsch and Ian McAllister

In contrast with many of the other advanced democracies, Australia has been relatively immune from acts of terrorism. The terrorist acts that have occurred in Australia over the past half-century generally involved attacks on foreign diplomats by ethnic extremists intent on publicising grievances within their home country. The most significant terrorist act on Australian soil took place in February 1977 during the Commonwealth Heads of Government meeting, when a bomb exploded outside the Hilton Hotel in Sydney, claiming three lives. By contrast, between 1968 and 1998 about 125 people were killed in mainland Britain by Irish republican violence, and in the United States, six were killed in the February 1993 World Trade Center bombing, 198 died in the Oklahoma City bombing and 2998 in the 9/11 attacks. In relative terms, to date Australia has escaped the major effects of domestic terrorism that have been felt in many other countries.

Notwithstanding the absence of a terrorist attack within Australia, public opinion has been subjected to the effects of terrorism by way of the Bali bombings on 12 October 2002. Taking place in a popular tourist destination, the bombings killed 202 people, 88 of them Australian. An Islamist group, Jemaah Islamiyah, was responsible and said that it had mounted the attacks as retaliation for Australian support for the US-led 'War on Terror'. While the Bali attacks occurred outside Australia, the event brought home to the Australian public the potential terrorist threat that exists from radical Islamic groups. It also highlighted the potential domestic threat from terrorist activity and began a debate about the countermeasures that might be required to reduce that threat.

This chapter looks at the way the Australian public has responded to increased threats of terrorism in Australia and across the region. Using the 2007 Australian Survey of Social Attitudes (AuSSA), we examine public concern about terrorism and support for curtailing civil and political rights to deal with terrorist suspects who are considered to be a threat to national security. We also examine the extent to which concerns about terrorism and how to counter it influence political ideology and political behaviour. Before we begin our empirical investigation of these questions, we examine the different understandings of terrorism and outline some of the underlying causes.

Terrorism and political violence

What constitutes an act of terrorism, and how does it differ from other acts of violence? There are many different understandings of what constitutes terrorism (see Lentini 2003, 2008). While the threat of terrorism is a relatively new phenomenon in Australia, different versions of terrorism have existed for centuries. Britain, for example, has experienced terrorism for at least four decades, but Irish republican violence in Britain, in particular, stretches back at least as far as the late nineteenth century (see Hayes and McAllister 2001, 2005). Similarly, Israel has been dealing with the challenges of terrorism since its foundation as a state in 1949. Since the 9/11 attacks in New York, however, the threat of terrorism has spread more widely across the advanced democracies and has taken on a global dimension with the expansion of rapid communication and transnational networks. In line with the increasingly global nature of terrorism, there has been a significant increase in the level of government and academic interest in the threat of terrorism.

There are numerous definitions of what constitutes terrorism. A consistent divide is whether states are capable of engaging in terrorism or whether it applies only to individuals. Beau Grosscup (2006), for example, argues that the strategic bombing that is often used in state-sanctioned military campaigns should be labelled as terrorism. In addition, Grosscup argues that those powers which use strategic bombing have been able to monopolise definitions of terrorism (Grosscup 2006). Other scholars of terrorism studies have focused solely on individuals, and argued that terrorism is the use of threats or violence against innocent victims from non-state actors who want to bring about political change or achieve political goals (Hoffman 1998; Lentini 2008). Given that terrorism has now taken on a global dimension in many different political contexts, some scholars argue that the concept of terrorism suffers from 'stretching', with different types of crime now viewed as terrorism (Weinberg, Pedahzur and Hirsch-Hoefler 2004).

Accounts examining the causes of terrorism are as varied as the definitions. Traditional explanations often regard terrorism as a legitimate political struggle by a minority group to secure their independence against a more powerful state or group of states. Such groups often feel they have suffered unfairly and they regard terrorism as the only means of drawing attention to their cause (Pedahzur 2005). For example, in a study of political violence in Thailand, Croissant (2007) observes that the causes of terrorism can be traced to a range of contentious religious, cultural, economic and political causes. He argues that in southern Thailand, the Muslim minority has only ever rebelled when the Muslims perceived their cultural identity as threatened by the Bangkok-based authorities. The rise of suicide terrorism has added a new dimension to explanations of terrorism, with Ami Pedahzur (2005) suggesting that terrorists who use suicide to kill innocent civilians often do so for redemption.

Many scholars have argued that the absence of orderly institutions and accountable governance in weak and failed states heightens the risk of terrorism (see Newman 2007). Failed states are viewed by the advanced democracies as raising both humanitarian and strategic concerns; however, there is also considerable evidence that terrorist organisations take advantage of stable democratic states. In fact, the evidence shows that open societies with democratic governments are highly susceptible to violent conflict (Eubank and Weinberg 2008), as the presence of terrorist groups in Europe, the United States, India and Japan has demonstrated. There are also many states that are characterised by weak policies, institutions and governance, yet do not play host to terrorist organisations. In research on the presence of terrorist groups in Afghanistan, Sudan and Somalia, Newman has observed that while terrorism may operate in weak or failed states, it does not necessarily follow that the condition of failed statehood explains their presence (Newman 2007).

The definitions of and explanations for terrorism therefore vary widely; however, from the perspective of public opinion, there is more clarity about what constitutes a terrorist act. The news is presented by the mass media and interpreted by governments and interest groups. Viewed through the lens of the mass media, what does or does not constitute terrorism is rather clearer than any discussion of the definitions might imply. Moreover, the surveys show that respondents are always willing to proffer an opinion about the threat of terrorism or about measures designed to reduce that threat. This suggests that the widespread elite discussions about terrorism that took place after the Bali bombings clearly impacted on mass public opinion.

Public concern about terrorism

While there are many definitions and elite discussions about what constitutes terrorism, the data from the 2007 AuSSA cannot fully analyse how the public understands the concept of a terrorist attack. Our research, however, shows that respondents have no difficulty answering questions about terrorism and whether they feel it is a real or unlikely threat. First, terrorism did not rank highly as a main concern for the Australian public in the 2007 AuSSA. When asked to choose their first and second most important concerns from a list of 18 issues, just 3 per cent of the respondents ranked terrorism as the most important concern, making it tenth on the list. The most highly ranked issues were health care and hospitals (mentioned by 14 per cent), environmental damage (13 per cent), an ageing population (11 per cent) and lack of affordable housing (10 per cent). Nor was terrorism seen as a second-ranked issue, again being mentioned by just 3 per cent of respondents, making it twelfth out of the 18 issues. These results are similar to those found in the Australian Election Study (AES), where terrorism was mentioned as the most important issue by 5 per cent in 2001 and 2004, and by 2 per cent in 2007 (McAllister and Clark 2008, 53).

Despite the public's low ranking of terrorism relative to other major issues, during 2007 it was still a concern for a significant proportion of the population. The 2007 AES found that 14 per cent of the respondents were 'very concerned' about being the victim of a terrorist attack, and a further 36 per cent was 'somewhat concerned'.[1] These estimates were very close to those found in the United States, where about 44 per cent of survey respondents interviewed in June 2007 said that they were 'very' or 'somewhat' concerned that they or someone in their family could become the victim of a terrorist attack.[2] Moreover, trend figures for the same question since November 2001 show that this proportion had remained remarkably consistent, varying little over the period, with the partial exception of a slight rise in public concern after the July 2005 London bombings.

By any standards, there is widespread public concern about the possibility of a terrorist attack. The 2007 AuSSA asked the respondents how likely they believed a terrorist attack was in South-East Asia and in Australia in the next 12 months. Table 6.1 shows that almost three-quarters of the respondents believed that it was likely that a major attack would take place in South-East Asia, with just 13 per cent seeing it as unlikely. This reflects concerns that South-East Asia during this period had become a regional centre for Islamic terrorism and an important hub for terrorist training and financial support. The 9/11 attacks appear to have been followed by an exponential growth in terrorist organisations dedicated to attacking the United States and other Western interests in the region. Substantially fewer respondents see an attack in Australia as likely; just more than one in three takes this view, with the largest proportion, 43 per cent, seeing such an attack as 'not very likely'.

Table 6.1 Likelihood of a Terrorist Attack

	Terrorist attack in...	
	South-East Asia	Australia
Very likely	18	4
Likely	56	30
Not very likely	11	43
Not at all likely	2	11
Don't know	13	12
Total	100	100
(N)	(2516)	(2523)

Note: The questions were—'Do you think that a terrorist attack somewhere in [South-East Asia/Australia] during the next twelve months is...?'; 'And how concerned are you that there will be a major terrorist attack on Australian soil in the near future?'

Source: Australian Survey of Social Attitudes 2007, questionnaire C.

---

[1] The question was: 'How concerned are you personally about you yourself or a family member being the victim of a future terrorist attack in Australia?'

[2] <http://www.pollingreport.com/terror.htm> accessed 5 March 2009.

Overall, then, an attack in South-East Asia was seen as more than twice as likely as one in Australia. Despite the disparity in the proportions, the likelihood of seeing an attack in one region is strongly correlated with the likelihood of seeing an attack in another region. The correlation between the two items is high, at 0.473 (p < 0.000), so the perception of a terrorist threat is only loosely related to a particular geographical region, in Australia or within the immediate region. This reflects the global nature of terrorism, and as terrorism has become transnational, so too have public perceptions about the threat that is associated with it. It also reflects the fact that the public's concern about terrorism has become what has been termed 'the new normal', or the sense that living with terrorism is an unavoidable part of everyday life (Bowman 2005, 4). For example, in 2003 about three-quarters of US respondents thought that living with terrorism would be a part of life in the future; the same figure in Australia in the 2007 AES was very similar, at 62 per cent.[3]

Are there any consistent patterns in the types of individuals who are more likely than others to be concerned about terrorism? Table 6.2 suggests that there are, at least with regards to gender, age and possessing a university education, and particularly with regards to the likelihood of an attack in South-East Asia. Women are more likely than men to see a terrorist attack in South-East Asia as likely—25 per cent of women thought it was 'very likely' compared with 17 per cent of men—as are those aged over fifty. This reflects underlying gender and generational differences in attitudes to defence and foreign affairs more generally, with women and older persons being more likely to see threats to Australia (McAllister 2005, 33). Possessing a university education is also associated with a reduced probability of seeing a terrorist attack as likely, in both South-East Asia and Australia.

After 9/11 and the Bali bombings there was a consistent underlying concern about terrorism. While the public had immediate socioeconomic priorities—mostly associated with health, education or the performance of the economy—the fear of terrorism appeared to be a consistent background theme. The absence of a major terrorist act in Australia also underlines the extent to which the public is responding to events that have occurred internationally, in the United States, Britain, Spain or Indonesia, and to the global reach of the terrorist threat. It also highlights debates about the use of additional legal measures to counter these threats, and we examine this in detail in the next section.

---

3   The US figures are from Bowman (2005). The AES question was: 'Please say whether you strongly agree, agree, disagree or strongly disagree with each of the following statements. Acts of terrorism in Australia will be part of life in the future.'

Table 6.2 Concern about Terrorism and Socioeconomic Status

	Very likely	Likely	Not very likely	Not at all likely
(Terrorist attack in South-East Asia)				
Gender				
Male	17	67	14	2
Female	25	60	13	2
Age				
18–34	14	62	21	3
35–49	19	66	13	2
50–64	26	63	9	2
65 or over	20	65	14	1
University education				
No university education	22	64	12	2
University education	16	65	17	2
(Terrorist attack in Australia)				
Gender				
Male	5	38	47	10
Female	4	29	52	15
Age				
18–34	3	31	51	15
35–49	5	33	51	11
50–64	6	37	45	12
69 or over	4	33	51	12
University education				
No university education	5	37	47	11
University education	3	25	55	17

Note: 'Don't know' responses have been excluded.

Source: Australian Survey of Social Attitudes 2007, questionnaire C.

Countering the threat of terrorism

Since the 9/11 attacks in the United States, most Western societies have introduced a range of counter-terrorism legislation to manage the risk of terrorist attacks and deter future attacks. There are two dominant approaches to counter-terrorism: one based on a criminal justice model where terrorism is viewed as a crime, the other approach a military model where terrorism is viewed as an act of warfare and the response requires the military and the curtailing of individual freedoms

(Chalk 1998). Historically, Australia's approach to counter-terrorism has been guided by the criminal justice model and the use of the police force; however, the boundaries between the criminal justice model and the military model are not always clear during times of heightened threat (Crelinsten 1998; Crelinsten and Schmid 1992; Pedahzur and Ranstorp 2001). Indeed, Australia expanded its military operations in Afghanistan to combat the threat of terrorism and the government has stated that the responsibilities of the military and the police force must be merged in order to respond to terrorist threats (Australian Government 2008; Smith 2008).

The expansion of a criminal justice model has seen the introduction of special anti-terrorism legislation giving police and other authorities greater powers and resources to respond to terrorism. Since the 9/11 attacks in the United States and the Bali bombings in October 2002, Australia has made substantial increases to its budget on counter-terrorism strategy, with nearly A$8 billion having been committed since 2001 (Fealy and Borgu 2005). The most controversial part of Australia's counter-terrorism strategy was the introduction of anti-terrorist legislation and amendments to existing acts passed since 2001. The new legislative measures involved expanded intelligence gathering and police powers, and an increase in the range of preventive detention and control orders that can be applied to terrorist suspects. The anti-terrorist legislation increased the powers of the State and federal police forces and security agencies such as the Australian Security and Intelligence Organisation (ASIO) to monitor, detain and charge suspected terrorists (see Goulder and Williams 2006; O'Neil 2007).

To what extent are these counter-terrorism measures supported by the public, and what part does concern about terrorism play in shaping those opinions? The answers to the first question appear in Tables 6.3 and 6.4, which show public opinion towards various measures designed to reduce the likelihood of a terrorist act occurring. A standard government response to terrorism is to allow for longer periods of detention than would be possible under normal criminal justice rules. The first parts of Tables 6.3 and 6.4 show that the majority of the survey respondents support this approach. Almost three in four agree that terrorist suspects should be imprisoned indefinitely, while 54 per cent believe that the government should have the right to detain suspects without trial. The slightly lower support for the latter reflects the fact that the question explicitly removes the requirement for a trial, while the former question does not.

Other powers that governments can take to counter terrorism include listening to telephone conversations and stopping and searching suspects. Again, in both cases, Table 6.4 shows that there is a majority in support of such measures, though more so for tapping telephones (which has support from 77 per cent of the respondents) than for stop and search (support from 54 per cent). Finally, interrogation methods used by the United States on terrorist suspects—notably, 'water-boarding', where prisoners have the sensation of drowning—have focused attention on the extent to which torture should be used to extract information from suspects. The second column in Table 6.3 shows that a majority see torture as never being justified, and only one in five sees torture as being justifiable to gain information.

Table 6.3 Support for Measures to Counter Terrorism

	Imprison suspects indefinitely	Torture never justified
Agree strongly	38	29
Agree	35	32
Neither	8	16
Disagree	12	13
Disagree strongly	5	7
Don't know	2	3
Total	100	100
(N)	(2522)	(2507)

Note: The questions were—'How much do you agree or disagree with the following statements? "If a man is suspected of planning a terrorist attack in Australia, the police should have the power to keep him in prison until they are satisfied he was not involved"; "Torturing a prisoner in an Australian prison is never justified, even if it might provide information that could prevent an attack".'

Source: Australian Survey of Social Attitudes 2007, questionnaire C.

Table 6.4 Support for Extending Legal Measures to Counter Terrorism

	If person is suspected of terrorism, government should...		
	Detain without trial	Tap telephones	Stop and search
Definitely should have right	27	38	23
Probably should have right	27	39	31
Probably should not have right	23	14	24
Definitely should not have right	20	7	20
Can't choose	3	2	2
Total	100	100	100
(N)	(2715)	(2701)	(2694)

Note: The questions were—'Suppose the government suspected that a terrorist act was about to happen. Do you think the authorities should have the right to...detain people for as long as they want without putting them trial?...tap people's telephone conversation?...stop and search people in the street at random?'

Source: Australian Survey of Social Attitudes 2007, questionnaire A.

These results show that a majority of the public will accept some infringement of their civil liberties in order to reduce the threat of terrorism. This contrasts sharply with similar results from the United States, which show that the American public is less willing than their Australian counterparts to accept restrictions on their civil liberties in the interests of countering terrorism. For example, when asked in a December 2006 survey 'In order to curb terrorism in this country, do you think it will be necessary for the average person to give up some civil liberties, or not?', 40 per cent said it would be necessary, but 54 per cent said that it would not be necessary, and 6 per cent were unsure.[4] Similarly, in a September 2008 survey, 51 per cent said that they were more concerned about restrictions on their civil liberties than about the failure of the government to enact anti-terrorism legislation. These differences reflect the essentially rights-based political culture of the United States, where individual liberty is paramount, compared with the utilitarian culture of Australia, where efficiency in dealing with problems takes precedence over individual rights.

To what extent are the public's views about curtailing liberty to deal with terrorism influenced by perceptions of an imminent terrorist threat? Table 6.5 shows the correlations between the two questions measuring concern about a terrorist attack in South-East Asia and in Australia, and the public's views about detaining suspects indefinitely, and about the use of torture. All four correlations are significant, but they are particularly strong for concern about a terrorist threat and the detention of suspects. By contrast, those who see torture as never being justified are less concerned about a threat, but the relationship is only about one-third of that for indefinite detention. Clearly, then, those who are concerned about a terrorist attack see it as justifiable to take legal measures to reduce that threat, such as the indefinite detention of terrorist suspects.

Table 6.5 Concern about Terrorism and Methods to Reduce the Threat

	Imprison suspects indefinitely	Torture never justified
Attack likely in South-East Asia	0.22 ($p < 0.000$)	–0.07 ($p = 0.002$)
Attack likely in Australia	0.33 ($p < 0.000$)	–0.10 ($p < 0.000$)

Note: Figures are Pearson correlations, with significance level in parentheses.

Source: Australian Survey of Social Attitudes 2007, questionnaire C.

Countering terrorism represents a trade-off between increased security and curtailing civil liberty. At the core of the dilemma is the degree to which a democracy can contain terrorism and manage the associated risks while at the same time preserving liberal-democratic values (Pedahzur and Ranstorp 2001; Wilkinson 1986). In general, the more intrusive the nature of the counter-terrorism strategy, the greater is the risk that democratic foundations will be compromised in the process (Pedahzur and Ranstorp 2001). Mani (2006) notes, however, that citizens will generally accept some restrictions on civil and human rights for the purpose of national security, but only if these restrictions are in conformity with the rule of law. The results shown here support that

---

4 <http://www.pollingreport.com/terror.htm> accessed 5 March 2009.

interpretation, and there is most public support for extending measures that already are in place, such as tapping telephones. Moreover, these opinions are substantially driven by concerns about a terrorist attack; should such an attack occur on Australian soil then we would expect substantially more public support for a wider range of measures.

Terrorism and political preferences

There is a growing body of scholarship on the relationship between the threat of terrorism and public opinion. A number of studies have shown that there is a strong relationship between threat perceptions and public opinion (Arian 1989; Huddy et al. 2002, 2005). Terrorist threat perceptions, public opinion and support for public policy are often linked to underlying factors such as high media exposure, global experience and political knowledge (Ridout, Grosse and Appleton 2008). Similarly, studies have demonstrated the ways in which threat perceptions associated with terrorism influence political preferences and support for public policy generally (see Hutchinson and Gibler 2007). For instance, Pape (2003, 2005) observes that in Western democracies, an electorate that is sensitive to terrorism may call for greater concessions to terrorist groups. Other scholars have shown there is direct evidence between the incidence or threat of terrorism and the electorate's political preferences and levels of support for public policy (Berrebi and Klor 2006; McAllister 2008).

Research has shown that the threat of terrorism may have direct effects on political attitudes. In a study of Israeli voter sensitivity to terrorism, Berrebi and Klor (2006) identified two main political consequences of terrorism. The first consequence was for policy voting, so that voters changed their policy preferences in direct response to terrorism. The second consequence was in the ideological polarising effects within the electorate. Berrebi and Klor found that terrorism caused an increase in the relative support for political parties from the right end of the political spectrum, which place more weight on terrorism-deterrence policies. In addition, their conclusions supported the idea that terrorism polarises the electorate (Berrebi 2008). For example, their study showed that terrorism causes an increase in support for the right bloc in all localities with right-leaning preferences and a decrease in support for the right bloc in all localities with left-leaning preferences.[5] Overall, their study provided strong empirical support for the hypothesis that the electorate is highly sensitive to terrorism.

---

5   The occurrence of a terrorist fatality within three months of an election is significantly associated with a 0.45 percentage point increase in the locality's relative electoral support for the right bloc of political parties. If the attack resulted in three fatalities, this would result in an increase of 1.35 percentage points. This could be enough to decide an electoral outcome (see Berrebi 2008).

In the United States, research has shown that the threat of terrorism can alter public opinions in much the same way as wars can evoke popular feelings of hope and national pride. This 'rally round the flag' effect, as John Mueller (1973) has termed it, can in turn shape levels of confidence in government institutions and garner support for public policy (Gross, Brewer and Aday 2009). In Australia, studies have also shown that there are important links between public perceptions of threats from terrorism and support for public policy. For example, drawing on results from 1987–2007 AES surveys, McAllister observes that those who see more threats existing are more likely to view the ANZUS alliance with the United States as important than those who see fewer threats. In addition, those who perceive more threats within the region are more likely to have specific views about defence policy and support an increase in defence spending (see McAllister 2008, 13–14).

Notwithstanding these studies, it is difficult to determine whether it is one's political orientation that shapes attitudes towards policies designed to counter terrorism or whether the fear of terrorism itself is enough to shift one's ideological position further to the left or right. In general, however, the results of the AuSSA show that there is a strong relationship between ideological position and attitudes towards terrorism, measured by the person's self-placement on a zero-to-10 scale.[6] For example, 21 per cent of those who see themselves on the political left view a terrorist attack in Australia as likely compared with 39 per cent who view themselves as centre-right. Those who put themselves in the political centre are most likely to see an attack as likely, at 46 per cent. In terms of whether terrorist suspects should be imprisoned indefinitely, those on the left are least supportive of the measure, with just 38 per cent supporting it. This compares with support for the measure from nine out of every 10 who place themselves on the political right. Very clearly, then, attitudes towards terrorism are influenced by political orientation.

---

6   The correlation between ideological position and the likelihood of a terrorist attack is 0.12 ($p < 0.000$) and with detaining terrorist suspects, 0.40 ($p < 0.000$).

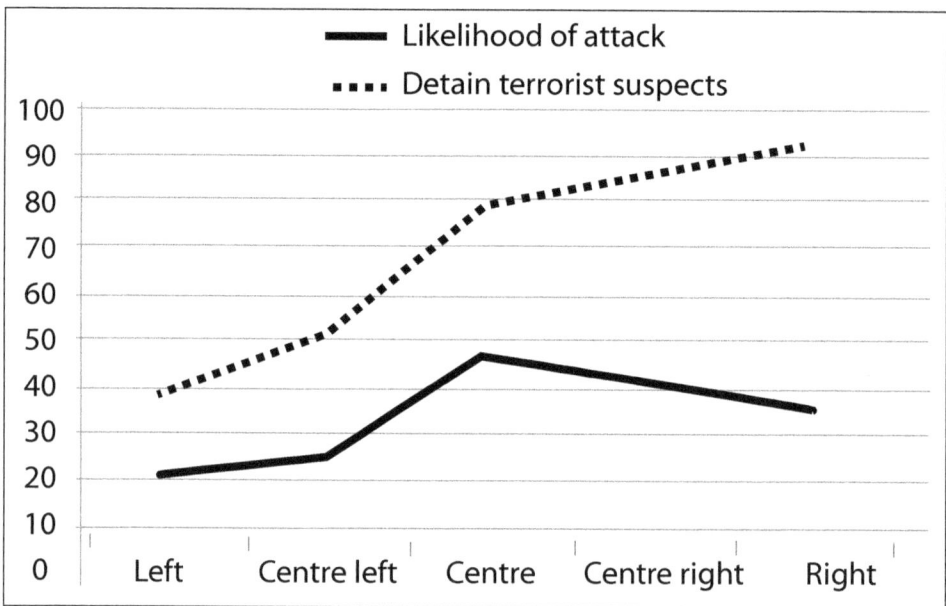

Figure 6.1 Ideological Position and Attitudes Towards Terrorism

Notes: Ideological location is left (1, 2, 3), centre-left (4, 5), centre (6), centre-right (7, 8), right (9, 10, 11). Likelihood of attack in Australia combined 'Very likely' and 'Likely', and detain terrorist suspects is 'Strongly agree' and 'Agree'.

Source: Australian Survey of Social Attitudes 2007, questionnaire C.

Conclusion

Following the 9/11 attacks and the Bali bombings, the Australian public rapidly became aware of the potential of terrorism. Like the mass publics of most other advanced democracies, in Australia terrorism became the 'new normal', and formed a low priority but nevertheless consistent concern for a large proportion of the population. Research shows that low-probability, high-risk events such as a major terrorist attack produce significant changes in attitudes and behaviours among mass publics (Gigerenzer 2006). Australia has been no exception to this pattern. Our findings show widespread public concern about terrorism, with relatively little distinction being made between terrorist events occurring within Australia and within the region. That may reflect the global reach of modern terrorism, but it is also a consequence of the Bali bombings, which occurred overseas but had major implications for public perceptions of the problem and for national security policy.

The survey results also show strong support for countermeasures to reduce the terrorist threat. There is most support for extending current legal measures, such as tapping telephones or the indefinite imprisonment of suspects, and least support for measures that could be construed as torture. Indeed, the Australian public seems more supportive of a wide range of legal countermeasures than the US public, with the latter more concerned about the risks such changes hold for their civil and political rights. These measures are strongly associated with perceptions of the potential threat of terrorism, so that the more the public sees there to be a threat—realised or not—the stronger is the support for measures to deal with it. Finally, our results confirm the strong influence of political ideology on attitudes towards terrorism, in the form of support for or opposition to the imprisonment of suspects. Those who support such moves are more likely to place themselves on the political right, while those who oppose them place themselves on the political left.

What implications do these findings have for public policy towards terrorism? First, there is widespread support for the steps that the government has already taken to reduce the threat. The 2007 AES found that 51 per cent of those interviewed said that the government was doing all it could, with 39 per cent saying that it could do more. That support could evaporate rapidly, however, if a terrorist attack occurred and if it was shown that the government could have done more to prevent it. A further complicating factor is the increasing unpopularity of the wars in Iraq and Afghanistan, which were originally justified as a means of reducing the terrorist threat to Australia. The 2004 and 2007 AES surveys both showed that a majority of the public actually believed that Australian participation in these wars had increased, not reduced, the terrorist threat (McAllister 2008, Table 3).

A second implication for public policy stems from the random nature of terrorism. Research conducted after World War II in both Britain and Germany found that it was the indiscriminate nature of the aerial bombing that produced the most fear within the civilian population, even though the risk of death or injury was comparatively small (Jones et al. 2006). Moreover, over-energetic attempts by the authorities to counter the threat only exacerbated that fear. Terrorism induces similar fears to aerial bombing within the mass public by virtue of its random, unpredictable nature and by public awareness campaigns by the authorities aimed at limiting its effects. Balancing the need for public awareness of the potential terrorist threat against the possible panic such measures can induce represents the heart of the public policy challenge for government.

References

Arian, Asher. 1989. 'A people apart: coping with national security problems in Israel'. *Journal of Conflict Resolution* 33(4): 605–31.

Australian Government. 2008. *The National Security Practice Note: The Rudd Government's evolving national security agenda*. Canberra: Australian Homeland Security Research Centre. <http://www.homelandsecurity.org.au/files/NSPN_Rudds_new_national_security_agenda08.pdf> accessed 22 February 2009.

Berrebi, Claude. 2008. 'Are voters sensitive to terrorism? Direct evidence from the Israeli electorate'. *American Political Science Review* 102(3): 279–301.

Berrebi, Claude and Klor, Esteban. 2006. 'On terrorism and electoral outcomes: theory and evidence from the Israeli–Palestinian conflict'. *The Journal of Conflict Resolution* 50(December): 899–925.

Bowman, Karlyn. 2005. *US Public Opinion and the Terrorist Threat*. Washington, DC: Canada Institute. <http://www.wilsoncenter.org/index.cfm?topic_id=1420&fuseaction=topics.public> accessed 5 March 2009.

Chalk, Peter. 1998. 'The response to terrorism as a threat to liberal democracy'. *Australian Journal of Politics and History* 44(3): 373–88.

Crelinsten, Ronald. 1998. 'The discourse and practice of counter-terrorism in liberal democracies'. *Australian Journal of Politics and History* 44(1): 389–413.

Crelinsten, Ronald and Schmid, Alex. 1992. 'Western responses to terrorism: a twenty-five year balance sheet'. *Terrorism and Political Violence* 4(4): 307–40.

Croissant, Aurel. 2007. 'Muslim insurgency, political violence and democracy in Thailand'. *Terrorism and Political Violence* 19(1): 1–18.

Eubank, William and Weinberg, Leonard. 2008. 'Terrorism and democracy: perpetrators and victims'. *Terrorism and Political Violence* 13(1): 155–64.

Fealy, Greg and Borgu, Aldo. 2005. *Local Jihad: Radical Islam and terrorism in Indonesia*. Canberra: Australian Strategic Policy Institute. <http://www.aspi.org.au/publications/publication_details.aspx?ContentID=79&pubtype=5.> accessed 20 January 2009.

Gigerenzer, Gerd. 2006. 'Out of the frying pan into the fire: behavioral reactions to terrorist attacks'. *Risk Analysis* 26(2): 347–51.

Goulder, Ben and Williams, George. 2006. 'Balancing national security and human rights: assessing the legal response of common law nations to the threat of terrorism'. *Journal of Comparative Policy Analysis* 8(1): 43–62.

Gross, Kimberly, Brewer, Paul and Aday, Sean. 2009. 'Confidence in government and emotional responses to terrorism after September 11, 2001'. *American Politics Research* 37(1): 107–28.

Grosscup, Beau. 2006. *Strategic Terror: The politics and ethics of aerial bombardment*. London: Zed Books.

Hayes, Bernadette and McAllister, Ian. 2001. 'Sowing dragon's teeth: public support for political violence and paramilitarism in Northern Ireland'. *Political Studies* 49(5): 901–22.

Hayes, Bernadette and McAllister, Ian. 2005. 'Public support for political violence and paramilitarism in Northern Ireland'. *Terrorism and Political Violence* 17(4): 599–617.

Hoffman, Bruce. 1998. *Inside Terrorism*. New York: Columbia University Press.

Huddy, Leonie, Feldman, Stanley, Capelos, Theresa and Provost, Colin. 2002. 'The consequences of terrorism: disentangling the effects of personal and national threat'. *Political Psychology* 23: 485–509.

Huddy, Leonie, Feldman, Stanley, Taber, Charles and Lahav, Gallya. 2005. 'Threat, anxiety, and support of antiterrorism policies'. *American Journal of Political Science* 49: 593–608.

Hutchinson, Marc and Gibler, Douglas. 2007. 'Political tolerance and territorial threat'. *The Journal of Politics* 69(1): 128–42.

Jones, Edgar, Woolven, Robin, Durodié, Bill and Wessely, Simon. 2006. 'Public panic and morale: Second World War civilian responses re-examined in the light of the current anti-terrorist campaign'. *Journal of Risk Research* 9: 57–73.

Kiewiet, Roderick. 1981. 'Policy-oriented voting in response to economic issues'. *American Political Science Review* 75(June): 448–59.

Lentini, Pete. 2003. 'Terrorism and its (re)sources: a review article'. *Australian and New Zealand Journal of Criminology* 36(3): 368–78.

Lentini, Pete. 2008. 'Understanding and combating terrorism: definitions, origins and strategies'. *Australian Journal of Political Science* 43(1): 133–40.

McAllister, Ian. 2005. *Attitude Matters. Public opinion towards defence and security*. Canberra: Australian Strategic Policy Institute.

McAllister, Ian. 2008. *Public Opinion in Australia Towards Defence, Security and Terrorism*. Canberra: Australian Strategic Policy Institute.

McAllister, Ian and Clark, Juliet. 2008. *Trends in Australian Political Opinion: Results from the Australian Election Study, 1987–2007*. Canberra: Australian Social Science Data Archive.

Mani, Rama. 2006. *The Relationship between Security and Democracy in Combating Terrorism*. Doha, Qatar: United Nations Development Programme.

Mueller, John E. 1973. *War, Presidents, and Public Opinion*. New York: John Wiley.

Newman, Edward 2007. 'Weak states, state failure, and terrorism'. *Terrorism and Political Violence* 19(4): 463–88.

O'Neil, Andrew. 2007. 'Degrading and managing risk: assessing Australia's counter-terrorist strategy'. *American Journal of Political Science* 42(3): 471–87.

Pape, Robert. 2003. 'The strategic logic of terrorism'. *American Political Science Review* 97(August): 343–61.

Pape, Robert. 2005. *Dying to Win: The strategic logic of suicide terrorism*. New York: Random House.

Pedahzur, Ami. 2005. *Suicide Terrorism*. Cambridge, Mass.: Polity Press.

Pedahzur, Ami and Ranstorp, Magnus. 2001. 'A tertiary model for countering terrorism in liberal democracies: the case of Israel'. *Terrorism and Political Violence* 13(2): 1–26.

Ridout, Travis, Grosse, Ashley and Appleton, Andrew. 2008. 'News media use and Americans' perceptions of global threat'. *American Journal of Political Science* 38(4): 575–93.

Smith, Ric. 2008. *Summary and Conclusions: Report of the review of homeland and border security*. Canberra: Australian Government.

Weinberg, Leonard, Pedahzur, Ami and Hirsch-Hoefler, Sivan. 2004. 'The challenges of conceptualising terrorism'. *Terrorism and Political Violence* 16(4): 777–94.

Wilkinson, Paul. 1986. *Terrorism and the Liberal State*. Basingstoke, UK: Macmillan.

7. Are We Keeping the Bastards Honest? Perceptions of corruption, integrity and influence on politics

Clive Bean

The words of the late Don Chipp, the founder of the Australian Democrats, have perennial relevance to politics. When Chipp talked about 'keeping the bastards honest', it related to a minor political party playing a role of keeping the major political parties true to their word (Warhurst 1997). Yet it is also a democratic role that citizens play on an ongoing basis, particularly through the mechanism of elections. At the ballot box, governments that are widely perceived to have acted with a lack of integrity are roundly punished. This chapter explores public opinion on issues of integrity, corruption, influence and trust in politics and politicians in Australia. The evidence paints a differentiated picture of a public which sees little sign of overtly corrupt political practices but on the other hand does not feel terribly influential and is not always confident of fair treatment from public officials.

Corruption and corrupt practices occur in a variety of manifestations and contexts (Heywood 1997). Australia is not known for the widespread institutional corruption prevalent in some nations. Although there has been no shortage over the years of instances of minor misdemeanours, corrupt practices tend to occur more in the form of individual or personal corruption rather than in a systematic, institutionalised form within structures of governance. In other words, a politician seeks to gain an illegitimate advantage from his or her position in a particular instance, not as an ongoing practice. Institutional corruption, involving systematic abuse of process, is certainly not unknown in Australia, particularly at the level of State politics (Beresford 2010), but it could not be said to be common practice in the way it is in some societies.

There are also, of course, degrees of dishonesty when it comes to the behaviour of politicians and the Australian public appears to have some level of resigned acceptance of political deceit and perhaps even an expectation of it. We are all used to politicians who promise something without qualification and then claim that circumstances have changed when they fail to deliver. A well-known example is that of former Prime Minister John Howard who, as Leader of the Opposition in the mid-1990s, claimed that the Coalition would 'never, ever' introduce a goods and services tax (GST), following its failure to win election on a GST platform in 1993. A few years later, having won office, the Howard

Government did in fact introduce a GST (Warhurst and Simms 2002). To a large extent, the Australian public took this change of mind in its stride on this occasion. Indeed, a clever politician can sometimes promote a change of heart as a virtue: they have seen the shortcomings of their prior position and are now acting squarely in the public interest.

Yet there is little doubt that integrity is regarded as an integral facet of good governance. Previous research into citizen perceptions of honesty and integrity in Australian politics has found, among other things, that the public expects higher ethical standards from politicians than politicians expect from themselves (McAllister 2000). It has also been shown that elections are widely regarded as serving their purpose well and ensuring that voters' views are represented, and further that corruption is not seen as very widespread (Bean 2009). On the other hand, as in so many countries, in Australia trust in politicians is modest at best (Bean 2005), and indeed some have argued that it has reached levels low enough to be of real concern (Martin 2010).

This chapter reviews evidence from the 'Role of Government' module in the 2007 Australian Survey of Social Attitudes (AuSSA) on questions of perceived corruption in politics and experiences of corruption, on questions of fair treatment and personal influence and on questions of efficacy and trust. Particular questions it will consider include how widespread political corruption is perceived to be, direct experience of corrupt practices, how fairly and honestly public officials deal with ordinary citizens, the amount and nature of influence members of the public have on political decision making and on politics and governance in general. The chapter will also consider the extent to which dispositions on these matters are related to a variety of other factors—for example, whether education generates greater political confidence and reduced scepticism. Importantly, it will also look at whether a person's sense of societal connectedness relates to views about political corruption and fairness of political treatment.

Perceptions of corruption, integrity and influence

The 'Role of Government' module in the 2007 AuSSA contains a series of questions probing public perceptions of the extent of political corruption and personal experience of it. The survey respondents are asked: 'In your opinion, about how many politicians in Australia do you think are involved in corruption?' The question is then asked again for public officials. The results are displayed in Table 7.1. The pattern of responses is fairly similar for the two and it is loaded towards a perception of relatively little corruption in Australian politics. Some 9 per cent say almost none and another 35 per cent say a few politicians are involved in corruption (making a total of 45 per cent who more or less dismiss the issue as a problem in Australia). When the 38 per cent who say 'some' are added, this leaves only 17 per cent (one in six) who believe that quite a lot (14 per cent) or almost all (3 per cent) politicians are involved in corruption.

Table 7.1 Perceptions of Corruption in Australian Politics, 2007 (per cent)

	Almost none/ a few	Some	Quite a lot/almost all	Total	(N)
Politicians involved in corruption	45	38	17	100	(2492)
Public officials involved in corruption	41	41	18	100	(2492)
	Never	Seldom	Occasionally/quite often/very often	Total	(N)
Instances of public official wanting bribe or favour	88	8	4	100	(2637)

Note: No. = 2781.

Source: Australian Survey of Social Attitudes 2007.

Switching the focus to appointed public officials, rather than elected politicians, makes little difference to the pattern of responses, although the attitude towards public servants is if anything slightly less benign: 41 per cent say almost none or a few public officials are involved in corruption and 18 per cent say quite a lot or almost all are. But overall, as befits a political system in which known cases of corruption are much more the exception than the rule, the balance of public opinion is stacked heavily against any notion of political corruption being commonplace in Australia.

When the questioning becomes more specific and refers to respondents' own experiences of instances of public officials wanting a bribe or favour (in the past five years) the response is even more emphatic (Table 7.1). The question reads: 'In the last five years, how often have you or a member of your immediate family come across a public official who hinted they wanted, or asked for, a bribe or favour in return for a service?' Almost nine out of 10 (88 per cent) say they have never been subjected to such a situation in the past five years, while virtually no-one says it has happened 'very often'. Indeed, we can add three differentiated answer categories together ('Very often', 'Quite often' and 'Occasionally') and still only make 4 per cent of the sample. In sum, corruption does not appear to be seen by the public as a major problem in Australian politics.

That citizens are not overly concerned about the level of corruption, though, does not necessarily mean that they are not concerned about integrity in

Australian politics. Acting with integrity can obviously be a more subtle matter than simply not being overtly corrupt. The initial questions in Table 7.2 are about how people feel they are treated by public officials. The first question—'In your opinion, how often do public officials deal fairly with people like you?'—shows a less benign view of political dealings. Fewer than half (46 per cent) feel that public officials deal fairly with people like them 'almost always' or 'often'. One-third think that public officials only deal fairly with people like them 'occasionally' and another 22 per cent say 'seldom' or 'almost never'. In other words, more than half the sample feel that in general they are not treated fairly by public officials.

Table 7.2 Perceptions of Fair Dealing and Influence in Australian Politics, 2007 (per cent)

	Almost always/ often	Occasionally	Seldom/ almost never	Total	(N)
Public officials deal fairly with people like you	46	32	22	100	(2497)
	Definitely	**Probably**	**Probably not/ definitely not**	**Total**	**(N)**
Treatment from public officials depends on who people know	29	51	20	100	(2566)
	Never	**Seldom**	**Occasionally/ often**	**Total**	**(N)**
How often asked to influence important decisions in other people's favour	39	33	28	100	(2674)
	Nobody	**A few**	**Some/a lot**	**Total**	**(N)**
People you could ask to help influence important decisions in your favour	40	44	15	100	(2607)

Note: No. = 2781.

Source: Australian Survey of Social Attitudes 2007.

In addition there is a strong sense of the 'it's not what you know but who you know' syndrome. In response to the question 'Do you think that the treatment people get from public officials in Australia depends on who they know?', 29 per cent of AuSSA respondents say that it definitely does and another 51 per cent say it probably does— four out of five, in other words, think who you know matters. And within the 20 per cent with a more positive outlook, only 2 per cent are confident that treatment people receive from public officials definitely does not depend on who they know.

The bottom two questions in Table 7.2 are about respondents' relationship to the 'who you know' category. The first question is: 'Some people, because of their job, position in the community or contacts, are asked by others to help influence important decisions in their favour. What about you? How often are you asked to help influence important decisions in other people's favour?' Most people have little if any experience of being asked to wield political influence. Just less than four in 10 say they are never asked and another third say seldom. Another 24 per cent say occasionally and only 4 per cent say they are often asked to help influence important decisions in other people's favour. Most people are not asked and most people do not know anyone they could ask to wield influence for them. In response to the second question—'And are there people you could ask to help influence important decisions in your favour?'—40 per cent say 'no, nobody', a further 44 per cent say 'a few', while only 15 per cent say 'some' or 'a lot' (and those who say 'a lot' number only 1 per cent). Thus, while respondents believe that receiving good treatment depends on having the right connections, most do not feel that they have such connections.

If these data suggest a sense of powerlessness, such a sense is further reinforced when we explore perceptions of political efficacy in Table 7.3. Research has shown that there are two forms of political efficacy: external efficacy, which is about how responsive governments and politicians are to the public; and internal efficacy, the sense of ability to participate in politics competently and effectively (Abramson 1983; Craig and Maggiotto 1982; Hayes and Bean 1993). More than half the AuSSA 2007 respondents agree with the proposition that 'People like me don't have any say about what the government does', while only a little more than one-quarter disagree, with the remainder neither agreeing nor disagreeing. A related question produces a similar result: nearly six in 10 (58 per cent) disagree with the notion that 'the average citizen has considerable influence on politics' with only one in five agreeing and the rest (22 per cent) sitting in the middle.

Table 7.3 Perceptions of Efficacy and Trust in Australian Politics, 2007 (per cent)

	Strongly agree/ agree	Neither agree nor disagree	Disagree/ strongly disagree	Total	(N)
People like me don't have any say about what the government does	53	19	28	100	(2484)
The average citizen has considerable influence on politics	20	22	58	100	(2672)
I feel I have a pretty good understanding of the important issues facing our country	65	22	13	100	(2674)
I think most people are better informed about politics than I am	18	36	46	100	(2665)
People we elect as MPs try to keep the promises they have made during the election	27	29	44	100	(2670)
Most public servants can be trusted to do what is best for the country	30	34	36	100	(2671)

Note: No. = 2781.

Source: Australian Survey of Social Attitudes 2007.

The sense of citizen efficacy is much stronger, however, when the focus is on political information and understanding. Nearly two-thirds (65 per cent) feel that they 'have a pretty good understanding of the important issues facing our country', while only 13 per cent feel that they do not (with a further 22 per cent being unsure). This expression of competence is reinforced by the fact that only 18 per cent think that 'most people are better informed about politics than I am'. Some 46 per cent disagree with this proposition with a further 36 per cent unsure. These findings replicate the results from earlier rounds of the AuSSA (Bean and Denemark 2007).

When it comes to questions of trust and honesty, opinion is divided and tends towards the sceptical. When asked whether they agree that 'people we elect as MPs try to keep the promises they have made during the election', 44 per cent disagree, 29 per cent neither agree nor disagree and only 27 per cent agree. A slightly greater proportion agree that 'most public servants can be trusted to do what is best for the country', while 34 per cent neither agree nor disagree and 36 per cent disagree. The AuSSA respondents, then, are ambivalent about how much trust they can place in politicians and public officials and many feel lacking in political influence, but they are fairly confident of their own political knowledge and understanding.

Societal underpinnings

Previous studies have shown that certain key socio-demographic variables influence perceptions of political integrity, efficacy and trust. A frequent finding is that education plays a crucial role in breaking down public suspicion of the political elite (Bean 2005; Bean and Denemark 2007; McAllister 2000). Gender and age often seem to play a role in shaping such attitudes as well. Another important factor is social capital—the sense of connectedness or integration into society that grows out of community networks, norms and trust (Putnam 2000). In this instance societal connectedness is represented by a question on social trust, in which respondents are asked to what extent they agree or disagree that 'if you are not careful, other people will take advantage of you'. Social trust, by this measure, is not high in Australia, with more than two-thirds of the sample (69 per cent) agreeing that there is a danger of other people taking advantage, while 17 per cent neither agree nor disagree and only 14 per cent adopt a confidently trusting stance by disagreeing with the proposition.

Each of Tables 7.4, 7.5 and 7.6 takes a key variable from Tables 7.1, 7.2 and 7.3 and breaks it down by these four socio-demographic indicators. Table 7.4 looks at perceptions of how many politicians are involved in corruption. A small amount of variation by sex is apparent, but it is very modest. Women are slightly less likely than men to say that almost none or only a few politicians are involved in corruption and very slightly more likely to say that quite a lot or almost all are. If anything women are thus marginally more concerned about the prevalence of political corruption in Australia, but there is very little in it. Age does not differentiate the respondents to any great degree either. Older people, however, are a little more benign and the young a little more suspicious. The university educated are somewhat more inclined to say that none or few politicians are involved in corruption than those without a university degree, but again the differences are modest.

Table 7.4 Perceptions of Corruption by Socio-Demographic Characteristics (per cent)

Politicians involved in corruption:	Almost none/ a few	Some	Quite a lot/ almost all
Sex			
Female (n = 1272)	43	39	18
Male (n = 1202)	47	38	16
Age			
Under 35 (n = 456)	41	40	19
35–49 (n = 711)	43	38	19
50–64 (n = 766)	47	36	17
65 and over (n = 527)	47	40	13
Education			
No university degree (n = 1829)	43	39	17
University degree (n = 599)	49	36	15
Social trust			
If you are not careful, other people will take advantage of you			
Agree (n = 1688)	40	39	21
Neutral (n = 393)	53	37	10
Disagree (n = 338)	56	36	8

Note: No. = 2781.

Source: Australian Survey of Social Attitudes 2007.

Differentiation is more apparent by social trust. Those who are most trusting of people generally are also substantially more likely to give politicians the benefit of the doubt than those who score lower on social trust. Some 56 per cent of those who display trust say few or no politicians are involved in corruption and only 8 per cent say most are. By contrast, 21 per cent of those who lack trust think most politicians are involved in corruption—two-and-a-half times the proportion of the trusting—and only 40 per cent say virtually none is.

Next we return to the issue of how people are treated by public officials, specifically the question of whether the treatment people get depends on who they know. Table 7.5 shows that on this question there are no gender differences to speak of and relatively small differences by age. The oldest cohort of respondents—those sixty-five and over—seems somewhat more committed than the remainder to the view that who you know matters.

Table 7.5 Perceptions of Treatment from Public Officials by Socio-Demographic Characteristics (per cent)

Treatment from public officials depends on who people know:	Definitely	Probably	Probably not/ definitely not
Sex			
Female (n = 1324)	29	53	19
Male (n = 1222)	28	51	21
Age			
Under 35 (n = 469)	27	54	19
35–49 (n = 726)	27	52	21
50–64 (n = 791)	30	48	23
65 and over (n = 542)	30	54	16
Education			
No university degree (n = 1893)	31	52	17
University degree (n = 605)	19	51	30
Social trust			
If you are not careful, other people will take advantage of you			
Agree (n = 1778)	34	51	15
Neutral (n = 402)	16	57	27
Disagree (n = 358)	15	46	39

Note: No. = 2781.

Source: Australian Survey of Social Attitudes 2007.

Both education and social trust make a marked difference to responses on this question. Whereas 30 per cent of those with a university degree state that who you know probably or definitely does not make a difference to the treatment received from public officials, only 17 per cent of those without university education think likewise. The figures are more or less reversed for those who say who you know definitely does make a difference: 31 per cent of those without a university degree give this response, while only 19 per cent of those with a degree do also. The contrast is even greater between those who differ on social trust. Nearly four in 10 of the trusting (39 per cent) say that treatment from public officials probably or definitely does not depend on who you know compared with 15 per cent of the untrusting. And again the balance is reversed for the group saying treatment definitely does depend on who you know: 34 per cent of the untrusting say it does compared with only 15 per cent of the trusting.

Table 7.6 Perceptions of Political Efficacy by Socio-Demographic Characteristics (per cent)

People like me don't have any say about what the government does:	Strongly agree/agree	Neither agree nor disagree	Disagree/strongly disagree
Sex			
Female (n = 1393)	52	20	29
Male (n = 1270)	55	19	26
Age			
Under 35 (n = 498)	50	20	30
35–49 (n = 768)	48	20	32
50–64 (n = 822)	54	18	29
65 and over (n = 559)	63	19	18
Education			
No university degree (n = 1981)	58	19	23
University degree (n = 632)	38	18	44
Social Trust			
If you are not careful, other people will take advantage of you			
Agree (n = 1809)	59	17	24
Neutral (n = 439)	43	28	29
Disagree (n = 366)	34	19	47

Note: No. = 2781.

Source: Australian Survey of Social Attitudes 2007.

A cynic might be tempted to say that the university educated and the socially trusting have more benign views because they have the right kinds of political connections to ensure good treatment, so they can afford to say who you know does not matter. Indeed, the AuSSA data show that there is some correlation, though small, between holding a degree and knowing people who may be able to help influence political decisions. A corrective to this perspective, however, is that even among the university educated and socially trusting sizeable majorities still hold the view that treatment from public officials does depend on who you know: seven in 10 of the university educated and six in 10 of the trusting. Thus, while concern about political treatment is reduced among those with a university degree, for example, it is far from completely transformed.

Last, we focus again on political efficacy, with Table 7.6 showing the socio-demographic breakdown of the question about how much say ordinary citizens have about what the government does. Again, gender differences are slim, although women appear to have a slightly stronger sense of efficacy than men. Age, however, does make a difference to feelings of efficacy. Younger people are considerably more likely to feel efficacious than older people. The clearest contrast is between those under the age of fifty and those sixty-five and over.

About half of those under fifty agree that 'people like me don't have any say about what the government does' but of those sixty-five and over nearly two-thirds do. And while 30 per cent or more of those under fifty disagree with the proposition, only 18 per cent of those sixty-five and over disagree.

Once again education and social trust give rise to the most marked differences. Nearly six in 10 of those without a university degree lack a sense of political efficacy while less than four in 10 of those with a university qualification express a similar lack of efficacy. On the other hand, 44 per cent of the university educated display a sense of efficacy compared with only 23 per cent of those who are less well educated. Similarly, those who are not socially trusting also tend to lack political efficacy (59 per cent display a lack of efficacy and only 24 per cent show a sense of efficacy), while those who do trust others are much more inclined to feel politically efficacious (47 per cent display a sense of efficacy and only 34 per cent lack a feeling of efficacy). In the sample as a whole the ratio of the non-efficacious to the efficacious is almost two to one (53 per cent versus 28 per cent). But for both the highly educated and the socially trusting, this balance is overturned so that more people in these groups express a sense of efficacy than a lack of efficacy.

Conclusion

The evidence in this chapter paints a mixed picture. While there is no indication that political corruption is perceived to be a major problem among the Australian public, there is a good deal of concern about how fairly people are treated by public officials and about a perceived lack of external political efficacy—that is, a lack of governmental responsiveness and a sense of inability to have any influence. On the other hand, internal efficacy—feeling politically competent—is very high. This contrast between low external efficacy and high internal efficacy is not an isolated finding (Bean and Denemark 2007).

Perhaps the most important finding to emerge from this study is the difference that education and social capital make to perceptions about politics. This is not the first time that the significance of education has been highlighted, both in Australia and elsewhere (Bean 2009; Hayes and Bean 1993; McAllister 2000). The implications for governance and for public policy development are important and worth discussing. Education appears to lessen the sense of suspicion and negativity inherent in many people's orientations towards politics. Governments thus have a vested interest in pursuing policies to enhance the educational stocks of the nation. The more people who undertake a university education the more barriers will be broken down between the political elite and the public;

likewise with social capital. Building strong communities in which citizens feel connected with and trusting of each other has many benefits, one of them being that it will help improve public perceptions of the political realm.

Yet neither education nor social capital is a panacea. The data show that education generally changes attitudes to an extent, not completely. Many well-educated people remain unconvinced of the benignity of the political world. And there are no doubt good reasons for this, reasons that would relate among other things to actual experiences of governmental non-responsiveness. Taken to its extreme, the argument about education would suggest that the problem is entirely one of perceptions, and with a thoroughly well-educated community no-one would have a low sense of political efficacy, for example. In reality of course governments and politicians are far from totally responsive to every citizen's political requirements and it would be almost impossible for them to be so. Nonetheless, education and the knowledge it generates do help make the realm of politics more accessible and less daunting for individuals.

Are we keeping the bastards honest? The evidence suggests that the answer is a qualified 'yes'. Corruption in politics is not widely perceived to be rampant and, perceptions aside, very few individuals have personal experience of corruption. Yet at a more diffuse level, many Australians feel relatively powerless in the political arena, they are concerned that people with the right connections will get more favourable treatment from public officials and they are not confident that elected politicians and appointed public officials can be trusted.

References

Abramson, Paul R. 1983. *Political Attitudes in America*. San Francisco: W. H. Freeman.

Bean, Clive. 2005. 'Is there a crisis of trust in Australia?'. In *Australian Social Attitudes: The first report*, eds Shaun Wilson, Gabrielle Meagher, Rachel Gibson, David Denemark and Mark Western. Sydney: UNSW Press.

Bean, Clive. 2009. 'Public perceptions of elections: an Australia–New Zealand comparison'. In *In the Public Interest: Essays in honour of Professor Keith Jackson*, eds M. Francis and J. Tully. Christchurch: Canterbury University Press.

Bean, Clive and Denemark, David. 2007. 'Citizenship, participation, efficacy and trust in Australia'. In *Australian Social Attitudes 2: Citizenship, work and aspirations*, eds David Denemark, Gabrielle Meagher, Shaun Wilson, Mark Western and Timothy Phillips. Sydney: UNSW Press.

Beresford, Quentin. 2010. 'Corporations, government and development: the case of institutional corruption in Tasmania'. *Australian Journal of Political Science* 45: 209–25.

Craig, Stephen C. and Maggiotto, Michael A. 1982. 'Measuring political efficacy'. *Political Methodology* 8: 85–110.

Hayes, Bernadette C. and Bean, Clive S. 1993. 'Political efficacy: a comparative study of the United States, West Germany, Great Britain and Australia'. *European Journal of Political Research* 23: 261–80.

Heywood, Paul (ed.). 1997. *Political Corruption*. London: Blackwell.

McAllister, Ian. 2000. 'Keeping them honest: public and elite perceptions of ethical conduct among Australian legislators'. *Political Studies* 48: 22–37.

Martin, Aaron. 2010. 'Does political trust matter? Examining some of the implications of low levels of political trust in Australia'. *Australian Journal of Political Science* 45: 705–12.

Putnam, Robert D. 2000. *Bowling Alone: The collapse and revival of American community*. New York: Simon & Schuster.

Warhurst, John (ed.). 1997. *Keeping the Bastards Honest: The Australian Democrats' first twenty years*. Sydney: Allen & Unwin.

Warhurst, John and Simms, Marian (eds). 2002. *2001: The centenary election*. Brisbane: University of Queensland Press.

8. A New Role for Government? Trends in social policy preferences since the mid-1980s

Shaun Wilson, Gabrielle Meagher and Kerstin Hermes

Three big problems—an economic crisis, failing infrastructure and adverse climate change—are reminders of the limits of market coordination and the need for active government, a role anticipated by the public and acknowledged by former Prime Minister Kevin Rudd (2009a). How have public expectations of government adjusted in awareness of these new challenges? Have voters come to expect a larger, or perhaps differently focused, role for government? Fortunately, more than 20 years of comparative survey research data provide opportunities to judge shifts in public opinion—over time and against trends evident in other countries (see, for example, Smith 1987). They also provide basic indicators of support for government activity at a time when the public's expectations of government are likely to be transformed by the economic crisis that emerged in 2008.

Our chapter looks closely at the International Social Survey Program's 'Role of Government Module 2006',[1] placing Australia over time and comparatively. We begin by examining Australian preferences for government to spend more or tax less. Data on this question go back to the 1960s, allowing us to explore changes in fiscal mood. We are also able to track the shift in fiscal mood against other social indicators that move over time: attitudes to the death penalty, immigration and union power. The second part of the chapter examines spending preferences between 1985 and 2006 to discover what policy areas the Australian public most wants government to spend more on now, and how our priorities have changed over the past two decades. In the third part of the chapter, we examine what Australians believe are the government's responsibilities in key areas such as controlling prices, finding people jobs, and providing housing and for people in retirement. We look at how these beliefs have changed—or not changed—over time, and compare Australian perspectives with those of citizens of other International Social Survey Program (ISSP) member countries.

---

1 The ISSP has fielded a Role of Government (RoG) module four times: in 1985, 1990, 1996 and 2006. In Australia, RoG was fielded with the AuSSA 2007.

Australians want more social spending

The Australian Survey of Social Attitudes (AuSSA) series has tracked spending and taxing preferences since 2003. Over this period, preferences for more social spending have increased and, correspondingly, preferences for cutting taxes have continued to weaken. This trend coincides with a number of political and policy developments during a long period of fiscally conservative government led by John Howard (1996–2007), which tends to produce a shift in public opinion in favour of spending (for the general argument, see Stimson 2004, 76–87). In real terms, this shift in mood coincided with a slowing expansion of welfare spending—after a period of rapid increase under the previous Labor government (see Table 8.1). Indeed, between 2000 and 2005, Organisation for Economic Cooperation and Development (OECD) figures suggest a significant slowdown in welfare spending increases in Australia. Additionally, a series of income tax cuts, which have continued under the Labor Government (2007–), have limited demand for further reductions at a time when voters believe public infrastructure is deteriorating (OECD 2008). Let's take a closer look.

Trends in welfare spending and taxation

Table 8.1 presents evidence of the shifting fiscal situation since 1985. The table shows social spending by government across a range of policy areas, as a proportion of gross domestic product (GDP). Overall, Australia's public welfare spending remains below OECD averages; in 2005, it was ranked twentieth out of a list of 29 (mostly wealthy) democracies. In comparative terms, Australia is most generous in the area of family income support, with spending at 2.8 per cent of GDP, and a rank of eighth out of 29. This is the result of active policy change: the Hawke and Keating Labor governments (1983–96) expanded this area of assistance and the Howard Government preserved this program. This additional spending has had a real impact on overall and child poverty rates (Harding and Szukalska 1999), although child poverty is still significant; a recent UNICEF study ranked Australia thirteenth out of 23 OECD countries and below average on a composite index of child material wellbeing (UNICEF 2007, 4).

Meanwhile, poverty among older Australians remains very high by international comparisons; in 2000, Australia was exceeded only by transitional Ireland in a study of 17 rich democracies (Mishel, Bernstein and Shierholz 2008, 384). It is easy to understand why: comparatively low spending (twenty-third out of 29) on old-age benefits evident in Table 8.1. This remains true even if we had included private spending on superannuation in the comparisons. It is not surprising, then, that Australians have strong preferences for spending more on age pensions; a recent Australian Election Study (AES) finding suggests 63 per cent of respondents believe that retired people with no superannuation deserve more assistance from the government (see Wilson, Meagher and Hermes 2012). Moreover, compared with 25 years ago, now older Australians have emerged as a strong constituency for more social spending. This new constituency for a more generous welfare state has made its impact: upon its election in November 2007, the new Labor government almost immediately faced demands to raise basic pension rates.

Table 8.1 suggests a slowing trend in social spending under the Howard Government compared with the previous Labor governments: compare the 4.1 per cent increase between 1985 and 1995—10 years of Labor—with just a 0.5 per cent increase between 1995 and 2005, 10 years of the Coalition. All the increase in welfare spending under Howard occurred during the first two terms of his government. The slowdown since is partly accounted for by labour, housing and asset markets that remained buoyant until 2007 and which, in turn, reduced fiscal pressures on unemployment, family and pension programs. But slower innovation in welfare policy compared with the previous government—Labor introduced Medicare, a new system of family payments and new benefits for students and for people living with disabilities—also contributed to the slowing of spending growth as well. By contrast, the Coalition's innovations concentrated on middle-class benefits—financed as tax expenditures—to subsidise private health care, child care and private retirement incomes (see Spies-Butcher and Stebbing 2008).

Table 8.1 also tells something of the tax story—at least in aggregate terms. Overall the tax take barely rose under Labor between 1985 and 1995 (0.5 per cent). Clearly, the Labor administration accepted a hard tax constraint, and attempted to reorganise welfare and government along 'Labor lines' within this constraint. The aggregate tax take under Howard actually increased, from 29 to 31 per cent—not a trend that would prompt voters to lose interest in tax reductions. Here, some extra detail helps to interpret the possible role of tax policy in the shifting fiscal mood in favour of spending. First, the tax expansion under Howard appears to have been more cyclical than discretionary. True, his government did broaden the tax base by introducing the goods and services tax (GST) in 2000, which helped finance a series of well-publicised income tax cuts that mostly benefited higher income earners and reduced the redistributive impact of income taxes (Vu, Harding and Percival 2008). But consumption and income taxes remained—measured as a share of GDP—fairly steady over the Howard years (see OECD 2007, p. 80). Instead, revenue growth came from rising corporate tax receipts produced by strong profitability in the private economy (OECD 2007, p. 81). Given this, the tax 'burden' faced by voters either stayed the same or decreased for higher income earners—despite growing tax revenues.

Table 8.1 Social Spending and Taxation Trends in Australia, 1985–2005 (per cent of GDP and rank in OECD)

	1985	1990	1995	2000	2005	Change 1985–95	Change 1995–2005	Rank 2005
Old-age	3.0	3.4	4.0	4.9	4.4	1.0	0.4	23/29
Incapacity	1.1	1.8	2.4	2.6	2.4	1.5	−0.2	10/29
Health	4.6	4.6	4.9	5.5	5.9	0.3	1.0	20/29
Family	1.2	1.5	2.8	3.0	2.8	1.6	0.0	8/29
Active labour-market programs	0.4	0.2	0.7	0.4	0.4	0.3	0.0	17/29
Unemployment	1.2	1.1	1.2	0.9	0.5	0.0	−0.7	16/28
Housing	0.3	0.3	0.2	0.1	0.3	−0.2	0.2	12/25
Public social spending (% GDP)	12.5	13.6	16.6	17.8	17.1	4.1	0.5	20/29
Tax revenue (% GDP)	28.3	28.5	28.8	31.1	30.9	0.5	2.1	23/30

Note: Public social expenditure totals include other program spending not included in the row items listed above.

Sources: OECD (2007, 2008).

Second, when the tax expansion under the Howard Government is viewed comparatively, it was relatively modest anyway: between 1995 and 2005, the average tax take among OECD countries increased about 4 per cent of GDP compared with Australia's 2 per cent. In general terms, most OECD governments were busy expanding tax revenues to meet similar challenges as those Australia faced, only at a faster rate. Moreover, when the comparisons are pushed a bit further—and Australia's rank in the OECD over time is considered—we see that Australia continues to fall in the tax stakes, from sixteenth (out of 26 countries) in 1985 to twenty-third (out of 30) in 2005 (see Table 8.1). None of the new entrants between 1985 and 2005 could be considered a 'high tax country' and a number overtook Australia over the 20-year period surveyed (Iceland, Spain, Portugal, Switzerland and Turkey) while others (South Korea and Greece) closed the gap (see OECD 2007, p. 19). Given pressures on governments that led to the growth of revenues elsewhere, the Australian Government managed to contain the growth of government—at least in comparative terms—more than the headline figures suggest.

The upward shift in spending preferences is probably more than a symbolic reaction against the 'fiscal conservatism' of the Howard years. Social spending grew slowly, and fell in GDP terms between 2000 and 2005; the focus was on cutting income taxes and broadening the tax base. Our argument is this: policy settings have led to public pressures to improve services that now strongly exceed pressures to deliver tax relief. This policy backdrop, we think, provides the best context in which to read public opinion. The AuSSA 2007 did not include the standard item on tax and spending preferences, so here we use a similar AES measure for which we have a time series dating back to 1987. The question asked is: 'If the government had a choice between reducing taxes or spending more on social services, which do you think it should do?' The five options are: strongly favour/mildly favour reducing taxes; depends; and mildly/strongly favour spending more on social services (see Table 8.2).

Table 8.2 Fiscal Mood, 1987–2007 (per cent in columns)

	1987	1990	1993	1996	1998	2001	2004	2007	Change 1987–2007
Strongly favour reducing taxes	44		38	41	33	27	22	21	-23
Mildly favour reducing taxes	22		18	16	14	15	14	13	-9
Total favouring tax cuts	66	80	56	57	47	42	36	34	-32
Depends	20	-	27	26	28	29	28	19	-1
Mildly favour spending more on social services	8		10	10	12	14	17	20	+12
Strongly favour spending more on social services	7		7	7	13	15	21	27	+20
Total favouring spending increases	15	20	17	17	25	29	38	47	+32
Spending preference ratio*	0.19	0.20	0.23	0.20	0.35	0.41	0.51	0.58	
	(n = 1740)	(n = 6084)	(n = 2942)	(n = 1727)	(n = 1804)	(n = 1951)	(n = 1711)	(n = 1816)	

* Net spending preferences divided by the sum of net spending and tax reduction preferences.

Sources: AES 1987–2007.

On the AES measure, the public continues to prefer attention to the spending side of government. The AES 2007 records the strongest preferences in favour of greater spending (on social services) in the series that commenced in 1987, with 47 per cent preferring more spending and 34 per cent now interested in tax cuts. This contrasts with just 10 per cent seeking more spending in 1987, when Labor (and others) were advocating spending constraint. To put spending trends in historical perspective, we have calculated a measure of spending preferences (see note to Table 8.2) and, on that score, Australians are now the most pro-spending they have been since the late 1960s (for earlier data, see Wilson, Meagher and Breusch 2005, p. 105). The fiscal mood provides opportunities for the Gillard Labor Government to increase social spending with one less constraint at least—that of general public opinion. And, with the scale of the global economic crisis, we can anticipate that the mood for spending has some way to run yet. We turn to the more specific question of what Australians prefer government to spend more on in the next section.

Are Australians seeking greater social protection? Spending preferences compared

We can compare trends in preferences for social spending against other social trends for which there are comparable time points. Here, we choose three others: attitudes to the death penalty, attitudes to union power and attitudes to immigration levels. The data points are for 1987 to 2007, taking account of 20 years of public opinion. We would expect attitudes to union power and immigration levels to be cyclical or 'mood' variables—that is, to fluctuate as the public moves through more liberal and more conservative moods (Stimson 1991, 2004). Over time, unions go through periods of power and influence as well as weakness and marginalisation—both are eventually registered by the public. Equally, support for immigration varies with the economic and employment cycle: as employment rises, economic resistance to immigration falls and vice versa. Attitudes to the death penalty are more complicated: they exhibit elements of a *secular* trend with a cyclical component—that is, long-term social change is probably *permanently* reducing support for capital punishment, but trends in the crime rate and publicity about serious crimes will have an impact on support or opposition at the margins.

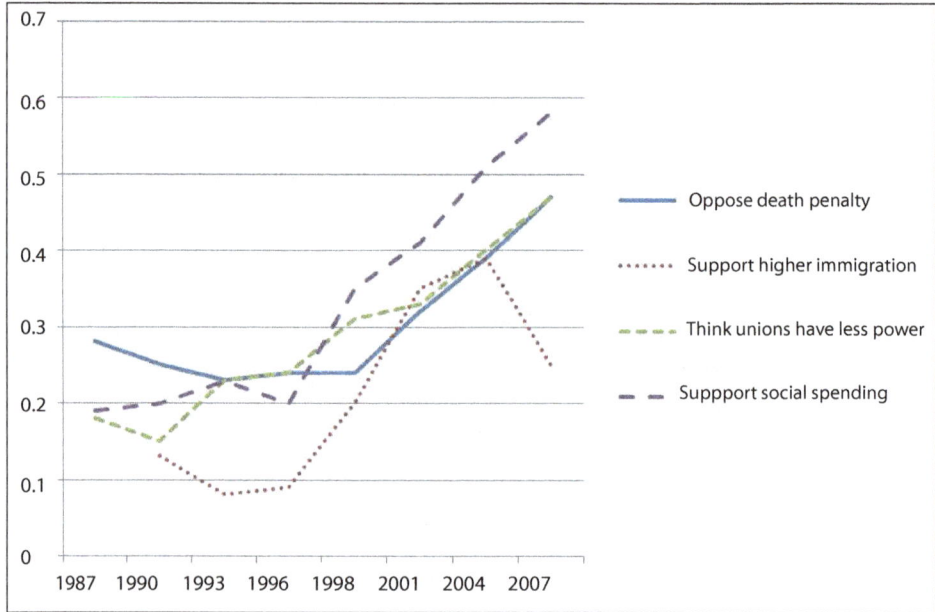

Figure 8.1 Pro-Spending Preferences: Part of a more liberal mood, 1987–2007

Notes: Figure 8.1 reports scores between 1987 and 2007 measuring: preferences for greater social spending, reduced support for the death penalty, support for more immigration, and perceptions that unions *do not* have too much power. Rising scores, on a scale between 0 and 1, indicate a more liberal aggregate response to each item. The scores have been calculated as ratios of support against opposition for each proposition specified above (see Appendix Table A8.2 for details of the calculations and the scores).

Sources: AES 1987–2007.

Do any of these social trends follow closely the trend for spending? Figure 8.1 reports scores between 1987 and 2007 measuring: preferences for greater social spending, reduced support for the death penalty, support for more immigration, and perceptions that unions *do not* have too much power. The scores have been calculated as ratios of support against opposition for each proposition specified above (see Appendix Table A8.2 for details of the calculations and the scores). We find that, between 1987 and 2004, all four variables tend to trend together. We can conclude that, taken together, they suggest a latent 'liberal' or even social-democratic mood gathered strength during the Howard years, most likely as a balancing response to that government's perceived fiscal and social conservatism.

In 2007, however, support for immigration started to fall, departing from the continuing upward trend for the other three variables. This downward turn in support for immigration levels suggests that, as recent high immigration intakes began to coincide with rising living standard pressures, the public tempered their generosity towards immigration levels, reversing a very liberal mood apparent since the early 2000s. But this decline in support for immigration may well correspond with a trend that supports social spending and recognises the weakness of unions. One possible reading of the combined trend is that, after the Howard years, Australians want governments to deal with pressures on living standards, with a greater emphasis on *social protection* in welfare and providing a strengthened voice and rights in the workplace. The same stresses on living standards that stimulate demand for social protection may also account for the more protectionist (that is, restrictive) stance towards immigration evident in 2007.

Declining support for the death penalty reflects the more liberal mood prevailing in Australia, but secular decline in support for capital punishment will probably mean that this trend will continue long after a broader trend back to political conservatism is established. On that score, it will be interesting to see how long it takes for a more political conservative mood to emerge—as a response to the Rudd Government's increases in welfare spending (partly in response to the economic crisis of 2008 and 2009) and its restoration of a role for unions in new industrial laws (Gillard 2008; Rudd and Gillard 2007). The mitigating impact of the global economic crisis, however, will probably mean that the public seeks more protection from government, and for longer, than the political mood cycle would normally accommodate.

Public priorities: Where do Australians most want additional spending?

As we have suggested, in 2007 Australian voters were in the mood for fiscal expansion. Combined with Labor in office and reduced elite opposition to fiscal activism at a time of crisis, conditions supported an expansion in the size and role of government. But voters have supported more spending for quite some time, so it is useful to identify those areas where voters expect the largest 'catch-up' from politicians. As part of the regular Role of Government module, the ISSP has asked respondents in member countries since the mid-1980s to nominate areas of government where they would prefer more or less spending—the areas are listed in Table 8.3. Although samples over time depended on different weighting methods, we report basic trends without re-weighting data. Instead, we conducted a series of regression models to confirm the validity of the changes we report below.[2]

---

2 Comparing survey results over time involves additional complications when the survey series changes; the earlier ISSP results (1985, 1990, 1996) were weighted by population characteristics while the 2006 data are unweighted. We needed to be sure the trends we identified were not distorted by sample bias. To resolve this problem, we merged the samples and performed regressions for each of the spending areas, obtaining coefficients for each of the years of the survey results (1985 was the base category). These models allow us to control for gender, age and education—the most likely, straightforward sources of sampling differences

As we can see in Table 8.3, there are three spending areas where Australians seek more spending than they did in the mid-1980s: the environment, health and education. Spending on the environment reflects the reality, and growing awareness, of dangerous climate change and the public's willingness to support major efforts by government to deal with this. Readers might be surprised to learn, however, that most of this shift in preferences took place back in 1990, during the first widespread awakening of ecological consciousness. By 2006, preferences for greater spending on the environment were much higher than they were in 1985, but perhaps disturbingly—given the state of the problem—have not fully recovered to 1990 levels.

Responses to health and education spending are equally interesting, but one could argue that these results, seeking greater public spending, reflect more polling 'noise' than real substance: voters of all persuasions consistently tell pollsters that governments don't do enough in these two huge portfolios. But trends are what matter here: Australians have become *increasingly* supportive of education and health spending. What explains this? For health, one possibility is that an older population will demand more health care—almost automatically. Yet our regression models did not find that support for more spending on health care increases with age. More likely is that population ageing increases perceptions in all age groups of the power of, and necessity for, more and more sophisticated medical care. Related, an affluent society—such as Australia—has increasingly high expectations of health care (Glennerster and Hills 1998; but see also Taylor-Gooby 1998). At the same time, perceptions of underfunding and poor maintenance and investment in hospital infrastructure have a bearing on public preferences. To explain increasing support for spending on education, it is reasonable to expect that as the skills, or at least the credentials, required to enter and advance within the labour market increase, so too will expectations of the education system, and of government spending. Again, other factors intervene: publicity about the quality of schooling, and neglect of the public school system, are likely factors in explaining support for more spending.

---

between weighted and unweighted data. How did results compare with the ones reported in Table 8.2? The trends in favour of greater spending on the environment, health and education were maintained—that is, these trends are real, and not products of sample bias. To compare the preferences of government spending in different years, the surveys of the years 1985, 1990, 1996 and 2006–07 were merged.

Table 8.3 Australian Spending Preferences by Policy Area, 1985–2007 (percentage preferring more)

	1985	1990	1996	2007	Change
Environment	32	64	48	59	+27
Health	62	68	80	90	+28
Law enforcement	67	68	67	67	0
Education	64	70	70	80	+16
Defence	46	25	27	25	−21
Retirement	55	55	50	54	−1
Unemployment benefits	13	10	12	12	−1
Culture and the arts	10	13	13	14	+4
	(n ≥ 1448)	(n ≥ 2356)	(n ≥ 2086)	(n ≥ 2618)	

Sources: Australian Survey of Social Attitudes 2007; ISSP Role of Government module 1985, 1990, 1996, 2006.

We have some evidence from previous surveys to support the argument that perceptions of the declining quality of health care and public education are widespread. In 2003 and 2005, the AuSSA asked respondents whether they thought the standard of health services, including Medicare, and of public education had increased or decreased in the previous two years. In 2003, 59 per cent of respondents thought health service standards had decreased a little or a lot, and 42 per cent thought standards in public education had decreased (Gibson et al. 2004). Two years later, 51 per cent thought health standards had fallen, and 48 per cent thought public education standards had fallen (Wilson et al. 2006). (In both surveys, relatively small minorities of between 14 and 18 per cent of respondents believed that either health or education standards had improved.) Although we should interpret the perception of precipitous decline in standards over four years with caution, these findings clearly demonstrate that Australians have been concerned about the quality of health and public education in recent years. These perceptions—more than, say, perceptions of the generosity of government to the unemployed—are driving support for greater government investment.

What have *not* changed much are preferences for spending in other areas of the welfare state: unemployment spending and retirement. Falling unemployment between 1992 and 2006 most likely accounts for this lack of change; while broader welfare-supporting attitudes have been rising, falling joblessness (until recently) has pushed the unemployment problem down the list of public priorities. But, even when joblessness is high or rising, the Australian public remains fairly cool about spending more on the unemployed, although regression results suggest Australians are marginally warmer towards spending on unemployment than they were in the 1980s. Still, the Labor Government did not direct any of two 2008 spending packages—totalling $14.4 billion and aimed at boosting the economy—towards the unemployed. The February 2009 stimulus plan also focused mainly on working families, small business and single parents. The goal clearly has been to prevent rising unemployment rather than to lift living standards for the already unemployed.[3]

More puzzling is the failure for preferences towards spending on retirement income to rise. As we mention above, other survey evidence from the AES 2007 data suggests strong support for spending more on pensions. Perhaps the 'retirement' label is too undifferentiated to capture an underlying reality: strong support for more spending on pensioners, but more limited support for spending on non-pensioner retirees (whom the public recognises benefited a good deal from tax expenditures available to self-funded retirees in the late Howard years) (Wilson, Meagher and Hermes 2012).

The only spending item to record a dramatic fall is defence. Recall that, in 1985, Cold War fears still held major currency with voters, doubtless adding to support for defence spending (for an overview of trends in defence attitudes, see Gibson and McAllister 2007). Notice that all of the fall in preferences occurred at the end of the Cold War period, in 1990. Although a number of post–Cold War conflicts have stimulated defence spending ambitions, none has been strong enough or long-lasting enough to return preferences for greater defence spending to Cold War levels.

Before we move on, it is worth noting one policy problem demanding significant spending that public discussion has recently centred on: the poor state of Australia's 'infrastructure'. This means different things to different people; for the public, poor infrastructure means rundown or inadequate schools, transport, hospitals and roads, while for business, it means inferior ports and telecommunications. The ISSP survey data do not directly ask about spending preferences on infrastructure but it appears from other sources that the local discussion of infrastructure problems does resonate in comparative survey research. Australians were much more likely to seek additional spending on infrastructure than respondents in India, China, the United States, Japan and Russia—as measured by the most recent AsiaBarometer (see Park 2008).

---

3 These are the $10.4 billion 'economic security strategy' announced in October 2008 (Rudd and Swan 2008), the $4 billion 'business investment partnership' announced in January 2009 (Rudd 2009b) and the $42 billion 'Nation building and jobs plan' announced in February 2009 (Rudd and Swan 2009).

Government responsibility and government performance

In the previous section, our focus was spending preferences—on what policy areas Australians prefer government to spend more or less on. In this section we explore some related, but more basic, questions about the role and performance of government. What social and economic activities do Australians believe the government should take responsibility for? Have Australians changed their views on the role of government over the past two decades? And how well do Australians rate the success of government action in some key areas? This section also takes advantage of ISSP data to compare what Australians think about the role of government with the views of citizens in other countries.

One important context for these questions is the political contention over the size of government that emerged in the wake of the economic crisis of the 1970s, and that has continued, if not raged, ever since. That economic crisis came towards the end of four decades of substantial growth in public spending in rich democracies. Governments had both expanded programs in areas in which they had previously been involved and taken on new responsibilities, and spending on social security and on human services, such as health and education, grew faster than spending in other areas (Lindert 2004; Wilensky 2002). Many of those on the 'small government' side of the debate blamed rising public spending, particularly social spending, for the economic crisis, and called for a reduction in the size and scope of government.

Debate about the size and scope is inevitably debate about whether the government should or should not be responsible for this or that activity, and if so to what extent. Accordingly, social researchers began to ask citizens about their perceptions of the role of government with the question: 'On the whole, do you think it should or should not be the government's responsibility to… [undertake the activities listed in the first column of Table 8.4].' Findings from these studies can be used to assess support for the redistributive activities of the welfare state, since several questions deal with social policy; to understand whether the public has taken up arguments for reducing the size and scope of government; and to explore the relationship between public opinion and policy structures in different welfare regimes (Jæger 2009; Svallfors 2003).

Do Australians want a reduced role for government?

Our analysis of spending preferences suggests that Australians do not seek a drastically reduced role for government, at least as measured by their willingness to pay more taxes and their desire to see more spending in some key policy areas.

Table 8.4 shows Australians' responses on the related question of government responsibility over two decades. The survey invites respondents to choose whether an activity 'Definitely should be', 'Probably should be', 'Probably should not be' or 'Definitely should not be' the government's responsibility. To make it easier to compare years (and groups of countries later in the chapter), we have converted responses into a 10-point mean scale. On this scale, a higher score (above five) means that, on average, respondents think the government *should* take responsibility and a lower score (below five) means that, on average, respondents think the government *should not* take responsibility. The higher (lower) the score, the more (less) people think the government should take more responsibility.

Table 8.4 Australian Beliefs about the Role of Government, 1985–2007 (mean scores)*

	1985	1990	1996	2007	Change 1985–2007**
Provide a job for everyone who wants one	5.2	4.7	4.9	4.5	–0.7
Keep prices under control	7.8	6.8	6.7	7.6	–0.2
Provide health care for the sick	8.4	7.7	7.9	9	0.6
Provide a decent standard of living for the old	8.6	7.7	7.7	8.3	–0.3
Provide industry with the help it needs to grow	7.2	6.7	6.8	7	–0.2
Provide a decent standard of living for the unemployed	5.5	5.1	5.6	5.2	–0.3
Reduce income differences between rich and poor	5.3	5.1	5.3	5.9	0.6
Give financial help to university students from low-income families	n.a.	6.9	7	7.6	0.7
Provide decent housing for those who can't afford it	n.a.	6.3	6.1	6.6	0.3
Impose strict laws to make industry do less damage to the environment	n.a.	n.a.	8.2	8.5	0.3
	(n ≥ 1440)	(n ≥ 2292)	(n ≥ 2038)	(n ≥ 2618)	

* 10-point scale; higher values = more responsibility.

** For items added to the ISSP survey in 1990 (housing, student support) and 1996 (environmental laws), comparison over time takes the relevant first survey year as the starting point.

Sources: Australian Survey of Social Attitudes 2007; ISSP Role of Government module 1985, 1990, 1996.

Focusing first on findings for 2007, we see very strong support among Australians for the government taking responsibility in some key social and economic policy areas: providing health care and environmental protection stand out, with scores of 9 and 8.5 out of 10 respectively, closely followed by a decent standard of living for the old (8.3). Support is considerably weaker when it comes to providing a decent standard of living for the unemployed (5.2) and reducing income differences (5.9). And on the question of government responsibility for providing jobs, Australians are, on balance, opposed (4.5). These three lowest-scoring activities are related, and responses show how much Australians frame the operation of the labour market, and a person's success or failure in it, in individualistic/market rather than social/government terms (see also Meagher and Wilson 2008).

Because these questions have been asked four times since, we can assess whether Australians have become less supportive of government involvement in economic and social life overall, in the context of calls for smaller government. One way to do this is to compare the scores on each activity between 1985 and 2007. Looking down Column 6 of Table 8.4, it is difficult to see evidence of a general preference for reducing government involvement among Australians: for some activities, support for government taking responsibility has grown (health care, financial help to students, environmental protection); for others it has fallen (providing jobs, industry assistance, price control). Most show a pattern of mild fluctuation across the decades. Another approach is to compare a combined average score for all activities, which forms a simple measure of overall support for government intervention. In 1985, the combined average score for the seven activities included in the survey was 6.9. The combined average score for the same seven activities in 2007 is 6.8. If we include all 10 activities asked about in the 2007 survey, we get an average score of 7.0. These findings suggest that, on balance, Australians' orientation to the role of government has been fairly positive and stable. The findings also accord with Michael Pusey and Nick Turnbull's (2005) conclusions about public opinion on market-oriented economic reform in Australia.

Government responsibilities: How does Australia compare?

Our task now is to put Australian beliefs about the role of government into international perspective. Figure 8.2 compares Australian beliefs with those of people in seven groups of countries, drawn from the rich democracies of East and West as well as from Eastern Europe and Latin America.[4] (Values charted

---

4 Researchers have long been interested in the relationship between public opinion and the institutional structures of welfare states, and a rich body of research has accumulated in recent decades. Debates about the extent to which attitudes vary as much *within* as *between* welfare regimes have been important. Within the scope of a survey chapter such as this, we are not able to engage deeply with these debates. Recent work has confirmed that systematic differences both within and between regime types can be expected (Jæger 2009); our focus here is on between-regime differences. We extend previous work by including groups of Latin American and rich East Asian countries.

for Australia are those from Column 5 of Table 8.4.) Western European, North American and Antipodean rich democracies are grouped into welfare regimes, following Esping-Andersen's (1990) typology, while the remaining countries are grouped geographically.[5] Again, we use a 10-point scale and calculate mean scores for each activity for each group of countries.[6] What does this comparison reveal? First, Australia and the other liberal welfare regimes stand out in their relative opposition to government intervention in the labour market and redistribution. Indeed, mean scores on 'provide a job for everyone' in Australia and in the group of other liberal countries are the only ones registering majority opposition to government involvement in any activity in any group of countries.[7] This is not surprising: an individualistic and market-oriented approach to the labour market and income distribution is a defining characteristic of liberal welfare regimes, and is reflected both in attitudes and institutions.

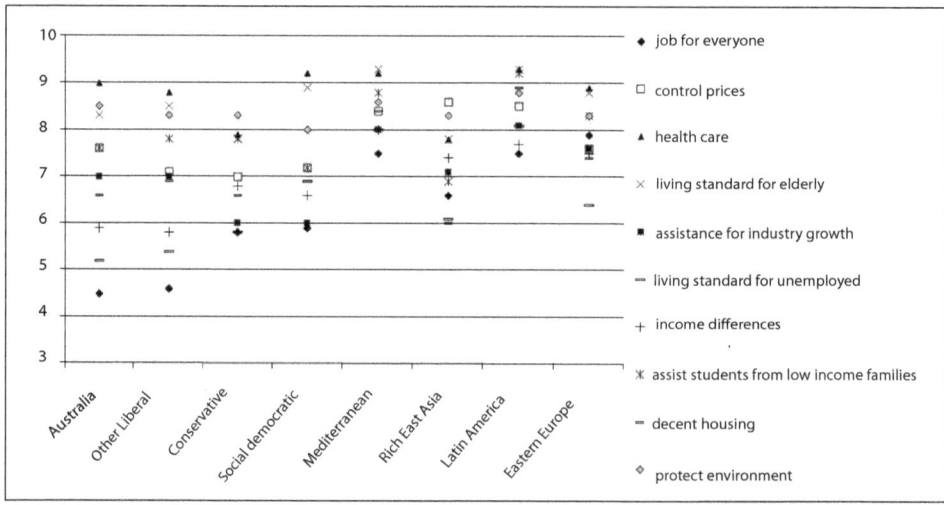

Figure 8.2 Beliefs about Government Responsibility, Australia and Other Welfare Regimes/Country Groups, 2006 (mean scores)

Sources: Australian Survey of Social Attitudes 2007; ISSP Role of Government module 2006.

Despite low scores on activities related to the labour market and redistribution in other liberal countries, respondents from these countries are, like Australians, on balance strongly supportive of a role for government in some activities—notably in health care, environmental protection and providing a decent living

---

5   We use Esping-Andersen's typology, but can include only those countries that participated in the ISSP 2006. Esping-Andersen classifies Australia as a liberal welfare state, although this has been contentious (Castles and Mitchell 1993). Appendix Table A8.1 shows the countries included in each group.
6   The means for country groups are not weighted for the size of the member countries.
7   Among the 30 individual countries included in the groups presented in Figure 8.2 only three had mean scores lower than five on any of the 10 activities surveyed in 2006: 4.1 for government responsibility for housing in Japan, 4.6 for providing a decent standard of living for the unemployed in the Czech Republic, and 4.8 for assistance to industry in Switzerland.

standard for old people. This wide dispersal of scores—from 4.6 (jobs) to 8.8 (health care)—in liberal regimes suggests the lack of a general position on the role of government. By contrast, the distribution of scores in Mediterranean, Latin American and Eastern European countries is much more compressed. Respondents in these country groups strongly support government responsibility in all activities surveyed (minimum score overall is 7.4 for housing in Eastern Europe), with the single exception of lower support for providing a decent standard of living for the unemployed in Eastern Europe (6.4). Other groups of countries fall somewhere in between. Dispersal is moderate in rich East Asia and conservative countries, but support for government involvement is also moderate, with few scores exceeding 8.0 in either group. Perhaps surprisingly, dispersal is quite wide in social-democratic countries, which show very strong support for government involvement in health care and providing for older people, but quite low support, on average, for providing jobs and assisting industry.

Explaining these patterns is not entirely straightforward. In some cases, high scores express respondents' desire for governments to *increase* their responsibility in a given area—this is likely to be the case for most activities in Latin American and Mediterranean countries, where universal institutional supports for social and economic development are weak. In other cases, high scores are likely to express citizen support for, and desire for further commitment to, significant existing government responsibility; health care and provision for the elderly in social-democratic countries are examples here. When it comes to low scores, we have already pointed out how little support there is for intervention in the labour market and redistribution in liberal countries, and noted how these beliefs accord with comparatively low levels of government involvement in these activities. Yet support for government responsibility for job creation and supporting the living standards of the unemployed is also relatively weak in social-democratic countries. In these countries, governments have taken very significant responsibility in these policy areas, and so are likely to have more fully met demand for labour-market intervention.

We can explore these ideas a little further using a question the Role of Government survey asks respondents about how successful they think their government is in a range of activities. Four of the activities asked about correspond directly with those included with the question about government responsibility: health care, living standards for the old, fighting unemployment and protecting the environment. Figure 8.3 compares mean scores for these four activities for measures of both government responsibility and government success.

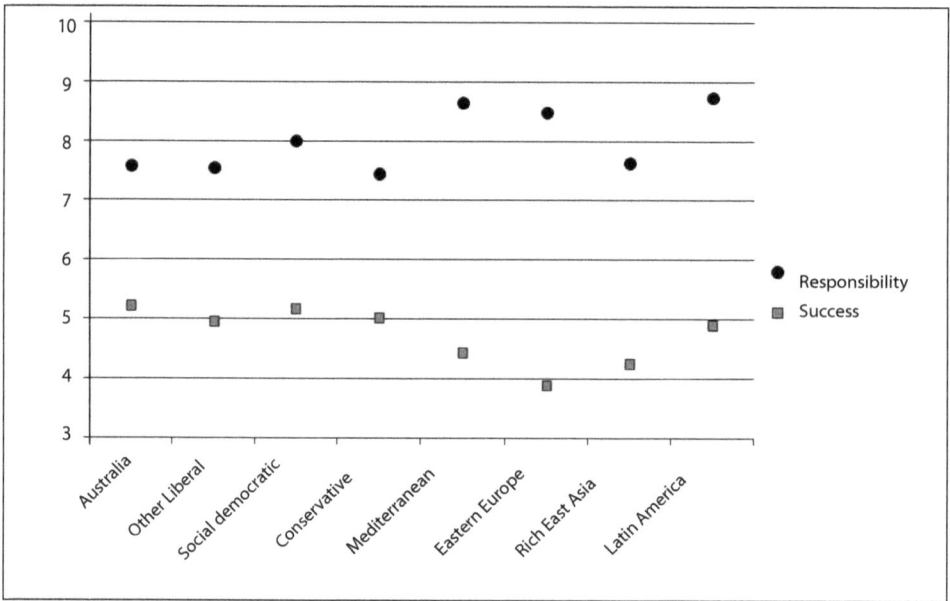

Figure 8.3 Beliefs about Government Responsibility and Perceptions of Government Success, Mean Scores by Regime Type, 2006

Sources: Australian Survey of Social Attitudes 2007; ISSP Role of Government module 2006.

First, note the rather lacklustre assessment respondents make, on average, of the success of government in these four activities. Just as for the government responsibility scale, a higher score (above five) means that, on average, respondents think the government *is* successful and a lower score (below five) means that, on average, respondents think the government *is not* successful. On average, government is considered *unsuccessful* in all groups of countries except the conservative and social-democratic regimes and in Australia, where it is considered only very marginally successful. Second, note the larger gap between perceptions of success and beliefs about responsibility in the groups we previously identified as having underdeveloped supports for social and economic development: Latin American and, to a lesser extent, Mediterranean countries. There is also a large gap between perceived success and beliefs about responsibility in Eastern European countries, where institutional supports have been greatly reduced since the fall of communism. This suggests at least some attachment among citizens to the supports developed in communist states, if not to the political repression they also experienced.

Clearly, attitudes and institutions are related in complex ways, and to understand these relationships we need knowledge of policy structures and institutional histories (Brooks and Manza 2007, 30–2). For example, we have mentioned the individualist orientation of liberal welfare states. This orientation is not simply a matter of values or culture; these are also countries where left-wing parties and unions had the most trouble, during the twentieth century, establishing institutions that would guarantee full employment and high levels of social protection for the unemployed, usually through active labour-market programs. Where left-wing parties and unions gained a strong foothold, as they did in social-democratic countries, they were able to establish institutions, such as the Ghent system. Under Ghent systems, unions control unemployment insurance. This institution encourages very high levels of union participation and high levels of support for collective welfare arrangements that are organised separately from the mainstream tax system.

In English-speaking countries, such institutions have not been established, and so the public, without experience of them, 'defaults' to private solutions. Further reducing pressure on English-speaking democracies to spend more on labour-market solutions are falling rates of unemployment in recent years; supporters say this is the result of labour-market deregulation, but some economists have observed—for some time now—that debt-driven growth is behind this success (Schmitt 2000). How the economic crisis tests public orientations in liberal regimes about dealing with unemployment will be interesting to observe.

The role of government: Does political orientation matter?

Detailed analysis of the social structure of beliefs about the role of government is beyond the scope of this chapter;[8] however, we conclude this section by briefly exploring whether political orientation makes a difference to beliefs about the role of government.

Figure 8.4 sets aside the issue of international variation to examine what relationship there might be between political orientation and beliefs about the role of government. The chart compares the mean scores between respondents identified with political parties across the spectrum from extreme left to extreme right with the average response overall.[9] (In other words, the mean score overall for each activity is set at zero for the purposes of this comparison.) Two findings stand out. First, and unsurprisingly, there is a stark divide between the far left and the conservative right on government intervention in the labour market and redistribution; after all, these are the economic and social policy issues that define left and right orientations. We see, then, that those on the far left have higher than average scores in favour of government redistributing income,

---

8 For comparison of countries within welfare regime groups, see Evans (1998); Jæger (2009); and Svallfors (2003). Svallfors (2003) and Jæger (2009) also analyse variations between social groups, such as class and gender, within and between regimes.
9 Respondents to the ISSP are asked about which party in their country they affiliate with. To enable researchers to make cross-national comparisons, the ISSP derives a new variable by coding political parties in each country on the left–right scale (shown in Figure 8.5) when preparing the combined file with data for all countries.

providing jobs and providing a decent standard of living for the unemployed, while those on the conservative right have lower than average scores for all activities measured here, but particularly for these three. Second, we see that the far right and the conservative right do not seem to cluster together, and that those on the far right are closer to the average, and even to the left, than they are to the conservative right. This finding likely reflects class cleavages on the right, such that the far right is dominated by disaffected working and lower middle-class voters, while the centre right is dominated by the wealthier middle class. The finding is also likely to reflect differences between countries in the political orientations of class groupings—far-left and far-right parties are virtually non-existent in most liberal countries, for example.

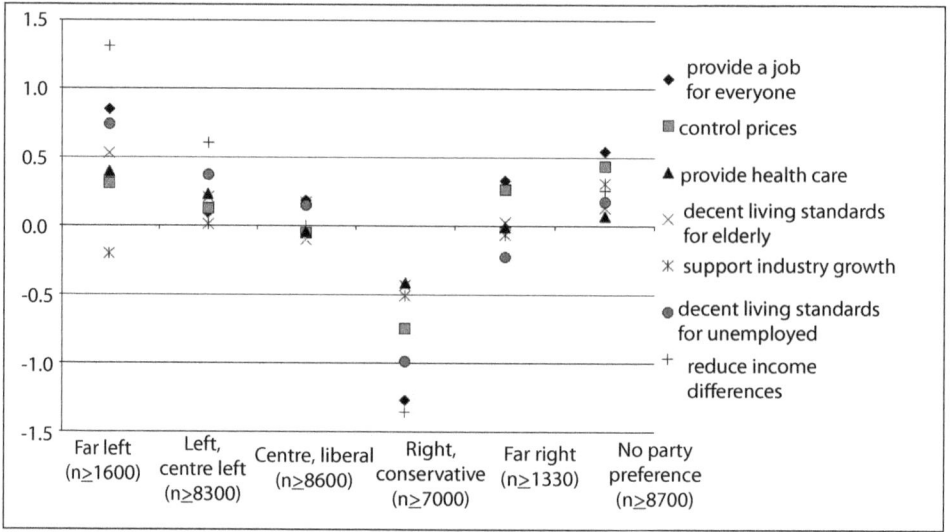

Figure 8.4 Perceptions of Government Responsibility, Difference from Mean Scores Overall by Political Party Orientation, All Respondents, 2006

Sources: Australian Survey of Social Attitudes 2007; ISSP Role of Government module 2006.

Conclusion

This chapter makes three claims. First, the mood for fiscal expansion—evident in survey findings for about 10 years—continues. The Rudd Labor Government's economic stimulus packages (December 2008 and February 2009), though designed to address an economic crisis, have chosen to reflate through spending rather than tax reductions—in accord with public preferences. Second, when we compare spending priorities of Australians today with those researchers found in the mid-1980s, we find that voters want more spending on education, health care and the environment. We speculate that perceptions of rundown education and health systems are major factors driving the strong spending preferences that have become a longer-term trend. Third, we find that Australian expectations of government look similar to other liberal welfare states: highly supportive of government provision of pensions and health care, *increasingly* supportive of assistance for low-income students, reducing income inequality and providing public housing, but less supportive of assistance to the unemployed and finding people jobs. But market solutions to maintaining employment have come under severe strain as a result of the economic crisis. How publics and governments across liberal regimes respond to these new threats will reveal something about the durability—or perhaps, adaptive dynamics—of the liberal model.

References

Brooks, Clem and Manza, Jeff. 2007. *Why Welfare States Persist: The importance of public opinion in democracies*. Chicago: University of Chicago Press.

Castles, Francis G. and Mitchell, Deborah. 1993. 'Worlds of welfare and families of nations'. In *Families of Nations: Patterns of public policy in Western democracies*, ed. F. G. Castles. Aldershot, UK: Dartmouth Publishing Company.

Esping-Anderson, Gøsta. 1990. *The Three Worlds of Welfare Capitalism*. Princeton: Princeton University Press.

Evans, Geoffrey. 1998. 'Britain and Europe: separate worlds of welfare?'. *Government and Opposition* 33: 139–270.

Gibson, Rachel and McAllister, Ian. 2007. 'Defence, security and the Iraq war'. In *Australian Social Attitudes II: Citizenship, work and aspirations*, eds David Denemark, Gabrielle Meagher, Shaun Wilson, Mark Western and Timothy Phillips, pp. 37–57. Sydney: UNSW Press.

Gibson, Rachel, Wilson, Shaun, Meagher, Gabrielle, Denemark, David and Western, Mark. 2004. Australian Survey of Social Attitudes 2003. Data file. Canberra: Australian Social Science Data Archives, The Australian National University.

Gillard, Julia. 2008. Introduction of the Fair Work Bill today. Media release. Canberra: Deputy Prime Minister's Office, Parliament House. <http://www.deewr.gov.au/Ministers/Gillard/Media/Releases/Pages/Article_081128_144403.aspx>

Glennerster, Howard and Hills, John. (eds). 1998. *The State of Welfare: The economics of social spending*. Oxford: Oxford University Press.

Harding, Anne and Szukalska, Aggie. 1999. *Making a Difference: The impact of government policy on child poverty in Australia, 1982 to 1997/9*. Discussion Paper no. 42. Canberra: National Centre for Social and Economic Modelling.

Jæger, Mads Meier. 2009. 'United but divided: welfare regimes and the level and variance in public support for redistribution'. *European Sociological Review* (12 January).

Lindert, Peter. 2004. *Growing Public: Social spending and economic growth since the eighteenth century*. Cambridge: Cambridge University Press.

Meagher, Gabrielle and Wilson, Shaun. 2008. 'Richer, but more unequal: perceptions of inequality in Australia 1987–2005'. *Journal of Australian Political Economy* 61: 220–43.

Mishel, Lawrence, Bernstein, Jared and Shierholz, Heidi. 2008. *The State of Working America 2008/9*. Ithaca, NY: Cornell University Press.

Organisation for Economic Cooperation and Development (OECD). 2007. *Revenue Statistics 1965–2006*. Paris: Organisation for Economic Cooperation and Development. <http://oberon.sourceoecd.org/vl=1004325/cl=26/nw=1/rpsv/cgi-bin/fulltextew.pl?prpsv=/ij/oecdthemes/99980169/v2007n3/s4/p84.idx>

Organisation for Economic Cooperation and Development (OECD). 2008. *Growing Unequal? Income distribution and poverty in OECD countries*. Paris: Organisation for Economic Cooperation and Development.

Park, Chong-Min. 2008. Public attitudes toward government spending in advanced and emerging market economies. Paper prepared for the AsiaBarometer 2008 Workshop, Chuo University, Tokyo, 17–18 December.

Pusey, Michael and Turnbull, Nick. 2005. 'Have Australians embraced economic reform?'. In *Australian Social Attitudes: The first report*, eds Shaun Wilson, Gabrielle Meagher, Rachel Gibson, David Denemark and Mark Western, pp. 161–81. Sydney: UNSW Press.

Rudd, Kevin. 2009a. 'The global financial crisis'. *The Monthly* (42)(February).

Rudd, Kevin. 2009b. Building Australia's future—a $4 billion Australian business investment partnership to support Australian jobs. Media release, 24 January. Canberra: Parliament House. <http://www.pm.gov.au/media/Release/2009/media_release_0771.cfm>

Rudd, Kevin and Gillard, Julia. 2007. *Forward with Fairness: Labor's plan for fairer and more productive Australian workplaces*. Canberra: Australian Labor Party. <http://www.alp.org.au/download/now/forwardwithfairness.pdf>

Rudd, Kevin and Swan, Wayne. 2008. Economic security strategy. Joint press release with the Treasurer, Wayne Swan, 14 October. Canberra: Parliament House. <http://www.pm.gov.au/media/release/2008/media_release_0550.cfm>

Rudd, Kevin and Swan, Wayne. 2009. $42 billion nation building and jobs plan. Joint press release with the Treasurer, Wayne Swan, 3 February. Canberra: Parliament House. <http://www.pm.gov.au/media/Release/2009/media_release_0784.cfm>

Schmitt, J. 2000. 'Demand drives US jobs success'. *The Guardian*, 4 September. <http://www.epi.org/publications/entry/webfeatures_viewpoints_demand_usjobs/>

Smith, Tom. 1987. 'The polls—a report: the welfare state in cross-national perspective'. *Public Opinion Quarterly* 51: 404–21.

Spies-Butcher, Ben and Stebbing, Adam. 2008. Beyond the targeted welfare state? How recent developments in tax expenditures are transforming Australian welfare. Paper presented to the conference on A Future for the Australian Welfare State? Continuity and Change from Howard to Rudd, Macquarie University, Sydney, 25 July.

Stimson, James. 1991. *Public Opinion in America: Moods, cycles, and swings*. Boulder, Colo.: Westview Press.

Stimson, James. 2004. *Tides of Consent: How public opinion shapes American politics*. New York: Cambridge University Press.

Svallfors, Stefan. 2003. 'Welfare regimes and welfare opinions: a comparison of eight Western countries'. *Social Indicators Research* 64: 495–520.

Taylor-Gooby, Peter. 1998. '"Things can only get better": expectations and the welfare state'. *Policy & Politics* 26: 471–6.

UNICEF. 2007. *Child Poverty in Perspective: An overview of child well-being in rich countries, Innocenti report card 7*. Florence: UNICEF Innocenti Research Centre. <http://www.unicef-irc.org/publications/pdf/rc7_eng.pdf>

Vu, Q. N., Harding, A. and Percival, R. 2008. A growing gap? Trends in economic wellbeing at the top of the spectrum in Australia. Paper prepared for the 30th General Conference of the International Association for Research on Income and Wealth, Portoroz, Slovenia, 29 August. <http://www.iariw.org/papers/2008/harding.pdf>

Wilensky, Harold. 2002. *Rich Democracies: Political economy, public policy, and performance*. Berkeley: University of California Press.

Wilson, Shaun, Gibson, Rachel, Meagher, Gabrielle, Denemark, David and Western, Mark. 2006. *The Australian Survey of Social Attitudes, 2005: User's guide*. Canberra: Australian Social Science Data Archive, The Australian National University.

Wilson, Shaun, Meagher, Gabrielle and Breusch, Trevor. 2005. 'Where to for the welfare state?' In *Australian Social Attitudes: The first report*, eds Shaun Wilson, Gabrielle Meagher, Rachel Gibson, David Denemark and Mark Western, pp. 101–21. Sydney: UNSW Press.

Wilson, Shaun, Meagher, Gabrielle and Hermes, Kerstin. (2012). 'The social division of welfare knowledge: policy stratification and perceptions of welfare reform in Australia'. *Policy and Politics 40: 323-46.*

Appendix 8.1

Table A8.1 Country Groups

Liberal	[Australia], Canada, Ireland, New Zealand, United Kingdom, United States of America
Social democratic	Denmark, Finland, Norway, Sweden, Netherlands
Conservative	France, Germany (West), Switzerland
Mediterranean	Portugal, Spain
Eastern Europe	Croatia, Czech Republic, Germany (East), Hungary, Latvia, Poland, Russia, Slovak Republic, Slovenia
Rich East Asia	Japan, South Korea, Taiwan
Latin America	Chile, Uruguay, Venezuela

Source: ISSP Role of Government module 2006.

Table A8.2 Ratios for Figure 8.1

	1987 (n ≥ 1774)	1990 (n ≥ 1999)	1993 (n ≥ 2913)	1996 (n ≥ 1749)	1998 (n ≥ 1802)	2001 (n ≥ 1933)	2004 (n ≥ 1695)	2007 (n ≥ 1815)
Death penalty	0.28	0.25	0.23	0.24	0.24	0.32	0.39	0.47
Immigration levels	n.a.	0.13	0.08	0.09	0.20	0.35	0.39	0.25
Union power	0.18	0.15	0.23	0.24	0.31	0.33	0.40	0.47
Social spending	0.19	0.20	0.23	0.20	0.35	0.41	0.51	0.58

Notes: 1987—death penalty item (agree/disagree, five-point scale), 'Bring back the death penalty'; union item (too much/not too much, three-point scale). 1990—death penalty item (agree/disagree, five-point scale), 'Death penalty reintroduced for murder'; 'Number of migrants allowed into Australia' (much too far to not nearly far enough, five-point scale); union item—'Trade unions have too much power' (agree/disagree, five-point scale). Items remain the same from 1990 onwards. The scores are simple, unstandardised ratios that express aggregated support for the propositions listed divided by combined support and opposition for the proposition. They allow us simple comparisons over time, and between variables, that account for different response category structures used in some surveys.

Sources: AES 1987–2007.

9. WorkChoices: An electoral issue and its social, political and attitudinal cleavages

Murray Goot and Ian Watson

From the moment John Howard announced his plans to reshape industrial relations, WorkChoices changed the political debate. The legislation represented the biggest shake-up of industrial relations policy since Stanley Bruce's ill-fated attempt, nearly 80 years earlier, to repeal the *Commonwealth Conciliation and Arbitration Act* (Lee 2010, Ch. 6). Yet, as the Treasurer's press secretary would later lament, WorkChoices 'seemed to come out of nowhere' (Savva 2010, 214; also Lewis 2008, 178–9). It provoked the trade union movement into mounting 'one of the most brilliant campaigns in Australia's history' (Kelly 2009, 306), failed to mobilise large parts of the business community in its defence (Howard 2011, 580, 585) and, with Labor committed to dismantling the legislation, began to spell the end of the Howard Government; like Bruce, Howard lost both the prime ministership and his own seat.

In this chapter we show how—thanks to the government, the trade union movement and the Opposition—the issue of industrial relations was transformed, virtually overnight. More precisely, we show how it went: from an issue of low electoral importance to an issue of high importance; from a policy, or series of policies, over which electors were divided to a policy on which opinion ran largely one way; and from something of a political strength for the government to something that loomed as a fatal weakness. Had respondents not rated the issue highly, WorkChoices would not have shifted votes, no matter how widespread the opposition. Had respondents been divided over the merits of the legislation, the government might have gained as many voters as it lost. Had respondents not seen a real difference between Labor and the Coalition on industrial relations it would not have affected their support for either party no matter how the issue was regarded (see Butler and Stokes 1969, Ch. 15 for the *locus classicus* of this model; for an earlier analysis of survey data on WorkChoices that omits the second condition, see Wilson 2005, 294).

Nonetheless, as this chapter shows, data from the Australian Survey of Social Attitudes (AuSSA) together with data from public opinion polls commissioned by the press and surveys commissioned by others—notably the Australian Council of Trade Unions (ACTU)—need to be handled with care. Indeed, there were moments where the outcome of the party battle might have depended on what the diverse data on public opinion—from polls, focus groups and the feedback from MPs—were taken to mean. Just how survey respondents regarded the legislation in relation to their vote very much depended on the other issues they were asked to rate. In responding to the issue, the options open to respondents also mattered; for example, the size of the opposition to the legislation was partly a function of whether the relevant question encouraged a non-committal response. In some cases, a reframing of the issue changed the balance of opinion; reactions to the unfair dismissal legislation were a spectacular instance of this. And on a number of the issues associated with the legislation the government was able to claw back some of the lost ground: whether the legislation would lead to higher wages, whether it would be bad 'for the average worker', and whether union powers in the workplace should be enhanced are examples of this. In the end, while the modification of the legislation made some aspects of the Coalition's reforms more acceptable to the electorate and while the gap over which of the two parties would best handle industrial relations might have narrowed, neither may have done much to stem the flow of votes to Labor.

WorkChoices brought to the surface a number of deep-seated cleavages in Australian society. In terms of social structure, there was the cleavage between young and old as well as the cleavage between unionists and non-unionists. Politically, there was the cleavage between respondents who thought of themselves as 'left' or 'right' as well as the cleavage around how respondents intended to vote. And in terms of attitudes to industrial relations there were cleavages over the classic issues of class: union power and employer prerogatives—a reflection of the attempt to remove what Howard characterised as 'the privileged position of the trade union movement' by means of 'aiding', as Paul Kelly put it, 'one side of the class divide' (Kelly 2009, 304, 307; also Norrington 2006, 102).

The rise of industrial relations as an election issue

The Howard Government's announcement to the parliament, on 26 May 2005, that it intended to introduce new industrial relations legislation—officially known, from November 2005, when it was introduced to the House of Representatives, as WorkChoices (Stewart and Williams 2007, 31) and rushed through the Senate in early December (Singleton 2008, 80–1)—transformed industrial relations from an issue of relatively low importance to an issue of high importance. In the Australian Election Study (AES) conducted after the October 2004 election, fewer than one-third (30 per cent) of the respondents named industrial relations as 'extremely important' when 'deciding about how to vote'; in a ranking of 12 issues, industrial relations tied for tenth. After the 2007 election, when the AES went back into the field, no fewer than two-thirds (67 per cent) of the respondents said industrial relations had been 'extremely important' when 'deciding about how to vote'; out of 11 issues, industrial relations tied for first. Asked, directly, in the 2004 survey to say which issue on the list 'was most important to you and your family during the election campaign', just 2 per cent named industrial relations; no issue on the list was less important. Asked after the 2007 election which issue had been most important, 16 per cent named industrial relations; only one issue, 'health and Medicare' (20 per cent) outranked it.

The rise of industrial relations as a voting issue was not something that simply happened in the course of the 2007 campaign. Nor was it a 'sleeper issue', as Roy Morgan Research suggested (cited in Muir 2008, 77), stirred into wakefulness in mid-2006 after the bulk of the new, wide-ranging legislation came into effect (see Lewis 2008, 177). Its rise dates from the government's announcement of WorkChoices and the ACTU's mobilisation against it. From an issue that at the end of 2004 had virtually disappeared from the range of concerns respondents volunteered to Morgan as among 'the three most important things the government should be doing something about' (Norton 2007–08, 25, for the data), industrial relations was rated 'very important' by many more respondents after the first of the ACTU's advertisements—most memorably, the 'Tracy' advertisement—went to air from Saturday, 18 June 2005 than it had been for years before (Muir 2008, 66–7, 217n.19). In a Newspoll conducted on the same weekend as the ACTU's advertising the proportion of respondents saying industrial relations was 'very important' to how they 'would vote in a federal election' was 41 per cent—a substantial rise from the 31 per cent registered by Newspoll in June 2004, the last time this question had been asked. By early October, as the government's campaign shifted up a gear, roughly half of the respondents (49 per cent) rated industrial relations 'very important'. In February 2006 the corresponding figure (48 per cent) was virtually unchanged. In October, however, it rose to 54 per cent after a second wave of ACTU ads had gone to air in June and the Labor leader, Kim Beazley, had promised to 'rip up' WorkChoices (Muir 2008, 71, 77). Two years later, in mid-October 2007, notwithstanding that the Senate had passed The Workplace Relations Amendment (A Stronger Safety Net) Bill in June (Muir 2008, 28), the figure (49 per cent) was still high.

While half the respondents may have thought the issue 'very important', how did industrial relations rank in relation to other issues? In June 2005, as in June 2004, out of the 17 issues listed by Newspoll, industrial relations ranked either second or third-last. Even in October 2006, when the list was cut back to just six issues, industrial relations ranked below health and Medicare (82 per cent), education (78 per cent), welfare and social issues (66 per cent), national security (64 per cent) and leadership (56 per cent). In November 2007, shortly before the election, a Galaxy survey across seven marginal seats found 'industrial relations' ranked fourth out of six issues: of those who had 'made up' their mind, 54 per cent said it had been the 'most influential' issue when they were 'choosing the party' for which they would vote.

But where respondents were restricted to naming the one issue that would be most important to them—or even the three issues that would the most important—industrial relations appears to have been more potent than the Newspoll or Galaxy data suggest. In October 2006, according to Nielsen, industrial relations (named by 17 per cent of its respondents) came second after health and hospitals (24 per cent) as 'the most important' issue (out of nine) helping respondents decide their 'vote at the next federal election'; even in March 2007, when industrial relations (nominated by 15 per cent) slipped to fourth it was no more important than health and hospitals (19 per cent), the economy (17 per cent) or the environment (16 per cent). In March 2007, 'the industrial relations laws' were nominated by 15 per cent as 'the single most important issue that will decide how you vote at the federal election this year' by those interviewed by Essential Research on behalf of the ACTU; only 'health care' (19 per cent) was nominated by more. Asked to nominate, from the same list of 12, the three issues that were 'likely to be the most important' in deciding 'how you vote', 'the industrial relations laws' (37 per cent) came in third behind health care (52 per cent) and education (45 per cent). And in late October 2007, across 25 of the Coalition's marginal seats, 'the industrial relations laws' (13 per cent) came in third as the most important issue (out of 11) and fourth (with 30 per cent nominating it) as one of the top three.

In an election-day poll, conducted by Auspoll, those who regarded 'industrial relations and WorkChoices' as 'very important' were 11 times more likely to vote for the Australian Labor Party (ALP) than for the Liberal-National Party (LNP); for 'global warming', the second-most important issue, the odds ratio was five (Watson and Browne 2008, 5–6). And in the AES, conducted by mail after the election, 'industrial relations' (16 per cent) came second to 'health and Medicare' (21 per cent); but for unionised respondents and Labor voters, industrial relations was the most important issue (Bean and McAllister 2009).

Fear of WorkChoices

Awareness

At first, word that the government was to legislate spread slowly. But after the Prime Minister outlined the legislative changes to parliament and the ACTU started to run its television ads, word spread quickly. Earlier, in May 2005, before Howard had addressed the parliament, more than half the employees interviewed for the ACTU said they had heard 'hardly anything' (37 per cent) or 'not much' (25 per cent) about the government's 'plans to make some major changes to the industrial relations laws'. But by the beginning of July, after the unions' campaign had commenced, 83 per cent of those interviewed by Nielsen said they had 'read or heard' something 'about the federal government's changes to industrial relations, known as WorkChoices'; in a Morgan poll taken later that month, 79 per cent reported having 'read or heard about the federal government's proposed industrial relations reforms'; and in August, three-quarters of the employees interviewed for the ACTU across 41 marginal seats said they had heard 'a lot' (41 per cent) or at least 'some' (36 per cent). In subsequent polling, the proportion saying they had 'read or heard' something hardly moved; Morgan repeated its question in October 2005, and Nielsen did so several times until March 2007. Those not made aware of the government's legislation soon after Howard had spoken, it seems, were destined never to be aware of it at all.

But having read or *heard* about it did not necessarily mean respondents felt they *knew* 'about it. In the AuSSA, conducted between August and December 2005, about half the respondents said they knew 'a lot' (10 per cent) or at least 'something' (42 per cent) about the 'changes' involved in the government's 'reforming' of 'the Australian industrial relations system'. Two years later, in the AuSSA conducted between July and November 2007, these figures—'a lot' (13 per cent) or at least 'something' (47 per cent)—had increased only slightly.

Opposition

With awareness came opposition—in part, Liberal polling is said to have shown, because 'people could not understand why the reforms were necessary' (Savva 2010, 214). Between July 2005 and March 2007 there was to be little change in either the size of the opposition or its strength. In the six Nielsen polls conducted in this period, the majority (57–59 per cent) of those who had 'read or heard' about the legislation either 'opposed' or 'strongly opposed' the 'changes', with those strongly opposed (34–41 per cent) outnumbering those in favour of the changes; few (5–8 per cent) were strongly in favour. Across the samples as a whole, roughly half (47–49 per cent) 'opposed' or 'strongly opposed' the 'changes'. Among those who told Morgan, in July and October 2005, that they had 'read or heard' about the 'reforms', similar proportions (59 and 61 per cent respectively) disagreed with the measures; no more than 22 per cent agreed with them. Again, once we include those who had not read or heard of the 'reforms', the proportion disagreeing with them is lower (47 and 49 per cent, respectively). In April 2006, when Morgan did not ask whether respondents had read or heard about the 'reforms', the proportion saying they disagreed with them rose to 55 per cent. Other polling, conducted for the ACTU in March

2006 (across 24 marginal Coalition seats) and in March 2007 (nationally)—this time with no attempt to filter respondents according to whether they had read or heard about the issue—showed fewer respondents 'not sure' (10–15 per cent) about 'the recent industrial relations measures introduced by the Howard Liberal government', but more (62–65 per cent) opposed to them. Revisiting Coalition marginal seats in October 2007, the ACTU discovered that opposition to the government's 'industrial relations measures' had slid to 56 per cent.

If filtering made a difference, so did response options. Responses to an AuSSA question in 2005, repeated in 2007, which included a neutral option, show the lowest levels of opposition (40 and 39 per cent, respectively) to the legislation, with levels of approval (19 and 24 per cent) similar to those reported by Nielsen and Morgan. The proportions that 'neither approve[d] nor disapprove[d]' (22 and 24 per cent) or said they couldn't choose (20 and 14 per cent) were greater than those reported as not having read or heard of the issue or not stating a view (about one-third of the Nielsen and Morgan samples). These differences confirm what the (unfiltered) ACTU polls and the 2006 Morgan poll suggest: where levels of opposition were relatively high, the 'don't knows' were relatively low; and where there were fewer 'don't knows', more respondents were opposed. But even in the AuSSA strong disapproval of WorkChoices (19 and 15 per cent) easily outweighed strong approval (5 and 6 per cent).

The more respondents thought they knew about WorkChoices the more likely they were to oppose it—if not in absolute terms then in relative terms. Of those in the 2007 AuSSA study who said they had 'a lot' of knowledge, 64 per cent disapproved of WorkChoices compared with 39 per cent (40 per cent in 2005) in the sample as a whole; 30 per cent approved of the legislation compared with 24 per cent (19 per cent in 2005) in the sample as a whole. This is a ratio of 1.7 to the benchmark for the opponents and only 1.3 among supporters. And the more respondents thought they knew, the stronger were their feelings. Of those with 'a lot' of knowledge, 43 per cent 'strongly' disapproved in 2007, while 15 per cent 'strongly' approved. Compared with the sample as a whole, the ratio for the strong opponents was 2.9 and for the strong supporters 2.5.

Other data suggest not only that respondents were much more likely to oppose WorkChoices than to support it; they thought it 'bad for Australia', 'bad for the average worker'—a finding that by April 2007 Howard (2011, 584) was especially worried about—and that it would 'make Australian society less fair'. In October 2005, 50 per cent of those interviewed by Morgan said that 'the industrial relations reforms' would be 'a bad thing for Australia'; only 29 per cent said they would be 'a good thing'. In April 2006, the corresponding figures were 52 per cent and 27 per cent. In May 2005, research for the ACTU found that—from what they knew of 'the government's general position on these types of matters'—38 per cent of the employees interviewed believed changes to the laws were likely to be 'bad for the average worker' rather than 'good' (16 per cent) or 'make no difference'. In August, following the start of the unions' Your Rights at Work campaign (Muir 2008, 66), 64 per cent of the employees interviewed in marginal seats believed the changes to 'the industrial relations laws' were likely to be 'bad for the average worker' rather than 'good' (10 per cent) or would 'make no difference'. In March 2007, the 'bad' figure was 62 per cent; but by October—after the government had advertised a new safety net in May and amended the legislation to incorporate it in June (Muir 2008, 28)—that figure had dropped to 51 per cent. It 'is a pity', said one supporter of the legislation, that 'the pollsters did not explore opinions about the reforms' fairness more' (Norton 2007–08, 23). They did. In October 2005, Ipsos Mackay reported that more than half (53 per cent) of its respondents thought 'the federal government's planned changes to the workplace relations system' would 'make Australian society less fair'; little more than one-third thought the legislation would generate 'no change' (10 per cent) to society or make it 'fairer' (19 per cent).

Self-regard versus solidarity

What about self-interest? Much of the polling focused on this. In July 2005, just 10 per cent of those interviewed by Morgan thought they would be 'better off'; 42 per cent thought they would not be 'better off', the remainder not having read or heard about the 'reform' (21 per cent) or not stating an opinion (27 per cent). In October the ratio of 'better off' to 'not better off' was 7:34 and, in April 2005, 13:49. Had Morgan asked whether respondents thought they might be left not only 'not better off' but 'worse off', the conclusion would have been quite different. In a poll conducted by Ipsos Mackay, in October 2005, 7 per cent said the planned 'changes' would leave them and their family 'better off'; 35 per cent said it would leave them 'worse off'. In a Nielsen poll, conducted that month, 7 per cent said 'the planned changes' would make them 'better off' and 31 per cent said they would leave them 'worse off'; as with the poll conducted by Ipsos Mackay, a plurality of respondents thought the changes would make 'no difference'. In subsequent surveys the corresponding ratios of 'better off' to 'worse off' were 8:27 (June 2006) and 7:19 (March 2007). A Newspoll series, from October 2005 to March–April 2007, restricted to respondents who were full-time or part-time workers, revealed a similar pattern, though both the proportion saying the changes would make them 'better off' and the proportion saying the changes would make them 'worse off' were slightly greater. And in a survey conducted in March 2007 for the ACTU, 10 per cent said 'the laws' would be 'good' for them 'personally', while 25 per cent thought the laws would be 'bad' for them 'personally'.

However, among those interviewed in late June 2007 by Ipsos Mackay, immediately after the 'Stronger Safety Net' amendment had become law, almost as many (40 per cent) agreed (7 per cent 'strongly') as disagreed (42 per cent; 22 per cent 'strongly') that the 'fairness test' 'for individual contracts known as Australian Workplace Agreements (AWAs)', applied 'to those earning up to $75,000', would 'ensure fairness for employees working under AWAs'. And while Howard (2011, 585) would lament that the restoration of the 'no disadvantage test' had little effect on public opinion, by October, in the ACTU surveys, opinions about what the laws meant personally—'bad' (19 per cent) and 'good' (16 per cent)—were almost evenly balanced.

The Coalition's framing

The ACTU's 'first mover' advantage—an advantage it used to set the terms of the debate (Lewis 2009, 208)—left the government in its wake. The 'positive' argument for WorkChoices, advanced by the government in early newspaper advertising to promote the changes—that the legislation would mean 'an even stronger economy, more jobs, and higher wages' (Muir 2008, 145)—was easily trumped. In an ACTU survey conducted across 24 Coalition marginal seats, in February–March 2006, less than one-third of respondents (30 per cent) agreed with the government's claim; half (50 per cent) disagreed. Among 'soft voters'—those who: intended to either vote for or give their second preference to the Liberals in a national election but to Labor at a State election or vice versa; weren't 'firm' about their party choice; didn't know their voting intention; or didn't know to which party they leaned—the distribution of opinion, 26:60, was even more lopsided.

Some elements of the argument were more persuasive than others. Asked in August 2005, on behalf of the ACTU, whether the 'proposed changes to employment laws will produce a stronger economy', 40 per cent of respondents agreed it would; a bare majority (50 per cent) disagreed (8 per cent did so 'strongly'). When the question was repeated in March 2007, the gap had narrowed: 42:45. In October and December 2005, Newspoll also reported a quite small gap between the proportion of respondents who thought the 'changes to the industrial relations system' were 'bad' or 'somewhat bad' for 'the Australian economy' (40 and 43 per cent, respectively) and those who thought the changes 'good' or 'somewhat good' (31 and 38 per cent). Subsequent surveys, however, showed a larger gap: 15 percentage points (April 2006), 13 (December 2006) and 19 (February–March 2007)—the last as big as the gap reported in February–March 2006 in relation to the government's more comprehensive claim.

Asked in July 2005 whether 'business will benefit' from 'the new laws' and 'this will lead to more jobs', only 33 per cent of respondents in a Galaxy poll agreed it would; very few (11 per cent) thought 'the government' had 'done enough to explain the new industrial relations laws so people do not feel their jobs and conditions are threatened'. In August, asked on behalf of the ACTU whether the 'proposed changes to employment laws will produce more jobs', one-third (32 per cent) of respondents again agreed it would; nearly two-thirds (62 per cent) said it wouldn't (17 per cent believing this 'strongly'). When the question was repeated in March 2007, the gap had narrowed hardly at all: 33:58. The Newspoll story is rather different. From October 2005 to March–April 2007 it reported a variable but smaller gap—between 3 and 12 percentage points—in the proportion of respondents who thought the 'proposed changes' would be 'good' rather than 'bad' for 'creating jobs'.

It was on the question of whether WorkChoices would lead to higher wages that the government's credibility was weakest. 'From what you understand about these proposed changes', Galaxy asked respondents in July 2005, 'are you worried that employers may use the new laws to force workers into accepting lower pay and worse conditions?' Nearly two-thirds (63 per cent) of respondents said they were 'worried'. Asked a month later, on behalf of the ACTU, whether the 'proposed changes to employment laws will produce better pay', no more than 20 per cent of those interviewed agreed it would; no fewer than 75 per cent said it wouldn't (20 per cent believing this 'strongly'). When the question was repeated in March 2007, the gap had narrowed—22:66—but was still large.

Opposition to WorkChoices was reflected, too, in opposition to other assumptions about, or aspects of, the new legislation. In 2005 and again in 2007, AuSSA data show two-thirds of respondents (69 per cent in 2005, 64 per cent in 2007) agreeing that 'award wages are the best way of paying workers and setting conditions'; few (12 and 15 per cent, respectively) disagreed. Respondents also agreed that 'individual contracts favour the employer over the employee': 47:18 (2003), 53:16 (2005) and 49:17 (2007). In the ACTU's surveys, in February–March 2006 and March 2007, more than two-thirds of the respondents agreed that 'individual contracts give too much power to the employer'—the difference between these and the AuSSA being largely explained by the absence in the ACTU polls of a 'neither agree nor disagree' option. Support in the AuSSA for the view that 'employers and employees should be able to negotiate pay and conditions directly' was even more one-sided: 64:18 (2003), 57:20 (2005) and 63:14 (2007). Some insight into the reasoning behind these responses may be afforded by the polling conducted for the ACTU. In February–March 2006 (across 24 Coalition marginal seats) and March 2007 (nationally), roughly two-thirds of the respondents agreed that: 'collective bargaining gives power back to workers, which is a good thing'; 'collective bargaining means better job security for workers'; and 'collective bargaining sets the standards for workers across the economy' (compare the discussion in Norton 2007–08, 23).

The unions

Marginalising collective bargaining through WorkChoices meant reducing the presence of unions; indeed, for leading members of the government, reducing the power of unions in the workplace mattered most (see Aubin 1999, 91ff; Errington and van Onselen 2007, 187, 270). But respondents rejected this goal too. With attitudes since the 1980s becoming more—not less—'pro-union' (Peetz 2006, 40), this should come as no surprise. In the 2005 AuSSA, half the respondents (52 per cent) disagreed that 'unions should have less say in how wages and conditions are set'; in 2007, the weight of opinion was still against it, 29:42. With 'studies around the world' showing 'unions obtain higher wages for their members' (Peetz 2006, 89), two-thirds (65 per cent) of those interviewed in Coalition marginal seats, in February–March 2006, agreed that 'union collective agreements deliver better wages and conditions for workers'—a figure that rose to 69 per cent in a national survey conducted in March 2007. Almost as many (62 per cent) agreed that 'union collective agreements are the best means of giving workers a say in their workplace'—the corresponding figure in March 2007 being 65 per cent. And little more than one-third (38 per cent) agreed that 'collective bargaining gives unions too much power in workplaces'—a figure, however, that rose to 48 per cent in March 2007. And in the face of a WorkChoices agenda designed both 'to make it easier for corporations to legally exclude union officers' and to discourage 'collective bargaining by exposing unions and their members to fines and damages' (Peetz 2006, 135–6, 193), two-thirds (67 per cent and 68 per cent, respectively) of those interviewed for the ACTU in February–March 2006 and March 2007 supported 'laws that allow unions to enter workplaces' while 64 per cent and 58 per cent, respectively, opposed 'laws making it easier for the government and employers to sue or fine unions and workers when they take industrial action'.

Unfair dismissal

Another point of contention—one with a much higher profile for small business, the Your Rights at Work campaign and for the media generally—was the unfair dismissal laws. Asked if they agreed with the proposal 'that unfair dismissal laws should be abolished for employers with 100 staff or less', two-thirds of those interviewed by Morgan in July 2005 (67 per cent) and again in October (71 per cent) said they disagreed. In the ACTU surveys, roughly three-quarters of the respondents in February–March 2006 (72 per cent in Coalition marginal seats) and March 2007 (76 per cent) supported 'unfair dismissal laws that protect workers'. In the AuSSA, an even greater proportion agreed in 2005 (79 per cent) and again in 2007 (85 per cent) that 'there should be a law to protect all workers in Australia against unfair dismissal'. In 2007, as the proportion disagreeing dropped to single figures (7 per cent), the proportion agreeing 'strongly' rose, from 29 to 38 per cent.

Some attributed the 'predictably low levels of support for change' to the inevitable outcome of 'pollsters' inquiries on unfair dismissal laws' that formulated 'at least partly leading questions' (Norton 2007–08, 24). Others were emboldened to see in the unfair dismissal laws the 'strongest and clearest' opposition to WorkChoices (van Wanrooy 2007, 198; Wilson 2005, 291). Argument and counterargument, reframing the issue in the ACTU's March poll, shifted the AuSSA figures but didn't turn them around—the majority of respondents (59:30) saying they were more inclined to agree with the unions' argument that 'every worker no matter what the size of the business should be protected from unfair dismissal' than with the government's argument that 're-introducing unfair dismissal laws would cost jobs and be an unnecessary burden on small business'. By March 2007, faced by 'almost daily adverse reports' in the media of the 'unpopular impacts' of WorkChoices (Lewis 2008, 180) and adverse polling (Howard 2011, 583), the government was forced to act. But Liberal Party research is said to have suggested that far from mollifying voters, the move was 'seen as a trick or ploy to win the election'—a sign that Howard cared about his 'battlers' not 'as people—just as voters' (Savva 2010, 217, 273). Sentiment was more evenly divided over the proposal 'that the probationary period for new employees be extended from three to six months': 43:47 in Morgan's July poll, 41:54 in October.

There was also support for the 'no disadvantage test'—dropped under the original WorkChoices (Peetz 2006, 9)—to be brought back. Of those interviewed for the ACTU in February–March 2006 and March 2007, the majority (55 and 61 per cent, respectively) supported 'a law to stop individuals from under-cutting award conditions'. Although in April a form of the 'no disadvantage test' was restored, on the evidence of the polls its absence does not appear to have been among the most objectionable features of the legislation.

Support

Notwithstanding widespread objection to most aspects of WorkChoices—and many aspects, far from not being 'truly put to the test publicly' (van Wanrooy 2007, 176), were tested in the polls before the legislation was introduced—some aspects did appear to meet with majority approval. One was the idea that employees would 'be able to cash in two weeks of their annual leave'. In the Morgan poll conducted in July 2005 this was supported, 55:39; in October, 55:40; but a fuller account of the consequences of this change may have changed the result (Wilson 2005, 291). Another was the idea of a 'single national industrial relations system', approved by 51 per cent of respondents in 24 Coalition marginal seats in February–March 2006, and by 58 per cent in a national poll conducted for the ACTU in March 2007. But for the ACTU a centralised system was not a bone of contention—whatever it might have said in public (Hartcher 2009, 60–1).

The government might have taken greater comfort from the fact that when the campaign against the new laws was cast as an issue of union credibility, opposition to WorkChoices lost a good deal of its bite. Thus, in July 2005, when asked by Galaxy if they thought 'the union campaign has been appropriate' or whether 'the unions have created undue fear in the community', respondents divided 43:41. Asked in March 2007 whether they agreed or disagreed that 'unions are scaremongering about John Howard's new industrial relation laws and the people will see in the next few years that things will not have changed for the worse'—a line of argument that some public opinion analysts sympathetic to the new laws had encouraged the government to accept (for example, Norton 2005, 38)—44 per cent of those interviewed on behalf of the ACTU agreed but less than half (48 per cent) disagreed.

Labor as the preferred party on industrial relations

Even if respondents opposed WorkChoices—including almost all its assumptions, features and perceived consequences—and rated the issue of high importance to the way they would vote, industrial relations would have made very little difference to the outcome of the election if the parties were not easily distinguishable, with voters preferring Labor over the Coalition on the issue, or vice versa.

At the time Howard announced WorkChoices, Newspoll suggested that Labor was the preferred party to handle the issue of industrial relations but its margin over the Coalition was not large. From October 2002 to June 2004, a few months shy of the 2004 election, Labor's lead over the Coalition, almost always in single figures, averaged about 7 percentage points. WorkChoices changed that. From June 2005, when it opened a lead of 12 percentage points, to October 2007, less than two months before the 2007 election, Labor's lead over the Coalition averaged more than 18 percentage points. On one view, it was business support for the Coalition's changes that had helped open the gap: 'You could hear them thinking, *Isn't Howard meant to be the mate of the battler? What's he doing running the same argument as the boss who happens to be screwing me?*' (Megalogenis 2008, 345; emphasis in the original).

That the gap wasn't larger may reflect one or both of two things: a sense that the Coalition had softened its position, perhaps through the introduction of a 'no disadvantage test' (noted above); or a sense that Labor's opposition to WorkChoices wasn't sufficiently clear—and not only under Kim Beazley (cf. Lewis 2008, 182–3). Though few respondents in the ACTU's polling in early 2006 or early 2007 thought 'federal Labor' supported 'the federal government's new industrial relations laws' (6 and 8 per cent, respectively, thought this), as the election approached a larger number thought 'Kevin Rudd and the Labor Party' had been 'not tough enough' (32 per cent) than thought they had been 'too tough' (12 per cent) 'in opposing the Howard Government's IR laws, such as unfair dismissal, removal of penalty rates and protecting conditions like four weeks' annual leave and public holiday pay'. While more than two-thirds of those interviewed in March rated Rudd 'good' (72 per cent), almost as many (68 per cent) said 'I would like Kevin Rudd to stand up more strongly for ordinary working people against John Howard's industrial relations laws'. If Rudd's 'industrial relations package, due for release before the May budget, fell short of public expectations', Megalogenis remarked, 'he could still blow the election' (2008, 342).

In the ACTU's August poll, the majority (55 per cent) endorsed the proposition that 'Rudd should maintain a strong stand against the Howard Government's IR laws, including issuing a pledge to fully restore unfair dismissal rights of workers, and holiday and other penalties'. In doing so, they rejected the proposition 'that Kevin Rudd and the ALP should moderate its [sic] position on the Howard Government's IR law and accept most of the changes Howard has instituted'; only 33 per cent endorsed this. The majority (58 per cent) also agreed they 'would like to see Kevin Rudd and the ALP stop waffling on the IR issue and take a strong, tough stand against the Howard Government's workplace policies'. The same proportion also agreed they 'would like to see Kevin Rudd clearly state that he will get rid of the Howard Liberal Government's IR laws and restore unfair dismissal protections and penalty rates the day he gets into office'.

However much respondents wanted Labor to be 'tougher' a connection between Labor's stand on WorkChoices and its improvement in the polls is difficult to gainsay. Seeking to explain 'the dramatic turnaround in Labor's fortunes' revealed by the results of the first Nielsen poll, taken on 1–3 July 2005, after the union movement's National Week of Action, John Stirton, the poll's director, noted that 'for the first time in a long time there is a clear point of differentiation between Labor and the Coalition on a matter that is very important to many voters' (ACNielsen 2005). In October 2005, Ipsos Mackay reported 35 per cent of its respondents saying 'the planned changes to the workplace relations system' had made them 'less likely to vote for the Coalition'; only 7 per cent said it had made them more likely to vote for the Coalition. And in mid-2006 a Morgan poll had Labor support jumping to 53.5 per cent after Beazley 'promised to "rip up" the industrial relations laws' (Muir 2008, 77). Asked, in a post-election poll for the ACTU, whether they had 'changed the party' they 'intended to vote for because of the IR laws', 13 per cent said they had.

Since the election a number of attempts, of varying sophistication, have been made to quantify the size of Labor's gain (see, for example, Bean and McAllister 2009, who use the AES; Lewis 2009, 205, 210, who cites ACTU research; Megalogenis 2008, 340,

362–3, who cites Labor research; and Spies-Butcher and Wilson 2008, 2011, who use the AES). While we doubt the size of Labor's gain can be calculated with any precision—attitudes to industrial relations may have been as much a consequence of favouring Labor as voting Labor was a consequence of the party's position on industrial relations—the fact that Labor did gain is undeniable; accounts of 'what went wrong' in the Howard years that have nothing to say about WorkChoices are clearly incomplete (for example, Manne 2008).

Structural, political and attitudinal cleavages

WorkChoices was one of the key issues in the 2007 election. It also raised the profile of the trade union movement after a long period of dormancy (Spies-Butcher and Wilson 2011) and with a membership in steep decline (Muir 2008, 9, 15; Peetz 2006, 54). Not since the 1998 waterfront dispute (Trinca and Davies 2000) had the sight of trade unionists marching in the streets and rallying around the countryside featured so strongly. In terms of the amount of money spent by the union movement on television advertising (Muir 2008, 39–40) not to mention market research, Australia had never seen anything like it.

Are the divisions that WorkChoices brought to the fore reflected in the survey data—in particular, divisions related to labour-market location and the workplace? Where in this do broader social divisions around income and class identity fit? Do voting patterns supplant or augment these divisions? And what other aspects of industrial relations mattered most when respondents assessed their opposition to—or support for—WorkChoices?

To answer these questions, we fit three models to responses to the 2007 AuSSA question on WorkChoices. In each case the outcome being modelled (using multinomial logistic regression)[1] is the approval scale, ranging from 'strongly approve' to 'strongly disapprove'. The first is a *structural* model, involving demographic variables—sex, age, education, income and occupation—and variables related to the workplace: employment sector (public/private), industry type, workplace status (supervisory/non-supervisory) and union membership. The second is a *political* model, incorporating not just voting intention but also class identity, social status and political self-placement (from left to right).

---

[1] Approval scales are often modelled using ordinal logistic regression, but particular statistical assumptions must be satisfied (the 'proportional odds assumption') to use this approach. The failure of this assumption with these data required that we fit either a multinomial logistic model (in which the ordinality of the data is ignored) or a binomial logistic model (with just two categories, for and against). We favoured the first option because it retained more information about the strength of opinion—something highly relevant in this context.

The third is an *attitudinal* model, which incorporates several other items on industrial relations issues from the AuSSA study. The top-line results from all the substantive items have been noted already.

The way in which these models relate to each other is important. Each model adds to the previous one, such that as one moves from structural to political to attitudinal, the net effect of each variable in the preceding model is weakened. Our interest lies in the extent to which the structural variables still have some purchase as we incorporate more of the political and attitudinal variables. Since the attitudinal variables are more highly correlated with the issue of WorkChoices, they are bound to become quite dominant in the third model. This model also has the usual problems of circularity, of trying to explain attitudes by recourse to attitudes, without being at all certain as to which attitudes come first (contrast van Wanrooy 2007, 183–4). Nevertheless, the strength of various associations—even when they cannot be deemed effects—is of value because it helps map the terrain on which the battle over WorkChoices was fought.

The multinomial models are shown in detail in Appendix 9.1 where both coefficients and standard errors are presented. Here the results are shown in Table 9.1 as relative risk ratios. As with odds ratios, they need to be understood in terms of two sets of contrasts. One contrast is between what respondents say about the dependent variable—those who 'strongly approve', 'approve', 'disapprove' or 'strongly disapprove' of WorkChoices are contrasted with the neutral position: 'neither approve nor disapprove'. This, in turn, is based on another contrast between the various categories of the explanatory variable; for example, in the structural model the figure '1.5' for retired persons in the 'strongly disagree' category means a person who was retired (compared with someone not yet retired) was 1.5 times or 50 per cent more likely to 'strongly disagree' with WorkChoices rather than to feel neutral about it. As it happens, the same person was 1.2 times more likely to 'strongly agree' with WorkChoices than to feel neutral about it. There is nothing illogical in this. Moreover, most of the small differences between the relative risk ratios and 1.0 are not statistically significant; as a glance at the standard errors in Appendix 9.1 shows, neither 1.2 nor 1.5 differs significantly from 1.0 (though since these are shown as coefficients what matters is the difference from 0.0). Where the ratios are larger, the most common pattern is for one end of the scale ('strongly agree' or 'strongly disagree') to be dominant; with union membership, for example, the ratios are 0.4 for 'strongly agree' and 6.2 for 'strongly disagree'. Generally, one looks for relative risk ratios that are large (more than 2.0) and, where the sentiment is unimodal, one reads off which category of the variable favours that sentiment.

Table 9.1 Approval Scale for WorkChoices, Combined Results for Models

	M1: Structural				M2: Political				M3: Attitudinal			
	SA	A	D	SD	SA	A	D	SD	SA	A	D	SD
(Intercept)	0.0	0.2	0.5	0.2	0.0	0.1	0.2	0.1	0.0	0.0	0.1	0.0
Sex: Male	2.1	1.2	1.0	1.9	2.7	1.5	0.9	1.7	2.9	1.5	0.9	1.5
Age: 25–34	2.9	1.4	0.8	0.7	3.4	1.2	0.9	0.7	3.0	1.1	0.8	0.6
Age: 35–44	2.6	2.0	0.9	0.9	3.5	1.9	0.9	0.8	2.9	1.6	0.8	0.6
Age: 45–54	4.5	2.8	1.0	1.1	4.9	2.3	1.0	1.0	4.8	2.2	0.8	0.7
Age: 55–64	8.8	3.9	1.1	1.1	7.2	2.5	1.3	1.1	6.9	2.2	1.0	0.7
Age: 65 and over	6.4	4.3	0.6	0.5	4.0	2.4	0.7	0.5	2.9	1.9	0.6	0.4
Workplace: Retired	1.2	1.1	1.5	1.5	1.1	1.2	1.4	1.3	1.4	1.3	1.3	1.2
Education: Early leaver	0.7	0.6	0.6	0.5	0.9	0.7	0.8	0.8	1.0	0.7	0.9	0.9
Education: Before year 12	1.2	0.8	0.6	0.5	1.2	0.8	0.8	0.8	1.3	0.8	1.0	0.9
Education: Year 12	0.6	0.9	0.6	0.4	0.7	0.9	0.7	0.5	0.6	0.8	0.7	0.4
Education: Trade qualifications	0.7	1.0	0.9	0.7	0.7	1.0	1.2	1.2	0.7	0.9	1.4	1.4
Education: Other TAFE	0.6	0.8	0.8	0.6	0.6	0.7	1.0	1.0	0.7	0.7	1.0	1.0
Income: $400 < $800 pw	1.0	1.2	1.3	0.9	0.8	1.1	1.3	0.9	0.8	1.0	1.3	0.9
Income: $800 < $1000 pw	0.9	1.0	0.8	0.8	0.7	0.9	0.8	0.8	0.8	0.9	0.8	0.7
Income: $1000 < $1500 pw	1.3	1.4	1.0	0.9	0.8	1.1	1.0	0.8	0.8	1.1	1.0	0.9
Income: $1500 < $2000 pw	1.6	2.3	1.3	1.0	1.0	2.0	1.2	0.9	0.9	2.0	1.2	0.9
Income: $2000 or more	1.5	1.8	0.7	0.7	0.6	1.2	0.8	1.0	0.6	1.0	0.8	1.0
Occupation: PMC	1.5	1.2	1.3	0.8	1.7	1.2	1.3	0.8	1.9	1.2	1.4	0.8
Occupation: Blue collar	0.6	0.8	1.2	1.2	0.7	0.9	1.1	1.1	0.7	0.9	1.1	1.1
Position: Supervisory	0.6	1.0	1.0	1.4	0.7	1.1	0.9	1.1	1.0	1.3	0.8	1.0
Position: Non-supervisory	0.5	0.7	1.2	1.5	0.6	0.9	1.0	1.1	1.0	1.2	0.9	1.1
Sector: Public	0.5	0.8	0.7	1.3	0.6	0.8	0.8	1.3	0.6	0.8	0.7	1.2
Union: Current member	0.4	0.6	2.9	6.2	0.5	0.8	2.6	5.3	0.8	1.1	1.7	2.7
Union: Previous member	0.4	0.8	1.7	2.3	0.5	1.0	1.4	1.9	0.6	1.0	1.2	1.5

9. WorkChoices: An electoral issue and its social, political and attitudinal cleavages

	M1: Structural				M2: Political				M3: Attitudinal			
	SA	A	D	SD	SA	A	D	SD	SA	A	D	SD
Class: Upper/upper middle					1.7	1.2	1.2	1.0	1.2	1.0	1.2	1.0
Class: Lower middle					1.0	1.0	1.3	1.3	0.7	0.9	1.1	1.2
Class: Working					2.0	0.8	1.4	1.1	1.6	0.7	1.2	0.9
Left–right: Left					0.9	0.9	2.7	5.1	1.0	0.8	2.5	4.3
Left–right: Right					4.0	1.9	0.8	1.0	3.6	1.8	0.9	1.0
Status: Low					0.7	0.7	1.3	1.3	0.8	0.8	1.3	1.3
Status: Top					1.5	0.9	1.2	1.0	1.4	0.9	1.1	0.9
Voting: Coalition					3.8	3.8	0.5	0.2	2.4	3.0	0.5	0.2
Voting: ALP					0.7	0.7	2.0	2.8	0.8	0.8	1.8	2.3
Voting: Other					1.1	1.4	0.9	1.3	1.1	1.4	0.9	1.2
Voting: Greens					0.4	0.7	1.5	1.8	0.6	0.9	1.4	1.5
Indiv.: Agree									0.6	0.9	4.1	7.6
Indiv.: Disagree									3.8	2.2	1.5	2.0
Direct: Agree									8.2	2.7	1.0	1.0
Direct: Disagree									1.5	1.0	1.6	3.1
UnionPower: Agree									11.2	2.9	1.1	1.3
UnionPower: Disagree									3.6	1.5	2.3	4.2

Notes: Models based on multinomial logit, with outcome being approval scale for WorkChoices ('neutral' as reference category). Models included industry as a control. This table does not show industry results, but the tables in Appendix 9.1 do. Omitted categories are: Female; Aged under 25; Not retired; University qualifications; Income under $400; Occupation other; Managerial position; Private sector; Never a union member; No class identification; Middle of left–right scale; Middle status; Voting informal; 'neutral' category for last three items. All categories (except 'Voting') are coded as treatment (or 'indicator'). Voting is coded using effect coding, such that the comparison is with the group mean. Abbreviations: WorkChoices = "Thinking about this new workplace relations system [WorkChoices], do you approve or disapprove of the reforms?'. PMC = professional-managerial class. Status = where place self on social scale (top, middle, bottom). Indiv. = 'individual contracts favour the employer over the employee'. Direct = 'employees and employers should be able to negotiate pay and conditions directly'. UnionPower = 'unions should have less say in how wages and conditions are set'. Population = all respondents in the IR module. Missing values replaced with imputed values, using multiple imputation by chained equations (MICE). N = 2698.

Source: Combined results shown as relative risk ratios (similar to odds ratios) based on models shown in Appendix 9.1.

Where possible, the omitted category, which forms the basis of the comparison, is a middle or neutral category or a category with little intrinsic interest—for example, 'other'. But some variables need to be treated with caution. For example, in Table 9.1 the high ratios for respondents aged fifty-five to sixty-four (8.8) and sixty-five or over (6.4) who 'strongly approve' of WorkChoices are derived by comparing their responses with those aged eighteen to twenty-five—a group that 'strongly opposes' WorkChoices. If a different age group had been chosen as the reference group, the ratios for the older groups would be considerably lower. Voting intention is different. The coding scheme used here ('effects coding') compares each category with the group mean. This is more meaningful for voting since a comparison with those who intend to vote 'other' (that is, for a minor party) is not particularly informative.

Multinomial logit results are best presented as predicted probabilities—an approach that presents figures in a more meaningful light. The probabilities are predicted by 'plugging' values into most of the variables in the model equation. These values are generally the modal value or the mean, while other variables in which we are interested are allowed to assume different values so as to illustrate the strength of particular effects. In Table 9.4, for example, the variables for union membership and occupation are allowed to vary across their range of values, with all other variables set at their modal value. Since the absolute predicted probabilities reflect the values plugged into the equation, these are not generally of great interest. Rather, the *changes in probabilities* are what matter: what happens, for example, as one moves from current union membership to never being a union member, or from what the Ehrenreichs (1979) call the professional-managerial class (PMC) to blue-collar work.

Structural model

Our interest lies in the extent to which various demographic differences explain attitudes to WorkChoices. In the case of the relative risk ratios (Table 9.1) it makes sense to present the divisions at their sharpest—hence, the contrast of oldest to youngest, lowest income to highest income, and so on. This allows us to illustrate the strength of these divisions most dramatically. It also allows us to examine how much these divisions weaken as additional variables (political and attitudinal) are included.

Beginning with age and the long version of the scale, we see a strong contrast in the level of agreement—especially strong agreement—between older respondents (fifty-five plus) and the youngest group (eighteen–twenty-four). This would be weaker had we chosen a middle-aged group as our reference; however, our choice of reference group helps draw attention to how wary younger respondents were of WorkChoices—its impact on the wages and working conditions of the young were highlighted in the media throughout the campaign (see Muir 2008, 188–90, for the unions' attempt to target young voters)—and how supportive older respondents were of it (contrast the discussion, based on bi-variate data, in Wilson 2005, 286). The retirement variable shows that the association with age is not wholly reducible to a lack of contact with the workplace. Neither is the association with age the result of job seniority, since managerial positions are also included in the model. The addition of a variable for voting intention shows older supporters of the Coalition were not the only ones causing the association with age (Goot and Watson 2007, Table A2), though they certainly influenced it (the relative risk ratio drops from 6.4 to 4.0 when voting is included).

Union membership is one of the strongest associations in the model; the differences across panels in Table 9.2 are quite pronounced. But within panels, there is still a considerable age association: for current union members disapproving of WorkChoices (short scale), it is 19 percentage points between the under twenty-fives and those aged sixty-five or more; however, except when compared with the over sixty-fives, the under twenty-fives are not all that different from the other age groups. For previous union members, the age gap between youngest and oldest is still very large (25 percentage points), but again the gap is much less evident in relation to the other age groups. Among those who were never union members the gap between youngest and oldest is just as large, but the distinctiveness of young people is more evident, with a gap of at least 8 percentage points between them and any other age group. The upshot of all this is that, irrespective of how one presents the relative risk ratios, the age association is a strong one, even in the presence of the variable with the largest impact in the model.

By way of contrast, consider Table 9.3, which focuses on position in the workplace—as a manager, supervisor or neither. This cleavage is not an important one (as the relative risk ratios in Table 9.1 show) and the differences across panels do not amount to much. But within panels the age effect (short scale) is again large: 25 to 27 percentage points (youngest respondents compared to oldest).

What of the labour-market divisions between the professional-managerial class, blue-collar workers and other (mainly clerical and 'pink-collar') workers? The relative risk ratios in Table 9.1 suggest only weak associations between occupation and responses to WorkChoices. The predicted probabilities confirm this: differences within panels (that is, between occupations) are trivial compared with the differences between panels (Table 9.4). In the case of workplace position, neither the differences between panels nor the differences within panels are substantial (Table 9.5). In short, divisions around the labour market and workplace do not count for much.

Table 9.2 Predicted Probabilities, Union and Age

	Full scale					Short scale	
	SA	App.	Neut.	Dis.	SD	App.	Dis.
Current union member							
Under 25	0	2	16	36	45	3	81
25–34	1	4	20	35	39	5	75
35–44	1	5	18	35	42	6	76
45–54	1	6	15	33	45	7	78
55–64	2	8	14	34	42	10	76
65 and over	2	14	22	29	33	16	62
Previous union member							
Under 25	0	5	29	36	30	6	66
25–34	1	9	33	33	24	10	57
35–44	1	11	29	33	26	12	59
45–54	2	13	25	31	29	15	60
55–64	3	17	23	32	25	20	57
65 and over	3	25	31	24	18	28	41
Never union member							
Under 25	1	9	41	30	18	11	49
25–34	4	14	43	26	13	18	39
35–44	3	18	39	26	15	21	40
45–54	5	21	33	25	16	26	41
55–64	8	26	29	24	14	34	37
65 and over	7	34	35	16	8	41	24

Notes: Absolute values reflect choice of values inserted into predictions. Relative values are most meaningful.

Source: Predicted probabilities based on structural model in Appendix 9.1.

Table 9.3 Predicted Probabilities, Union and Occupation

	Full scale					Short scale	
	SA	App.	Neut.	Dis.	SD	App.	Dis.
Current union member							
PMC	1	6	17	44	32	7	76
Blue collar	0	4	16	36	44	4	80
Other	1	5	18	35	42	6	76
Previous union member							
PMC	2	12	27	40	19	14	59
Blue collar	1	8	28	36	28	8	64
Other	1	11	29	33	26	12	59
Never union member							
PMC	4	19	35	30	11	24	41
Blue collar	2	13	38	30	17	15	46
Other	3	18	39	26	15	21	40

Notes: Absolute values reflect choice of values inserted into predictions. Relative values are most meaningful.

Source: Predicted probabilities based on structural model in Appendix 9.1.

9. WorkChoices: An electoral issue and its social, political and attitudinal cleavages

Table 9.4 Predicted Probabilities, Class and Union

	Full scale					Short scale	
	SA	App.	Neut.	Dis.	SD	App.	Dis.
Managerial							
PMC	3	18	29	36	14	21	50
Blue collar	1	12	31	34	22	13	56
Other	2	16	32	30	19	19	50
Supervisory							
PMC	2	17	28	34	19	19	53
Blue collar	1	11	29	31	28	12	59
Other	1	15	30	28	25	17	53
Non-supervisory							
PMC	2	12	27	40	19	14	59
Blue collar	1	8	28	36	28	8	64
Other	1	11	29	33	26	12	59

Notes: Absolute values reflect choice of values inserted into predictions. Relative values are most meaningful.

Source: Predicted probabilities based on structural model in Appendix 9.1.

Table 9.5 Predicted Probabilities, Class and Union

	Full scale					Short scale	
	SA	App.	Neut.	Dis.	SD	App.	Dis.
Current union member							
Upper/upper middle	1	10	29	28	33	11	61
Lower middle	0	8	26	27	39	8	66
Working	1	7	27	31	34	7	65
None	0	9	31	24	35	10	60
Previous union member							
Upper/upper middle	1	19	41	22	17	19	39
Lower middle	1	16	39	23	22	16	45
Working	1	13	41	26	19	14	45
None	1	17	44	19	19	18	38
Never union member							
Upper/upper middle	2	21	48	18	10	23	28
Lower middle	1	19	48	19	14	20	33
Working	2	15	49	22	12	17	33
None	1	20	52	16	11	21	27

Notes: Absolute values reflect choice of values inserted into predictions. Relative values are most meaningful.

Source: Predicted probabilities based on political model in Appendix 9.1.

Political model

With our second model, the results become more interesting, not least because they cast doubt on the claim that public opinion on industrial relations reform is 'unideological' (Norton 2005, 38) and confirm the importance—even in a 'post-ideological' age—of the categories 'left' and 'right' (Goot 2005, 108ff; Noel and Therien 2008, Ch. 2). While those identifying as 'working class' are more inclined than those with no class identification to support WorkChoices—as, more predictably, are the 'upper class'—neither result is statistically significant; and most of the relative risk ratios (around 1.0) among those who 'strongly disagree' with WorkChoices show no relationship either. As Table 9.1 also shows, however, when it comes to thinking of themselves as 'left' or 'right', the results are more striking. Those who place themselves on the right (7–10 on a 10-point scale) strongly support WorkChoices (a relative risk ratio of 4.0 compared with those in the middle of the scale), while those on the left (0–3 on the scale) are strongly opposed (a relative risk ratio of 5.1). These effects are independent of voting intention. The relative risk ratio for Coalition respondents who supported WorkChoices is 3.8; for Labor respondents who opposed it, 2.8.

Table 9.6 Predicated Probabilities, Left–Right Scale and Union

	Full scale					Short scale	
	SA	App.	Neut.	Dis.	SD	App.	Dis.
Current union member							
Left	0	2	8	23	66	2	89
Middle	0	8	26	27	39	8	66
Right	1	15	25	22	38	16	59
Previous union member							
Left	0	6	17	27	49	6	76
Middle	1	16	39	23	22	16	45
Right	2	27	35	17	19	29	36
Never union member							
Left	1	9	26	27	37	10	65
Middle	1	19	48	19	14	20	33
Right	4	30	41	14	12	34	25

Notes: Absolute values reflect choice of values inserted into predictions. Relative values are most meaningful.

Source: Predicted probabilities based on political model in Appendix 9.1.

We can illustrate these differences with predicted probabilities. For self-assigned class, stratified by union membership, there are trivial differences within panels but big differences between panels (Table 9.6). On the left–right scale, by contrast, the differences within panels are generally greater than between panels. For current union members, for example, the difference between left and right in terms of opposing WorkChoices (89 per cent compared with 60 per cent) is 29 percentage points. For someone on the left, by comparison, the difference between being a union member and never having been a union member is 25 percentage points (89 per cent compared with 64 per cent). However, this doesn't apply uniformly since for someone on the right the same difference is 34 percentage points (Table 9.7).

Table 9.7 Predicted Probabilities, Voting and Union

	Full scale					Short scale	
	SA	App.	Neut.	Dis.	SD	App.	Dis.
Current union member							
Coalition	1	31	38	20	10	32	30
ALP	0	2	15	33	50	2	83
Other	0	8	26	27	39	8	66
Greens	0	3	20	34	43	3	76
None	0	3	37	28	32	3	60
Previous union member							
Coalition	2	42	40	12	4	44	16
ALP	0	6	27	34	33	6	67
Other	1	16	39	23	22	16	45
Greens	0	7	35	32	26	7	58
None	1	5	54	23	17	6	40
Never union member							
Coalition	3	44	42	9	2	47	11
ALP	1	7	37	32	23	8	55
Other	1	19	48	19	14	20	33
Greens	0	9	45	29	18	9	46
None	1	6	64	19	10	7	29

Notes: Absolute values reflect choice of values inserted into predictions. Relative values are most meaningful.

Source: Predicted probabilities based on political model in Appendix 9.1.

Looking at voting intentions, there are strong differences within panels as well as between them. As Table 9.7 shows, even ALP respondents who were never union members opposed rather than supported WorkChoices—55 per cent to 8 per cent. Among Coalition respondents, union membership neutralises support for WorkChoices with virtually no gap between the proportions who approve (32 per cent) and disapprove (30 per cent). Greens are paler versions of Labor respondents. If they are union members, their opposition is close to that of ALP supporters (76 per cent compared with 83 per cent). Greens who were never union members are only a little more likely than Labor voters who were never union members to oppose WorkChoices (46:55) but no more likely to support it (9:8).

Table 9.8 Predicted Probabilities, Voting and Left–Right Scale

	Full scale					Short scale	
	SA	App.	Neut.	Dis.	SD	App.	Dis.
Placing self on left							
Coalition	3	33	35	20	9	36	29
ALP	0	3	15	34	48	3	82
Other	1	9	26	27	37	10	65
Greens	0	4	20	35	41	4	76
None	1	3	37	29	31	4	59
Placing self in middle							
Coalition	3	44	42	9	2	47	11
ALP	1	7	37	32	23	8	55
Other	1	19	48	19	14	20	33
Greens	0	9	45	29	18	9	46
None	1	6	64	19	10	7	29
Placing self on right							
Coalition	9	56	28	5	1	65	6
ALP	2	14	36	26	22	16	48
Other	4	30	41	14	12	34	25
Greens	1	16	43	23	17	18	40
None	4	11	60	15	10	15	24

Notes: Absolute values reflect choice of values inserted into predictions. Relative values are most meaningful.

Source: Predicted probabilities based on political model in Appendix 9.1.

Finally, consider Table 9.8, which shows voting and left–right self-placement. This table helps net out the unique effects of each. As one would expect, left-leaning ALP voters are almost uniformly opposed to WorkChoices (82 per cent disapprove) while right-leaning Coalition voters are just as uniformly in favour (82 per cent approve); however, respondents who placed themselves on the right but favoured Labor were anti-WorkChoices, 48:16. On the other hand, those who put themselves in the middle and who intended to vote for the Coalition were much more likely to be pro-WorkChoices: 47:11. Finally, for those on the left who intended to vote Coalition (an uncommon combination), the gap closes, but approval of WorkChoices is still slightly higher than opposition, 36:29. In short, voting intention is stronger than left–right self-placement, though the latter should not be discounted—its impact is still considerable. But whatever the importance of voting intention, as we shall shortly see, it is not (contrary to van Wanrooy 2007, 188) the variable that is most important. (For a very different way of segmenting the electorate, used in the Your Rights at Work campaign, see Lewis 2009, 212–13).

Attitudes model

The inclusion of attitudes to industrial relations to explain attitudes to WorkChoices is somewhat circular unless one can establish a pattern of causality. Nevertheless, a third model, based on attitudes to industrial relations issues other than WorkChoices, is useful for exploring the issues that shaped the terrain of the struggle.

In our third model the political dynamic becomes more transparent, at least for those respondents (nearly one-third of the sample) at the extremes: 'strongly' in favour of WorkChoices or (three times as numerous) 'strongly against'. Clearly, for the small proportion of respondents who 'strongly' approved of WorkChoices, the view that 'unions should have less say in how wages and conditions are set' was a dominant consideration; Model 3 shows a relative risk ratio of 11.2 for this issue (Table 9.1). For strong supporters, the ability of 'employees and employers…to negotiate pay and conditions directly'—understood, presumably, as a situation in which unions were absent—was also important (a relative risk ratio of 8.2). Among strong supporters of WorkChoices, disagreeing that 'individual contracts favour the employer over the employee' featured as well (a relative risk ratio of 3.8).

By contrast, those who 'strongly' disapproved of WorkChoices saw the fundamental issue as one of the powerlessness of employees vis-a-vis employers (a relative risk ratio of 7.6). The value of unions in determining 'how wages and conditions are set' was also important (a relative risk ratio of 4.2), as were the problems with direct bargaining (a relative risk ratio of 3.1).

Conclusion

Despite the long campaign around WorkChoices, there is no evidence that awareness of it grew between mid-2005 and mid-2007 or (contrary to the expectation of van Wanrooy 2007, 185) that views about it became increasingly polarised. On a number of issues the government was able to claw back lost ground. That support for some aspects of the legislation increased in the months leading up to the election may have reflected both the government's decision to amend its legislation and the limits of the unions' campaign. In the end, to say of the government's own advertising that 'the more the government spent, the more the public attitude turned negative' (Lewis 2009, 208) looks like triumphalism.

Opposition to WorkChoices was never the majority position of respondents in the polls, if we take into account the sizeable proportions who said they either had not read or heard about it or were aware of the legislation but had no view on it; but it was the majority position for those who had read or heard about it and they made up the bulk of the electorate. Nor, offered a middle option, was disapproval the majority position of respondents in the AuSSA. But as in the polls, respondents in the AuSSA were more likely to approve than disapprove and those who did disapprove were roughly three times as numerous as those who approved to do so 'strongly'. Not only was WorkChoices opposed in the polls; so too was almost every aspect of the legislation and the assumptions behind it. From mid-2005, when the legislation made its initial impact on the parties' standing in the polls, those who mentioned WorkChoices in connection with their party choice were much more likely to be (intending) Labor voters than (intending) Liberal voters.

Hugh Mackay, a qualitative researcher, acknowledges that, in the opinion polls, reaction to the legislation was 'deeply unpopular'. But in his research the 'initial [sic] response' in 2006 was 'rather muted', even 'acquiescent' (2008, 250–1). This is a puzzle the polls, in the nature of the case, can do little to solve. Howard, too, notes that in 2006 Liberal MPs 'suggested no great public resentment against WorkChoices'. He 'regularly telephoned' those in marginal seats and '[t]o a man and a woman virtually, they said that few people raised particular cases with their offices, and the general advice I continued to receive was that…we should stick it out and eventually public opinion would come around' (Howard 2011, 583). But by the time of the NSW election, in March 2007, Howard's biographer and Liberal candidate Pru Goward acknowledged that WorkChoices had done the Liberals damage—'that a discredited state government could campaign on a federal issue, and get away with it, surely meant that Work Choices was poison' (Megalogenis 2008, 339).

In the electoral battle over WorkChoices, the ACTU set the terms of the debate. Had the Liberals succeeded in framing the debate, much of the unions'—and Labor's—campaign might have been blunted. The extent to which the polls adopted one side's agenda rather than the other's is another matter. If Howard saw the new laws as a way of boosting employment (Howard 2011, 487, 547, 573, 583–4), perceptions of the impact WorkChoices might have on employment were something to which the newspaper polls paid little attention. On the other hand, 'fear of job insecurity'—the fear that 'would destroy WorkChoices' (Kelly 2009, 384; also Savva 2010, 223)—didn't figure much in the published polls either. That Labor adopted the ACTU's framing and was able to convince much of the electorate of its commitment to the abolition of WorkChoices is important. Among those who argue that since the early 1980s the economic policies of the Coalition and Labor have converged around neo-liberalism, not all are prepared to concede that WorkChoices—an issue that goes to the foundations of the Liberal and Labor parties—constitutes an exception (see, for example, Lavelle 2010, 61–2; Lewis 2008, 169, 184). Nonetheless, industrial relations along with education and climate change were the issues Rudd singled out as the key issues on which Labor sought to distinguish itself from the Liberals (van Onselen and Senior 2008, 24). While it may be an exaggeration to say that under Rudd WorkChoices was 'dismantled' (Dyrenfurth and Bongiorno 2011, 189; cf. Megalogenis 2008, 349), according to critics on the right, not only was WorkChoices swept away, the new broom left the labour market 're-regulated' (Howard 2011, 659).

Were respondents concerned more with the impact of the legislation on society as a whole or on their own self-interest? According to Andrew Norton (2007–08, 20–2, also 2005, 37)—from the right, ironically—social solidarity trumped self-interest. According to Shaun Wilson, ironically on the left, and Peter Wilson, a key player in the ACTU's advertising campaign, opposition to the legislation has to be understood in terms of the personal impact respondents thought the changes were likely to make (Wilson 2005, 285, 292, 294, 296, 297; Lewis 2009, 209). Much of the media's analysis also took it as self-evident that self-interest was the principal driver (see, for example, Megalogenis 2008, Snapshot #17). The survey evidence, however, supports the view that social solidarity was more important. While many respondents thought the legislation would leave them worse off—something Howard had not been able to deny (Megalogenis 2008, 341)—their numbers were not nearly as large as the numbers who said they opposed the legislation.

The presence of electoral cleavages—or their absence—around WorkChoices tells us a good deal about contemporary Australian politics and society. Younger respondents, many of them relatively new entrants to the workforce, felt especially vulnerable; they were one of the unions' target groups (Muir 2008, 65, 188–90). The importance of union membership itself in structuring views about WorkChoices should not surprise. As the strongest and certainly most consistent predictor of Labor voting (Goot and Watson 2007, 270), union membership was not only the legislation's most important workplace target; it was also its most important political target. That occupation, workplace position, income and education had little bearing on attitudes suggests not that blue-collar workers supported the legislation—an assumption consistent with the notion of 'Howard's battlers'—but that they were not strongly opposed to it. This, in turn, suggests the analytical shortcoming of inferring political interests from class location (class-in-itself) rather than seeing these interests as something fashioned in struggle (class-for-itself). In their own way, both the importance of how respondents intended to vote—Liberal-National, Labor and the Greens—and the importance of their left–right self-placement testify to this. The struggle around power and the perception of power are also evident in the importance of attitudes to unions and management in explaining the strong views about WorkChoices—both for and against. There were no deep social divisions that WorkChoices tapped into. Rather, it was an ideological struggle with the lines between left and right, Labor and the Coalition, unions and bosses drawn quite sharply. Views about WorkChoices mapped onto demographics only in relation to age and union membership; other class, labour-market and workplace divisions did not feature. The struggle itself—in particular, the mobilisation by the labour movement—was crucial. The terrain of power and individual vulnerability shows how industrial relations attitudes played out.

For the supporters of WorkChoices, the core issues were union power and the freedom to bargain. Individual powerlessness did not feature in this perspective. Among opponents of WorkChoices, by contrast, unions were seen not as part of the problem but as facilitators, with the key issue the vulnerability of individuals in the workplace—a vulnerability that required unions for protection and exposed the risk of individual contracts that WorkChoices sought to promote. This was a prominent theme in the ACTU television campaign, which emphasised the vulnerability of the individual worker. It is no surprise, then, that the ACTU was able to mobilise so effectively against WorkChoices by exploiting themes of fear: the fears were real, and were keenly felt by many.

Looking back to the 1980s and 1990s, the 'remarkable period in which economic policies could be implemented in defiance of public opinion but without causing electoral defeat', Norton suggests that 'the political conditions for further reform' will only re-emerge when economic conditions are 'sufficiently bad' (2007–08, 27). But while much of the prosperity that characterised the Howard years has disappeared, and calls for the resurrection of WorkChoices are not difficult to hear, the political conditions that might lead to the reintroduction of such legislation—a Coalition government in control of the Senate, a union movement without resources and a Labor opposition wholly indifferent to mobilised opinion—are not presently on the horizon.

References

ACNielsen. 2005. 'Majority of Australians oppose industrial relations reforms'. *National Opinion Report*, 4 July.

Aubin, Tracy. 1999. *Peter Costello: A biography*. Sydney: HarperCollins.

Bean, Clive and McAllister, Ian. 2009. 'The Australian Election Survey: the tale of the rabbit-less hat. Voting behaviour in 2007'. *Australian Cultural Studies* 27(2): 205–18.

Butler, David and Stokes, Donald. 1969. *Political Change in Britain: Forces shaping electoral choice*. London: Macmillan.

Dyrenfurth, Nick and Bongiorno, Frank. 2011. *A Little History of the Australian Labor Party*. Sydney: UNSW Press.

Ehrenreich, Barbara and Ehrenreich, John. 1979. 'The professional-managerial class'. In *Between Labor and Capital*, ed. Pat Walker. Boston: South End Press.

Errington, W. and van Onselen, P. 2007. *John Winston Howard: The biography*. Melbourne: Melbourne University Press.

Goot, Murray. 2005. 'Pauline Hanson's One Nation: extreme right, centre party or extreme left'. *Labour History* 89: 101–20.

Goot, Murray and Watson, Ian. 2007. 'Explaining Howard's success: social structure, issue agendas and party support, 1993–2007'. *Australian Journal of Political Science* 42(2): 253–76.

Hartcher, Peter. 2009. *To the Bitter End: The dramatic story behind the fall of John Howard and the rise of Kevin Rudd*. Sydney: Allen & Unwin.

Howard, John. 2011. *Lazarus Rising*. Revised edition. Sydney: HarperCollins.

Kelly, Paul. 2009. *The March of Patriots: The struggle for modern Australia*. Melbourne: Melbourne University Press.

Lavelle, Ashley. 2010. 'The ties that unwind? Social democratic parties and unions in Australia and Britain'. *Labour History* 98: 55–76.

Lee, David. 2010. *Stanley Melbourne Bruce: Australian internationalist*. London: Continuum.

Lewis, Peter. 2009. 'How unions brought the workers back to Labor'. *Labour History* 96: 205–14.

Lewis, Phil. 2008. 'Industrial relations and the labour market'. In *Howard's Fourth Government: Australian commonwealth administration, 2004–2007*, eds C. Aulich and R. Wettenhall. Sydney: UNSW Press.

Mackay, Hugh. 2008. *Advance Australia…Where?* Updated edition. Sydney: Hachette Australia.

Manne, Robert. 2008. 'What went wrong'. In *Liberals and Power: The road ahead*, ed. P. van Onselen. Melbourne: Melbourne University Press.

Megalogenis, George. 2008. *The Longest Decade*. Revised edition. Melbourne: Scribe.

Muir, Kathie. 2008. *Worth Fighting For: Inside the Your Rights at Work campaign*. Sydney: UNSW Press.

Noel, Alain and Thérien, Jean-Philippe. 2008. *Left and Right in Global Politics*. Cambridge: Cambridge University Press.

Norrington, Brad. 2006. 'Unfinished business'. In *The Howard Factor: A decade that changed the nation*, ed. N. Cater. Melbourne: Melbourne University Press.

Norton, Andrew. 2005. 'The politics of industrial relations reform'. *Policy* 21(2): 34–8.

Norton, Andrew. 2007–08. 'The end of industrial relations reform?' *Policy* 23(4): 20–7.

Peetz, David. 2006. *Brave New Work Place: How individual contracts are changing our jobs*. Sydney: Allen & Unwin.

Savva, Niki. 2010. *So Greek: Confessions of a conservative leftie*. Melbourne: Scribe.

Singleton, Gwynneth. 2008. 'The Senate a paper tiger?' In *Howard's Fourth Government: Australian commonwealth administration, 2004–2007*, eds C. Aulich and R. Wettenhall. Sydney: UNSW Press.

Spies-Butcher, Ben and Wilson, Shaun. 2008. 'Election 2007: did the union campaign succeed?' *Australian Review of Public Affairs*, <http://www.australianreview.net/digest/2008/02/spies-butcher_wilson.html> accessed 30 April 2009.

Spies-Butcher, Ben and Wilson, Shaun. 2011. 'When labour makes a difference: union mobilization and the 2007 federal election in Australia'. *British Journal of Industrial Relations* 49 (Supplement 2): s306–31.

Stewart, Andrew and Williams, George. 2007. *Work Choices: What the High Court said*. Sydney: Federation Press.

Trinca, Helen and Davies, Anne. 2000. *Waterfront: The battle that changed Australia*. Sydney: Doubleday.

van Onselen, Peter and Senior, Philip. 2008. *Howard's End: The unravelling of a government*. Melbourne: Melbourne University Press.

van Wanrooy, Brigid. 2007. 'The quiet before the storm? Attitudes towards the new industrial relations system'. In *Australian Social Attitudes 2: Citizenship, work and aspirations*, eds David Denemark, Gabrielle Meagher, Shaun Wilson, Mark Western and Timothy Phillips. Sydney: UNSW Press.

Watson, Ian and Browne, Peter. 2008. *The 2007 Federal Election: Exit poll analysis*. Report prepared for Australian Policy Online, September, <http://apo.org.au/research/2007-federal-election-exit-poll-analysis>

Wilson, Shaun. 2005. 'Any attention is bad attention? Public opinion towards the Howard Government's industrial relations reforms in 2005'. *Journal of Australian Political Economy* 56: 284–98.

Appendix 9.1

Details of Modelling

Table A9.1 Results for Multinomial Logit Model: Structural model (coefficients and standard errors in parentheses)

	Approve or disapprove of WorkChoices			
	S. approve	Approve	Disapprove	S. disapprove
(Intercept)	-3.454	-1.744	-0.684	-1.763
	(0.864)	(0.402)	(0.308)	(0.380)
Sex: 2	0.736	0.211	-0.011	0.650
	(0.224)	(0.140)	(0.130)	(0.151)
Age: 25-34	1.062	0.317	-0.219	-0.358
	(0.782)	(0.351)	(0.236)	(0.292)
Age: 35-44	0.959	0.698	-0.105	-0.159
	(0.779)	(0.335)	(0.227)	(0.274)
Age: 45-54	1.498	1.031	-0.000	0.078
	(0.770)	(0.333)	(0.229)	(0.272)
Age: 55-64	2.180	1.367	0.095	0.051
	(0.76t0)	(0.332)	(0.234)	(0.278)
Age: 65 and over	1.861	1.456	-0.490	-0.615
	(0.772)	(0.340)	(0.262)	(0.323)
Retired: Retired	0.150	0.136	0.414	0.382
	(0.297)	(0.190)	(0.196)	(0.237)
Education: Early leaver	-0.370	-0.545	-0.434	-0.638
	(0.422)	(0.266)	(0.239)	(0.281)
Education: Before year 12	0.210	-0.175	-0.581	-0.700
	(0.335)	(0.226)	(0.215)	(0.253)
Education: Year 12	-0.504	-0.109	-0.530	-0.830
	(0.419)	(0.244)	(0.222)	(0.270)
Education: Trade quals	-0.338	0.035	-0.098	-0.313
	(0.378)	(0.231)	(0.212)	(0.247)
Education: Other TAFE	-0.477	-0.280	-0.278	-0.468
	(0.288)	(0.181)	(0.164)	(0.195)
Income: $400 – under $800 pw	0.029	0.167	0.298	-0.095
	(0.275)	(0.158)	(0.137)	(0.168)
Income: $800 – under $1000 pw	-0.053	0.043	-0.198	-0.228
	(0.382)	(0.232)	(0.206)	(0.235)
Income: $1000 – under $1500 pw	0.260	0.345	0.019	-0.147
	(0.331)	(0.206)	(0.188)	(0.217)
Income: $1500 – under $2000 pw	0.471	0.834	0.234	-0.046
	(0.425)	(0.281)	(0.271)	(0.322)

	Approve or disapprove of WorkChoices			
	S. approve	Approve	Disapprove	S. disapprove
Income: $2000 or more	0.421	0.596	−0.332	−0.288
	(0.380)	(0.267)	(0.294)	(0.341)
Occupation: PMC	0.431	0.167	0.261	−0.222
	(0.250)	(0.159)	(0.153)	(0.187)
Occupation: Blue collar	−0.553	−0.284	0.142	0.140
	(0.321)	(0.178)	(0.155)	(0.178)
Industry: Agriculture	0.581	0.482	−0.553	−0.874
	(0.541)	(0.343)	(0.395)	(0.585)
Industry: Mining	0.695	−0.565	−0.006	0.082
	(0.545)	(0.429)	(0.358)	(0.428)
Industry: Manufacturing	0.485	0.484	0.227	0.483
	(0.481)	(0.276)	(0.257)	(0.310)
Industry: Utilities/construction	0.831	0.421	0.051	−0.447
	(0.468)	(0.280)	(0.259)	(0.336)
Industry: Wholesale/retail	0.394	−0.057	0.024	0.061
	(0.424)	(0.257)	(0.227)	(0.295)
Industry: Accommodation	−0.013	−0.082	−0.677	0.064
	(0.544)	(0.305)	(0.294)	(0.336)
Industry: Transport	0.761	−0.178	−0.165	−0.403
	(0.533)	(0.347)	(0.293)	(0.357)
Industry: Business services	0.969	0.182	0.015	0.357
	(0.402)	(0.246)	(0.225)	(0.281)
Industry: Government	0.181	0.511	0.448	0.161
	(0.619)	(0.295)	(0.261)	(0.312)
Industry: Education	0.043	0.016	−0.160	0.143
	(0.603)	(0.311)	(0.275)	(0.329)
Industry: Health	−0.171	0.042	−0.085	−0.008
	(0.528)	(0.270)	(0.241)	(0.304)
Position: Supervisory	−0.474	−0.023	−0.042	0.321
	(0.268)	(0.165)	(0.164)	(0.200)
Position: Non-supervisory	−0.769	−0.313	0.149	0.387
	(0.266)	(0.163)	(0.154)	(0.193)
Sector: Public	−0.625	−0.249	−0.290	0.243
	(0.363)	(0.188)	(0.165)	(0.189)
Union: Current member	−0.948	−0.432	1.072	1.820
	(0.437)	(0.224)	(0.166)	(0.190)
Union: Previous member	−0.837	−0.195	0.518	0.851
	(0.230)	(0.133)	(0.125)	(0.159)

Notes: Outcome (dependent) variable: approve or disapprove of WorkChoices, on five-point scale (with 'Neutral' and 'Can't choose' combined as reference category). Omitted categories are: Female; Aged under 25; Not retired; University qualifications; Income under $400; Occupation other; Industry other; Managerial position; Private sector; Never a union member.

Source: Australian Survey of Social Attitudes 2007.

Table A9.2 Results for Multinomial Logit Model: Political model (coefficients and standard errors in parentheses)

	Approve or disapprove of WorkChoices			
	S. approve	Approve	Disapprove	S. disapprove
(Intercept)	−5.167 (1.030)	−2.349 (0.488)	−1.448 (0.386)	−2.644 (0.478)
Sex: 2	1.006 (0.244)	0.384 (0.153)	−0.075 (0.137)	0.539 (0.163)
Age: 25–34	1.230 (0.811)	0.222 (0.372)	−0.141 (0.247)	−0.372 (0.313)
Age: 35–44	1.252 (0.807)	0.647 (0.354)	−0.099 (0.239)	−0.222 (0.295)
Age: 45–54	1.593 (0.799)	0.854 (0.352)	0.011 (0.241)	−0.039 (0.294)
Age: 55–64	1.974 (0.790)	0.905 (0.352)	0.252 (0.247)	0.096 (0.301)
Age: 65 and over	1.389 (0.802)	0.856 (0.359)	−0.339 (0.280)	−0.613 (0.353)
Retired: Retired	0.108 (0.323)	0.174 (0.202)	0.361 (0.209)	0.274 (0.262)
Education: Early leaver	−0.075 (0.459)	−0.385 (0.287)	−0.218 (0.259)	−0.168 (0.315)
Education: Before year 12	0.160 (0.368)	−0.275 (0.245)	−0.234 (0.231)	−0.210 (0.281)
Education: Year 12	−0.408 (0.444)	−0.145 (0.266)	−0.390 (0.237)	−0.719 (0.297)
Education: Trade quals	−0.400 (0.417)	−0.024 (0.253)	0.185 (0.228)	0.165 (0.277)
Education: Other TAFE	−0.487 (0.315)	−0.350 (0.198)	−0.003 (0.177)	−0.004 (0.216)
Income: $400 – under $800 pw	−0.201 (0.294)	0.115 (0.171)	0.281 (0.145)	−0.101 (0.183)
Income: $800 – under $1000 pw	−0.337 (0.412)	−0.066 (0.249)	−0.192 (0.217)	−0.225 (0.257)
Income: $1000 – under $1500 pw	−0.265 (0.366)	0.103 (0.230)	0.016 (0.201)	−0.171 (0.239)
Income: $1500 – under $2000 pw	−0.007 (0.468)	0.669 (0.303)	0.213 (0.291)	−0.118 (0.357)
Income: $2000 or more	−0.467 (0.433)	0.143 (0.293)	−0.248 (0.320)	−0.033 (0.384)
Occupation: PMC	0.557 (0.264)	0.209 (0.170)	0.262 (0.163)	−0.278 (0.208)
Occupation: Blue collar	−0.423 (0.346)	−0.117 (0.194)	0.083 (0.163)	0.075 (0.193)
Industry: Agriculture	−0.022 (0.580)	0.188 (0.371)	−0.616 (0.421)	−1.052 (0.628)
Industry: Mining	0.489 (0.592)	−0.755 (0.455)	0.186 (0.374)	0.414 (0.458)

	Approve or disapprove of WorkChoices			
	S. approve	Approve	Disapprove	S. disapprove
Industry: Manufacturing	0.264	0.296	0.213	0.518
	(0.511)	(0.301)	(0.270)	(0.334)
Industry: Utilities/construction	0.432	0.130	0.192	−0.136
	(0.501)	(0.305)	(0.270)	(0.357)
Industry: Wholesale/retail	0.177	−0.206	0.109	0.244
	(0.450)	(0.278)	(0.239)	(0.316)
Industry: Accommodation	−0.253	−0.305	−0.555	0.278
	(0.572)	(0.326)	(0.308)	(0.364)
Industry: Transport	0.242	−0.635	−0.051	−0.247
	(0.568)	(0.373)	(0.312)	(0.395)
Industry: Business services	0.892	0.067	0.049	0.384
	(0.430)	(0.266)	(0.237)	(0.303)
Industry: Government	−0.188	0.281	0.490	0.252
	(0.657)	(0.325)	(0.274)	(0.335)
Industry: Education	−0.227	−0.159	−0.167	0.120
	(0.648)	(0.340)	(0.290)	(0.353)
Industry: Health	−0.413	−0.150	−0.037	0.056
	(0.562)	(0.298)	(0.253)	(0.325)
Position: Supervisory	−0.331	0.096	−0.139	0.136
	(0.290)	(0.178)	(0.174)	(0.221)
Position: Non-supervisory	−0.516	−0.058	0.004	0.137
	(0.283)	(0.174)	(0.166)	(0.215)
Sector: Public	−0.531	−0.262	−0.286	0.263
	(0.383)	(0.205)	(0.174)	(0.206)
Union: Current member	−0.752	−0.241	0.946	1.667
	(0.457)	(0.241)	(0.175)	(0.207)
Union: Previous member	−0.606	0.014	0.360	0.659
	(0.247)	(0.144)	(0.132)	(0.171)
Class: Upper/upper middle	0.506	0.152	0.206	−0.020
	(0.464)	(0.262)	(0.249)	(0.304)
Class: Lower middle	−0.003	0.022	0.265	0.283
	(0.463)	(0.251)	(0.232)	(0.277)
Class: Working	0.711	−0.234	0.354	0.083
	(0.469)	(0.264)	(0.229)	(0.277)
Left–right: Left	−0.060	−0.102	0.988	1.628
	(0.570)	(0.287)	(0.169)	(0.184)
Left–right: Right	1.396	0.652	−0.177	−0.011
	(0.228)	(0.146)	(0.183)	(0.242)

| | Approve or disapprove of WorkChoices | | | |
	S. approve	Approve	Disapprove	S. disapprove
Status: Low	-0.328	-0.420	0.290	0.250
	(0.456)	(0.251)	(0.168)	(0.200)
Status: Top	0.401	-0.055	0.146	0.007
	(0.249)	(0.154)	(0.142)	(0.177)
Voting: Coalition	1.329	1.327	-0.707	-1.528
	(0.301)	(0.158)	(0.129)	(0.225)
Voting: ALP	-0.301	-0.310	0.711	1.028
	(0.364)	(0.182)	(0.098)	(0.126)
Voting: Other	0.113	0.354	-0.054	0.251
	(0.471)	(0.228)	(0.165)	(0.205)
Voting: Greens	-0.990	-0.317	0.421	0.562
	(0.841)	(0.320)	(0.172)	(0.210)

Notes: Outcome (dependent) variable: approve or disapprove of WorkChoices, on five-point scale (with 'Neutral' and 'Can't choose' combined as reference category). Omitted categories are: Female; Aged under 25; Not retired; University qualifications; Income under $400; Occupation other; Industry other; Managerial position; Private sector; Never a union member; No class identification; Middle of left–right scale; Middle status; Voting informal. All categories (except 'Voting') are coded as 'treatment' (or 'indicator'). Voting is coded using 'effect' coding, such that the comparison is with the group mean.

Source: Australian Survey of Social Attitudes 2007.

Table A9.3 Results for Multinomial Logit Model: Attitudinal model (coefficients and standard errors in parentheses)

| | Approve or disapprove of WorkChoices | | | |
	S. approve	Approve	Disapprove	S. disapprove
(Intercept)	-8.883	-3.604	-2.121	-3.967
	(1.314)	(0.543)	(0.426)	(0.567)
Sex: 2	1.078	0.422	-0.155	0.406
	(0.268)	(0.163)	(0.147)	(0.180)
Age: 25–34	1.114	0.084	-0.248	-0.522
	(0.885)	(0.385)	(0.263)	(0.342)
Age: 35–44	1.054	0.469	-0.285	-0.543
	(0.876)	(0.368)	(0.255)	(0.324)
Age: 45–54	1.574	0.786	-0.213	-0.423
	(0.869)	(0.364)	(0.258)	(0.325)
Age: 55–64	1.925	0.785	-0.047	-0.385
	(0.863)	(0.365)	(0.266)	(0.332)
Age: 65 and over	1.070	0.615	-0.505	-0.972
	(0.879)	(0.374)	(0.300)	(0.390)

	Approve or disapprove of WorkChoices			
	S. approve	Approve	Disapprove	S. disapprove
Retired: Retired	0.322	0.259	0.277	0.179
	(0.356)	(0.216)	(0.224)	(0.287)
Education: Early leaver	0.044	−0.398	−0.161	−0.145
	(0.495)	(0.304)	(0.277)	(0.347)
Education: Before year 12	0.234	−0.258	−0.003	−0.089
	(0.406)	(0.261)	(0.249)	(0.318)
Education: Year 12	−0.597	−0.240	−0.372	−0.801
	(0.485)	(0.282)	(0.251)	(0.328)
Education: Trade quals	−0.414	−0.063	0.323	0.325
	(0.449)	(0.267)	(0.244)	(0.306)
Education: Other TAFE	−0.380	−0.374	0.004	0.009
	(0.340)	(0.209)	(0.190)	(0.239)
Income: $400 – under $800 pw	−0.250	0.017	0.253	−0.126
	(0.318)	(0.180)	(0.156)	(0.201)
Income: $800 – under $1000 pw	−0.234	−0.071	−0.282	−0.324
	(0.444)	(0.261)	(0.231)	(0.284)
Income: $1000 – under $1500 pw	−0.276	0.123	0.035	−0.128
	(0.400)	(0.241)	(0.215)	(0.266)
Income: $1500 – under $2000 pw	−0.063	0.699	0.171	−0.130
	(0.522)	(0.320)	(0.310)	(0.393)
Income: $2000 or more	−0.540	0.040	−0.286	−0.032
	(0.473)	(0.308)	(0.340)	(0.427)
Occupation: PMC	0.659	0.209	0.325	−0.191
	(0.288)	(0.178)	(0.173)	(0.228)
Occupation: Blue collar	−0.320	−0.058	0.083	0.097
	(0.372)	(0.204)	(0.174)	(0.213)
Industry: Agriculture	0.016	0.281	−0.815	−1.350
	(0.645)	(0.400)	(0.448)	(0.665)
Industry: Mining	0.417	−0.783	0.160	0.182
	(0.667)	(0.483)	(0.403)	(0.520)
Industry: Manufacturing	0.562	0.343	0.124	0.294
	(0.542)	(0.317)	(0.289)	(0.366)
Industry: Utilities/construction	0.370	0.138	0.147	−0.307
	(0.548)	(0.325)	(0.285)	(0.390)
Industry: Wholesale/retail	0.521	−0.011	−0.003	0.063
	(0.489)	(0.299)	(0.255)	(0.342)
Industry: Accommodation	0.131	−0.143	−0.612	0.231
	(0.612)	(0.346)	(0.324)	(0.397)

	Approve or disapprove of WorkChoices			
	S. approve	Approve	Disapprove	S. disapprove
Industry: Transport	0.541	−0.569	−0.288	−0.679
	(0.632)	(0.394)	(0.337)	(0.433)
Industry: Business services	1.145	0.137	−0.037	0.188
	(0.469)	(0.286)	(0.254)	(0.329)
Industry: Government	−0.075	0.393	0.515	0.184
	(0.713)	(0.348)	(0.291)	(0.367)
Industry: Education	0.174	0.072	−0.190	−0.033
	(0.699)	(0.360)	(0.309)	(0.390)
Industry: Health	−0.416	−0.104	−0.050	−0.085
	(0.607)	(0.320)	(0.270)	(0.356)
Position: Supervisory	0.028	0.233	−0.216	0.017
	(0.317)	(0.189)	(0.186)	(0.243)
Position: Non-supervisory	−0.028	0.157	−0.060	0.057
	(0.317)	(0.186)	(0.177)	(0.235)
Sector: Public	−0.542	−0.265	−0.342	0.167
	(0.430)	(0.217)	(0.185)	(0.226)
Union: Current member	−0.163	0.052	0.542	0.981
	(0.498)	(0.257)	(0.190)	(0.232)
Union: Previous member	−0.530	0.048	0.216	0.374
	(0.268)	(0.152)	(0.141)	(0.189)
Class: Upper/upper middle	0.148	−0.014	0.204	0.043
	(0.506)	(0.279)	(0.267)	(0.343)
Class: Lower middle	−0.293	−0.141	0.128	0.145
	(0.497)	(0.269)	(0.250)	(0.315)
Class: Working	0.494	−0.359	0.178	−0.068
	(0.505)	(0.281)	(0.247)	(0.314)
Left–right: Left	0.034	−0.173	0.903	1.462
	(0.585)	(0.295)	(0.181)	(0.204)
Left–right: Right	1.281	0.560	−0.139	0.038
	(0.247)	(0.154)	(0.193)	(0.264)
Status: Low	−0.239	−0.279	0.284	0.231
	(0.498)	(0.263)	(0.180)	(0.223)
Status: Top	0.318	−0.142	0.053	−0.102
	(0.274)	(0.163)	(0.151)	(0.193)
Voting: Coalition	0.874	1.092	−0.637	−1.410
	(0.321)	(0.163)	(0.137)	(0.237)
Voting: ALP	−0.245	−0.246	0.566	0.834
	(0.389)	(0.187)	(0.105)	(0.139)

	Approve or disapprove of WorkChoices			
	S. approve	Approve	Disapprove	S. disapprove
Voting: Other	0.140	0.360	−0.067	0.199
	(0.502)	(0.235)	(0.175)	(0.227)
Voting: Greens	−0.578	−0.123	0.367	0.410
	(0.875)	(0.328)	(0.187)	(0.236)
Indiv.: Agree	−0.440	−0.092	1.419	2.024
	(0.328)	(0.161)	(0.137)	(0.210)
Indiv.: Disagree	1.326	0.783	0.423	0.708
	(0.254)	(0.168)	(0.218)	(0.329)
Direct: Disagree	0.423	−0.023	0.463	1.132
	(0.954)	(0.351)	(0.199)	(0.225)
UnionPower: Agree	2.417	1.059	0.099	0.293
	(0.380)	(0.160)	(0.178)	(0.272)
UnionPower: Disagree	1.286	0.433	0.832	1.425
	(0.459)	(0.188)	(0.138)	(0.194)

Notes: Outcome (dependent) variable: approve or disapprove of WorkChoices, on five-point scale (with 'Neutral' and 'Can't choose' combined as reference category). Omitted categories are: Female; Aged under 25; Not retired; University qualifications; Income under $400; Occupation other; Industry other; Managerial position; Private sector; Never a union member; No class identification; Middle of left–right scale; Middle status; Voting informal; 'Neutral' category for last three items. All categories (except 'Voting') are coded as 'treatment' (or 'indicator'). Voting is coded using 'effect' coding, such that the comparison is with the group mean.

Source: Australian Survey of Social Attitudes 2007.

10. How Do Australians Search for Jobs?

Xianbi Huang and Mark Western

Getting a job is one of the most significant events in people's lives. People's jobs substantially determine their financial circumstances and those of their families, can affect their psychological and physical health and wellbeing and may also influence their economic, social and political attitudes and behaviour. Getting a job is one of the important symbolic markers of becoming an adult and, conversely, not having a job, especially in households where no-one has a full-time job, is a major cause of poverty. In times of economic hardship and financial insecurity, getting and keeping jobs are also more difficult than when the economy is booming.

How people search for jobs has therefore been a vibrant and heated topic in international research since the seminal study of American sociologist Mark Granovetter in the 1970s. Granovetter (1974) conducted personal interviews and mail surveys with 282 professional, technical and managerial workers in a Boston suburb and published his book *Getting A Job: A study of contacts and careers*, which turned out to be a classic work that has been widely cited and highly influential. Granovetter's book refuted many of the taken-for-granted understandings about how people obtained their jobs. The key findings were the following: using personal contacts was the predominant method of obtaining jobs; job information secured through personal contacts was of higher quality than information obtained by other means; and better jobs with higher pay and prestige and affording greater satisfaction were more likely to be filled via personal contacts. Behind these findings is the crucial recognition that individuals are embedded in social networks and these networks influence how labour markets work. We cannot understand real labour markets without recognising this argument. Over the past three decades substantial research from this perspective about job searches has been stimulated in many capitalist and non-capitalist countries. Extensive research from Europe, North America and Asia has shown that, compared with other job-search methods, social networks play a significant role in accessing diverse social resources for securing jobs in different social contexts (Bian 1997; Bian and Soon 1997; De Graaf and Flap 1988; Lin, Ensel and Vaughn 1981; Yakubovich and Kozina 2000). So far, however, systematic research into this topic is rare in Australia.

In this chapter, we address the question of how Australians search for jobs by drawing on data from the Australian Survey of Social Attitudes (AuSSA) 2007 (Phillips et al. 2008). We first describe the different job-search methods used in Australia and then investigate who uses the different kinds of methods. Next, we explore what kinds of social resources job-seekers access through their social networks and what types of social ties or relationships individuals rely upon. We then look at how effectively different job-search methods 'match' individuals to jobs, and finally summarise our main research findings and discuss the implications of our research.

How do people search for jobs?

Australians, like others, rely on various job-search methods: looking at advertisements in newspapers or the Internet, using employment services, attending job and employer fairs, asking for help from friends or relatives, and so on. Researchers classify these different job-search methods in different ways such as non-personal means versus personal means (Bridges and Villemez 1986), formal channels versus informal channels (Boxman et al. 1991), personal contacts, formal channels and direct application (Lin et al. 1981). In essence, however, these job-search methods fall into three types: hierarchy, market and networks (Bian 2002; Granovetter 1995). Hierarchical methods of job searching refer to job assignments and organised transfers by a state authority or employing organisation. This is/was the most frequently used method in state socialist economies (Bian 1997) but is not confined to them. In Western societies, like Australia, organisational reallocations or transfers are also included under hierarchical methods. Market methods refer to job-search activities in which people individually seek jobs among employers, such as attending job fairs where employers gather to recruit employees, using formal employment services, applying directly to employers, responding to media advertisements, looking for jobs online, and so on. Network methods refer to any search activities in which people draw on personal assistance from others, mobilising social ties and connections to secure employment. We adopt this analytical scheme to examine Australians' job-search methods by using data from the AuSSA 2007.

The AuSSA 2007 asked which job-search method was mainly used in different stages of the process of finding a job. Respondents were asked three questions: 1) 'Of the following methods, which one did you mainly use in looking for your current or last job?'; 2) 'Among the methods you used to look for a job, which one was most helpful to get a job interview?'; and 3) 'On the whole, which one method was most important for getting your current or last job?' The job-search methods listed for their choice include: 'Looked at media advertisements', 'Used university career services', 'Used an employment agency', 'Used the Internet', 'Got help or information from family or relatives', 'Got help or information from friends', 'Got help or information from acquaintances', 'Approached an employer', 'An employer approached me', 'I was reallocated or transferred by the organisation I work for', 'I am self-employed', 'Other', and 'Don't know'. Since our research interest focuses on the effect of job-search methods, we do not include the self-employed or those who answered 'Other' or 'Don't know'. We group these job-search methods into three major types: *market-oriented methods*, *social networks* and *hierarchical methods*, as shown in Table 10.1.

Table 10.1 Methods Used in Job-Search Processes, AuSSA 2007 (per cent)

	Main method used in job search	Most important method for getting a job interview	Most important method for getting a job
Market-oriented methods	(74.2)	(75.5)	(73.7)
Looked at media advertisements	23.3	22.8	21.9
Used university career services	1.5	1.3	1.4
Used an employment agency	7.0	8.4	7.0
Used the Internet	8.5	9.8	6.6
Approached an employer	18.3	22.5	22.2
An employer approached me	15.6	10.7	14.6
Social networks	(21.0)	(21.1)	(21.6)
Got help or information from family or relatives	6.6	6.5	6.3
Got help or information from friends	11.1	10.8	11.2
Got help or information from acquaintances	3.3	3.8	4.1
Hierarchical methods			
Reallocated or transferred by the organisation I work for	4.8	3.4	4.7
	(n = 1681)	(n = 1669)	(n = 1752)

Source: Australian Survey of Social Attitudes 2007.

Two major results should be noted. First, similar numbers of people use the same methods at each stage of the job search. For example, similar percentages of respondents reported that they used social networks as the main method for job searching (21 per cent), as the most important method for getting a job interview (21.1 per cent) and as the most important method for getting a job (21.6 per cent). Market-oriented methods are the main methods used in job searching by 74.2 per cent of people, the most important method for getting a job interview by 75.5 per cent and the most important method for getting a job by 73.7 per cent. For hierarchical methods, the percentages are respectively 4.8, 3.4 and 4.7. Second, although market-oriented methods predominate in each stage of job searching, social networks also play a non-negligible role and hierarchical methods are noticeable as well.[1]

---

1 This result can be compared with that of the Job Search Experience Survey, which was conducted by the Australian Bureau of Statistics among employed people in 2007. The Job Search Experience Survey inquired about all steps taken to attain a job by employees who started their current job in the previous 12 months, so people may appear in more than one category of job-search methods. In this case, 27.5 per cent of respondents replied that they 'contacted friends or relatives' in their job searches (ABS 2007). In contrast, the AuSSA 2007 specifically asked which method was used as the main method in job searches; hence, in our coding, people do not fall into more than one category. The percentage of mainly using social networks turned out to be about 21 per cent. In addition, the AuSSA 2007 made a considerable contribution by exploring the utilisation of hierarchical methods in job-search processes.

Who uses which methods?

Given the different job-search methods used in Australian labour markets, do different groups of people use different methods? According to international research, the use of job-search methods varies for different people. Take the use of social networks, for example. Several factors may lead to variations in using networks to find jobs (Marsden and Gorman 2001). The first is gender. Some researchers argue that women make less use of social networks for finding jobs than men do because women's networks have more kin relations, more female ties and fewer colleagues than do men's; these kinds of networks are assumed to contain less valuable sources of job information than men's networks, which are potentially more diverse and less based in family and kinship ties (Marsden 1987, 1988). This argument has been supported by some research showing that women were less likely to secure jobs via contacts (Corcoran, Datcher and Duncan 1980; Hanson and Pratt 1991). Other research, however, finds that the gender difference in using contacts for job searches is negligible (Drentea 1998; Marx and Leicht 1992), or that social networks provide even higher returns to women than men (Aguilera 2008). Second, race and ethnicity have been found to affect the use of social networks in job searches (Fernandez and Fernandez-Mateo 2006). In the United States, racial and ethnic minorities are more likely to obtain jobs through social networks than non-minorities (Elliot 2000; Green, Tigges and Diaz 1999). Third, age differences in using social contacts for seeking jobs have been reported, with some studies showing a declining use of social networks with age (Corcoran, Datcher and Duncan 1980; Marsden and Hurlbert 1988) but others indicating very small age differences (Kirnan, Farley and Geisinger 1989). Finally, socioeconomic standing has been linked to using social networks in job searches. Most studies find that the use of social networks is more common among people in lower socioeconomic positions, such as the less-educated (Marx and Leicht 1992), blue-collar employees (Rees and Shultz 1970) and the poor (Green, Tigges and Browne 1995). There are, however, some contradictory findings pointing to the use of social networks by people in professional or managerial positions. Boxman, De Graaf and Flap (1991) found that managers secured their jobs largely through social networks in the Netherlands, but Falcón (1995) revealed that labourers and construction workers used social networks heavily in job searches while professionals or managers used them much less.

Bearing in mind these mixed findings, we examine who uses different job-search methods. Using AuSSA 2007 data, we explore relationships between job-search methods and the demographic and socioeconomic characteristics of Australians. Apart from the above factors, we also examine whether other factors, like union membership and residency in cities of different size, are correlated with the use of different job-search methods. We assume that being a union member is likely to be associated with greater use of social networks in job searches given that unions are membership-based organisations that enable individuals to pool their resources (Meagher and Wilson 2007). We also expect that people living in big cities will tend to more commonly use market methods in job searches because they will have greater access to employment services and other market mechanisms for obtaining job information and because more job opportunities are available in big cities resulting in higher rates of job mobility. As shown in Table 10.2, however, there are no significant statistical associations between job-search methods and gender, age, union membership, residency in a big city (more than 100000 people) or birthplace (Australia or overseas), respectively. To put it another way, in Australian labour markets, women and men, the old and the young, union members and non-members, residents in big cities and those in smaller cities or towns, native-born Australians and migrants do not differ in the kinds of job-search methods they use. For most of these social groups in Table 10.2 about 70–75 per cent of people use market methods, about 20–25 per cent use social networks and about 5 per cent use hierarchical methods.

On the other hand, the statistical associations between job-search methods and university degree, income and occupation are strongly significant. First, compared with people without a university degree, university degree holders are more likely to use market-oriented methods (78 per cent versus 72.2 per cent) and hierarchical methods (7 per cent versus 4 per cent) and less likely to use social networks (15.1 per cent versus 23.8 per cent). Second, compared with low-income people, middle and high-income people more commonly use market-oriented methods (75.5 per cent and 76.6 per cent versus 68.8 per cent) and hierarchical methods (3.9 per cent and 6.8 per cent versus 3.5 per cent), but their use of social networks is much lower (19.5 per cent and 17.7 per cent versus 27.7 per cent). Third, among eight major categories of occupations, labourers are least likely to use market-oriented and hierarchical methods (55.3 per cent and 0.7 per cent respectively) but have the highest use of social networks (44 per cent). In contrast, managers and professionals have the highest use of market-oriented methods (both more than 76 per cent) and hierarchical methods (both more than 7 per cent) but the lowest use of social networks (both less than 16 per cent).

Table 10.2 Associations between Job-Search Methods and Demographic and Socioeconomic Characteristics, AuSSA 2007 (per cent)

	Job-search methods		
Gender	Market methods	Social networks	Hierarchical methods
Male (n = 770)	74.4	20.4	5.2
Female (n = 975)	73.0	22.7	4.3
	$x^2 = 1.9$, p: ns		
Age	Market methods	Social networks	Hierarchical methods
34 and below (n = 375)	76.3	20.8	2.9
35–49 (n = 537)	70.6	22.9	6.5
50–64 (n = 521)	76.2	19.8	4.0
65 and above (n = 299)	72.2	23.1	4.7
	$x^2 = 10.0$, p: ns		
University degree	Market methods	Social networks	Hierarchical methods
Yes (n = 445)	78.0	15.1	7.0
No (n = 1275)	72.2	23.8	4.0
	$x^2 = 19.2$, $p < 0.001$		
Income	Market methods	Social networks	Hierarchical methods
Low (n = 452)	68.8	27.7	3.5
Middle (n = 610)	76.6	19.5	3.9
High (n = 514)	75.5	17.7	6.8
	$x^2 = 21.8$, $p < 0.001$		
Occupation	Market methods	Social networks	Hierarchical methods
Managers (n = 177)	76.8	15.3	7.9
Professionals (n = 403)	78.9	14.1	7.0
Technicians and trades workers (n = 215)	74.4	23.3	2.3
Community and personal service workers (n = 180)	70.5	23.9	5.6
Clerical and administrative workers (n = 343)	73.8	21.6	4.6
Sales workers (n = 146)	76.7	20.6	2.7
Machinery operators and drivers (n = 89)	70.8	27.0	2.2
Labourers (n = 141)	55.3	44.0	0.7
	$x^2 = 75.0$, $p < 0.001$		
Union member	Market methods	Social networks	Hierarchical methods
Yes (n = 1007)	72.8	21.5	5.7
No (n = 723)	75.0	21.6	3.5
	$x^2 = 4.6$, p: ns		

	Job-search methods		
Resident in big cities	**Market methods**	**Social networks**	**Hierarchical methods**
Yes (n = 1062)	73.8	21.7	4.5
No (n = 664)	73.9	21.1	5.0
	$x^2 = 0.2$, p: ns		
Birthplace	**Market methods**	**Social networks**	**Hierarchical methods**
Australia (n = 1375)	73.5	21.7	4.9
Overseas (n = 375)	74.4	21.6	4.0
	$x^2 = 0.5$, p: ns		

Source: Australian Survey of Social Attitudes 2007.

A pattern of using job-search methods by different people thus emerges. People who have a university degree, higher income or a professional and managerial occupation are more likely to use market-oriented methods and hierarchical methods in their job searches than people without a university degree, with low income or in labouring occupations. The last groups rely relatively strongly on social networks. These findings coincide with most extant studies revealing the use of social networks is more common among people in lower socioeconomic positions (Falcón 1995; Green, Tigges and Browne 1995; Marx and Leicht 1992; Rees and Shultz 1970). They also accord with information from the Australian Bureau of Statistics (ABS) on job-search experiences. About 46 per cent of unemployed persons contacted friends or relatives to find a job whereas only about 27 per cent of employed persons who started their current job in the previous 12 months did so (ABS 2007). As noted by Marsden and Gorman (2001), what these findings mean is not always explicit. To clarify these findings, we need to examine the institutional conditions of the Australian labour market.

Australia has one of the most open employment service markets in the world (Dockery 1999). Market mechanisms are highly developed or encouraged. Generally, information about job openings or employment opportunities is open to the public and allows equal access via different channels. A range of employment services or agencies, private and public, is available to provide advice and training to help people find and keep a job or make a career change. With the development of the Internet, online recruitment and applications are widely adopted, which are convenient for both employers and job-seekers. Employment processes are transparent and subject to policy and legislation that prohibit discrimination and emphasise formal and explicit hiring processes. Under such circumstances, people with higher levels of human capital such as a university degree are likely to have better access to information in labour markets and can also straightforwardly choose market-oriented methods for job searches because these formal market processes correspond with the formal processes of employment selection that characterise much of the Australian labour market. This is unlike the situation in some transitional economies such as China and Russia, where, due to underdevelopment of labour markets and institutional gaps embedded in employment processes, job information can be a scarce resource provided as a favour by influential helpers in job-seekers' mobilised social networks (Bian 1997; Yakubovich and Kozina 2000).

Our analysis of the AuSSA 2007 data also reveals that university degree holders have significantly higher incomes and are more likely to occupy professional or managerial positions than those without degrees[2]. Again, these jobs are subject to formal employment processes, educational qualifications, skills and experience are often requirements and market methods are therefore one way to match job-seekers appropriately to these jobs. In addition, since internal transfers commonly entail promotions, these kinds of hierarchy methods tend to be more frequently used by job-seekers who have relatively high income or a professional or managerial position within organisations. In contrast, labourers' jobs are more likely to be short-term or casual, lacking continuity and security; they have less in the way of formal requirements; and their unstable employment and peripheral status may inhibit investment in training from employers, causing the problem of limited opportunities for advancement in internal labour markets (Atkinson and Meager 1986). Without internal labour markets (that is, career ladders within an organisation), there are few opportunities for transfer or promotion. Labourers have opportunities to use market methods, but unlike those in more privileged occupations, informal social networks are also viable because there are almost no formal requirements for labouring jobs. Labourers may therefore choose to use social networks that are more flexible, convenient and relatively inexpensive to find jobs (Corcoran, Datcher and Duncan 1980). For instance, job information can be acquired from networks in the course of conversations about other things, which does not require either buying services or spending considerable time looking.

Network resources and social ties in job searches

Using social networks has been found to be a common job-search strategy in many countries (Franzen and Hangartner 2006). Australia is not an exception. In this section, we further investigate what social resources job-seekers use in their social networks and what types of social ties mainly help out.

---

2 Within our working sample, we calculated the association between a university degree and occupying a professional or managerial position as well as the association between a university degree and income levels. It turns out that both associations are statistically significant ($p < 0.001$). In detail, among 445 university degree holders, 76.2 per cent have a professional or managerial position. Again, among 430 university degree holders, 85 per cent belong to middle or high-level income groups.

The labour market is a competitive arena. Job-seekers bring various resources or forms of capital to compete for a vacancy and its expected returns. Three kinds of capital are especially relevant: financial capital (economic resources), human capital (skills, experience and education) and social capital (networks). Financial capital and human capital are individual resources while social capital is a relational resource, which arises from people's involvement in relationships with others. Human-capital theory (Becker 1993; Schultz 1960) in economics ascribes market returns (earnings) to individual productivity. By investing in education and technical skill training, people make themselves more productive and thus increase the economic returns they are able to earn. According to some sociologists, however, human capital is ineffective without social capital, which provides opportunities to apply human capital effectively. In an imperfect market, social capital (networks) helps people take best advantage of their human capital (Burt 1992, 1997) by finding appropriate jobs. The conceptualisation and measurement of social capital vary greatly in social research; we adopt the concept and measurement of social resources theory (Lin 2001). This argues that social capital is a feature of constraints and opportunities associated with social relationships between actors (individuals, organisations, and so on) and is a resource embedded in networks. Social capital is best understood by examining the mechanisms and processes by which embedded resources in social networks are used by actors to achieve certain objectives. As an example, searching for a job can be understood as a process by which the job-seeker employs social resources (resources based in social networks) in addition to his/her human capital and financial capital to realise the instrumental goal of getting a job.

Social networks provide different kinds of resources that are useful for job searching. Information and influence are widely recognised as two major kinds of resources (Bian 1997; Flap and Boxman 2001; Granovetter 1973, 1974). Generally speaking, economists who examine network resources emphasise the role played by information in addressing 'information asymmetry' or 'information gaps' in real labour markets (Akerlof 1970; Rees 1966). Information gaps occur when employers and/or potential employees do not have access to some of the information needed to make optimal decisions in relation to jobs and employment. Likewise, sociologists whose work is based on Western societies also typically emphasise the role of information. Granovetter's (1973) tremendously influential work, for instance, highlighted how people's weak ties (that is, ties outside their close personal relationships) allowed them access to new information that was very important for job searches. In contrast, scholars present a different view in Eastern countries like China, Singapore and Hong Kong and transitional state socialist countries like China and Russia (Bian 1997; Bian and Soon 1997; Clarke 1999; Yakubovich and Kozina 2000). These researchers claim that strong ties with norms of trust and obligation are more advantageous in accessing influence and favour for job attainment. Bian

(1997) put forward the hypothesis of the strength of strong ties, distinguishing between weak ties used to gather job information in a market economy and strong ties used to access influence from authority in a state socialist economy where labour markets are either greatly altered or nonexistent.

What kinds of social resources do Australian job-seekers get when they use social networks to help them find a job? The AuSSA 2007 asked respondents about the main help obtained from their social contacts (acquaintances, family members, relatives and friends) when searching for their current or last job. In addition to information and influence, we also examined whether job-seekers sought emotional support from their social contacts. We summarise the access to social resources by job searchers who had help from social networks in Table 10.3. Information is the major resource accessed by these job searchers; social contacts either 'provided employment information' (28.7 per cent) or 'helped to prepare a job application' (16.5 per cent). Emotional support is the second most common type of resource (34.6 per cent) while influence is least commonly provided by social contacts who 'approached people to exert influence' (10.5 per cent) or 'solved practical problems' (2.4 per cent).

Table 10.3 Network Resources Accessed by Job Searchers, AuSSA 2007 (per cent)

Network resources	
Information	
They provided employment information	28.7
They helped to prepare a job application	16.5
Influence	
They approached people to exert influence on my behalf	10.5
They helped to solve practical problems	2.4
Emotional support	
They provided emotional support	34.6
Other help	7.3
	(n = 1219)

Source: Australian Survey of Social Attitudes 2007.

As reviewed, the strength of ties is another aspect of significance in social network studies of job searches (Bian 1997; Granovetter 1973). Some researchers argue that strong ties (close personal contacts) are more effective in helping people find jobs, while other researchers argue that weak ties (contacts who are outside an individual's close personal relationships) are more effective. We measure the strength of social ties by using a question provided in the AuSSA 2007: 'Was there one particular person among those who helped you to get this job?' If a respondent answered that 'a friend, a family member or relative' helped out, we categorise this case as one that utilised strong ties. If a respondent chose to reply 'an acquaintance or other people', we categorise this case as one that used weak ties. As shown in Table 10.4, among 908 respondents who used social networks in job-search processes, more than 77 per cent used strong ties while about 23 per cent used weak ties.

Table 10.4 Types of Social Ties Mobilised by Job Searchers, AuSSA 2007 (per cent)

Types of social ties	
Strong ties	
Friends	38.1
Family members/relatives	39.2
Weak ties	
Acquaintances	15.2
Other people	7.5
	(n = 908)

Source: Australian Survey of Social Attitudes 2007.

The debate about whether strong or weak ties matter more in the job-search process (Bian 1997; Granovetter 1973) hinges on the kinds of social resources social contacts provide to job-seekers. Advocates of the 'weak tie hypothesis' argue that weak ties lie outside people's immediate social networks and therefore crosscut social circles to provide new information that people would not otherwise have. This new information helps to secure a job and achieve better employment outcomes. Proponents of the 'strong tie hypothesis' argue that close personal contacts are more useful for exercising influence. Are strong and weak ties connected to these resources in the Australian labour market as these ideas suggest? In Table 10.5, we continue to examine the association between social ties and network resources, which turns out to be slightly significant ($p < 0.1$); however, the finding differs somewhat from the above assumption in that strong ties were mainly used to access information (56.5 per cent) rather than influence (16.4 per cent) and weak ties helped to access influence to a considerable extent (21.3 per cent).

Table 10.5 Association between Network Resources and Social Ties, AuSSA 2007 (per cent)

	Network resources		
Social ties	Information	Influence	Other help
Weak ties (n = 169)	46.2	21.3	32.5
Strong ties (n = 646)	56.5	16.4	27.1
	$x^2 = 5.9, p < 0.1$		

Source: Australian Survey of Social Attitudes 2007.

Job-search methods and job match

Real labour markets are not perfect but full of uncertainty (Rees 1966). In economic theory, in perfectly competitive labour markets employers and employees would have complete and accurate information about all relevant characteristics of jobs, employers and job-seekers and this would allow optimal matches between jobs and individuals. Information asymmetries and gaps occur when employers and/or job-seekers lack relevant information. Job-seekers and employers try to minimise information gaps by finding out relevant information, but acquiring information requires spending time, effort and money (Stigler 1961); it is costly. Social ties are one relatively inexpensive way to obtain rich and trustworthy information (Marsden and Gorman 2001). Granovetter (1974, 1981) found that job-seekers and employers preferred information derived from weakly tied personal contacts. This kind of information is seen as less costly and of better quality than that obtained through other means. Other research has also shown that personal contacts and referral networks can promote better matches between individuals and positions because people hired through these network methods not only better understand their jobs and working environment at the start of employment but also are motivated to receive informal training from other employees (Fernandez, Castilla and Moore 2000; Manwaring 1984). Thus, for both sociologists (Fernandez and Castilla 2001; Granovetter 1981) and economists (Javanovic 1979; MacDonald 1980), job matching between individuals and positions has become an essential aspect of arguments about the effects of social networks on job-search and employment outcomes. Very little empirical research has, however, investigated job matching—that is, the fit between job-seekers and the requirements of skills or working experience for a job position. The AuSSA 2007 addresses this gap, making it possible to compare the quality of job matches arising from social networks with the quality of matches obtained through other means.

We look first at an overview of job matching in Australian labour markets. In the AuSSA 2007, respondents were asked how well their qualifications, skills and experience matched the jobs they obtained. About 13 per cent of job-seekers were overqualified for their positions, 72.4 per cent had a good match, 3.4 per cent were underqualified and 11.4 per cent said that there was no requirement in skills or experience for their positions (Figure 10.1). Overall, a majority of Australian jobs were matched well with qualified job applicants.

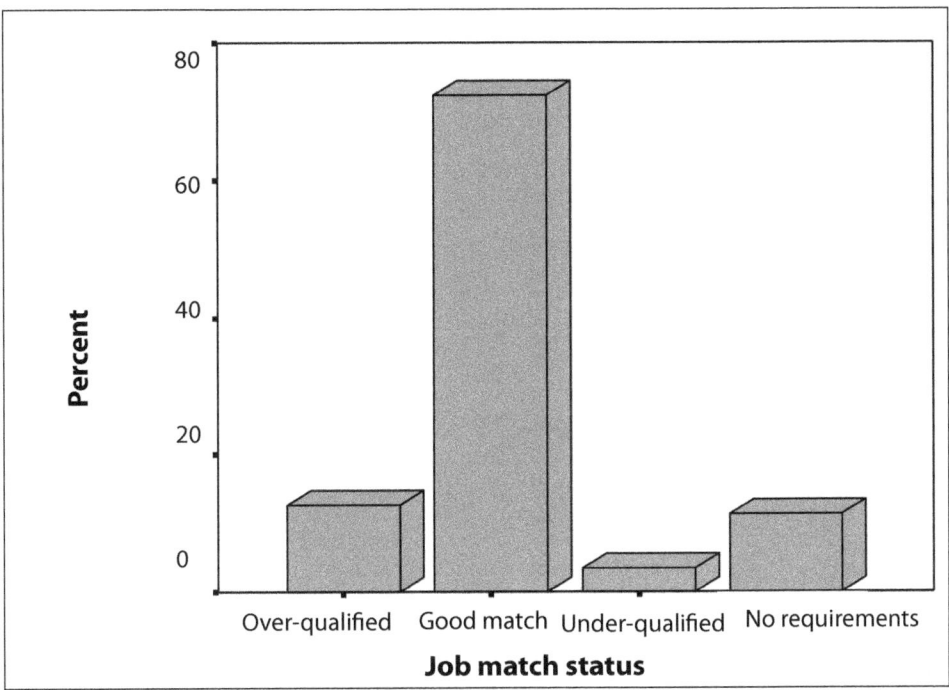

Figure 10.1 Job Matching between Job-Seekers and Positions, AuSSA 2007 (n = 1958)

Source: Australian Survey of Social Attitudes 2007.

We next examine whether different job-search methods produce different quality job matches (Table 10.6). It appears they do. Some 73.6 per cent of job-seekers who used market-oriented methods ended up in a good match between their qualifications and job positions, and 26.4 per cent were not matched well; however, only 67 per cent of job-seekers who used social networks realised a good match, with the rest (one-third) not matched well. Hierarchical methods were associated with the highest percentage of good matches, with 81.7 per cent; only 18.3 per cent of the users of hierarchical methods were not matched well.

These results suggest that in Australian labour markets, market methods and hierarchical methods outperform social networks in assisting a good match between applicants and job positions. To provide convincing support for this assertion, we look at the effect of using these job-search methods on job matches with other demographic and socioeconomic characteristics of job-seekers being held constant in a statistical model. A binary logistic regression is employed for this purpose (Table 10.7).[3]

---

[3] In this model, market-oriented methods, social networks and hierarchical methods are three dummy variables that are measured by using the question 'On the whole, which one method was most important for getting your current/last job?' in the AuSSA 2007 (see details in the section on 'Job-search methods'). Control variables include gender, age, years of schooling, university degree, professional or managerial position, income, union membership, birthplace and residency in a big city.

Table 10.6 Association between Job-Matching Status and Job-Search Methods, AuSSA 2007 (per cent)

Job-search methods	Job-matching status	
	Good match	Not matched well
Market methods (n = 1282)	73.6	26.4
Social networks (n = 379)	67.0	33.0
Hierarchical methods (n = 82)	81.7	18.3
	$x^2 = 10.0, p < 0.01$	

Source: Australian Survey of Social Attitudes 2007.

Table 10.7 Binary Logistic Regression in Predicting Effects of Job-Search Methods on Job Match, AuSSA 2007

Predictor variables	Job match (odds ratio)
Job-getting methods (ref. = hierarchical methods)	
Market-oriented methods	1.383*
Social networks	1.109
Control variables	
Gender (male = 1)	0.712**
Age	0.970
Age^2	1.000*
Years of schooling	1.012
University degree	0.843
Professional or managerial position	1.818***
Income (ref. = low income and other)	
Middle income	1.409*
High income	2.493**
Union membership	0.947
Birthplace (Australia = 1)	0.973
Resident in big city	1.086
Constant	1.712
Nagelkerke R^2	0.07
Number of cases	1739

*$p < 0.05$

**$p < 0.01$

***$p < 0.001$

Source: Australian Survey of Social Attitudes 2007.

This analysis shows that, compared with hierarchical methods, market-oriented methods have a higher probability of leading to a good job match but social networks do not. After controlling the demographic and socioeconomic characteristics of job-seekers, social networks do not have any statistically significant advantages over hierarchical methods or market-oriented methods in matching job applicants to positions. These findings differ from the positive effect of social networks on job matching found in previous studies (Fernandez, Castilla and Moore 2000; Manwaring 1984). How might we interpret them? First, information flows in Australian labour markets are highly marketised, as we have already seen. Thus, the information acquired through market channels can meet the needs of making a good match between applicants and job positions, leaving little room or necessity for social networks. Second, hierarchical methods may have positive effects on job matches because the internal transfer or reallocation within organisations is often based on employers' knowledge of the people and the positions with which they will be matched. Third, as shown above, Australian job-seekers heavily mobilised their strong ties instead of weak ties to find a job. If Granovetter (1973, 1974) is correct that strong ties do not provide high-quality job information, social networks may not lead to good job matches.

Conclusion

In this chapter, we have examined the question of how Australians search for jobs using AuSSA 2007 data. This is one of the first Australian analyses of this type. Our major findings are briefly summarised and discussed below.

Job-search methods coexist in Australian labour markets

We differentiate job-search methods into market-oriented methods, social networks and hierarchical methods (Bian 2002; Granovetter 1995). All these methods are used by Australians to search for jobs, to get job interviews and, finally, to locate a job. As in most Western countries, in Australia, market-oriented methods predominate. Social networks play a significant role in helping people look for jobs, and hierarchical methods are used to realise internal transfers or reallocation within work organisations.

The use of job-search methods varies by people's socioeconomic standing

Internationally, research has shown that the use of job-search methods is affected by the characteristics of job-seekers, such as gender, race, age, socioeconomic standing, and so on. We do not find differences between men and women, the old and the young, union members and non-members, residents in big cities and those in smaller cities or towns, the Australian born and migrants in terms of their use of job-search methods. Rather, socioeconomic standing is the main factor causing variations in using job-search methods. People who have a university degree, higher income or a professional and managerial occupation are more likely to use market-oriented and hierarchical methods in their job searches. People who do not have a university degree, have a low income or do a labouring job are more dependent on using social networks than other job-search methods. This finding is consistent with research from other Western countries (Falcón 1995; Green, Tigges and Browne 1995; Marx and Leicht 1992; Rees and Shultz 1970). There are at least two possible reasons why this occurs. First, successful applicants for high-status jobs may prefer formal market methods over informal methods that rely on social networks. Second, high-status jobs are more likely to have formal entry requirements associated with them than are low-status jobs. For high-status jobs, market methods will likely provide better information to employers and job-seekers about these requirements and the relevant characteristics of job-seekers than will social networks. Market methods will therefore produce better matches than social networks. Individuals who are poorly matched are more likely to be screened out during the selection process for high-status jobs than for low-status jobs because it is more likely to be apparent that they do not meet the formal criteria. In Australia the connections between market methods and high-status jobs probably reflect both these processes.

Strong ties are the main provider of information for job-seekers

Information and influence are widely recognised as two major kinds of resources flowing through social networks in job-search processes. As implied in the literature, the strength of weak ties (that is, acquaintances) lies in acquiring extensive and non-redundant information for locating a better job (Granovetter 1973), and the strength of strong ties (that is, friends, family members or relatives) lies in accessing influence from helpers who are either decisive in hiring or can provide favours to solve practical problems in job searches (Bian 1997). According to our data analysis, strong ties were mainly used to provide information for people who had contacted social ties in their job-search processes. Due to the 'homophilous' or 'like me' characteristics of social interactions associated with strong ties, people in low socioeconomic positions who heavily rely on strong ties may encounter difficulties in getting access to high-quality information when seeking jobs. This problem of reliance on 'unproductive networks' (Fernandez and Fernandez-Mateo 2006) deserves serious attention because it suggests that people who are socioeconomically disadvantaged may rely more heavily on poorer quality job-search methods, potentially compounding their disadvantage.

Social networks do not have relatively significant effects on realising good job matches

Job matching between individuals and positions is an essential element in the process of getting a job. Job-search methods contribute to the match. In Australia people who use market-oriented methods in their job searches are more likely to achieve good matches between their qualifications and employers' requirements compared with those who use hierarchical methods. In contrast, social networks do not have a significant effect on helping people to be well matched to job positions compared with hierarchical methods. This finding may reflect the high proportion of strong ties people use when drawing on social networks for job information. On the other hand, information flows via market channels or hierarchical methods appear to work well in the Australian labour market. Information flows are essential for making good job matches.

Two immediate implications follow from these results. First, relying on social networks is unproductive because these methods do not significantly increase the likelihood of getting a good job match. Second, if social networks are associated with comparatively poorer job matches than market and hierarchical methods, using social networks to get jobs could increase the employment insecurity associated with these jobs. Since social networks are more likely to be used by people without university degrees, with low incomes and in labouring jobs, the use of social networks could contribute further to the insecurity of people who are already vulnerable in the labour market. It is also possible that our results understate the extent to which social networks produce poor-quality matches, because some poor-quality matches will also be screened out during the employment process, although perhaps not as many as for higher-status jobs, as we have already noted.

One other implication derived from our research is also noteworthy. The study of job searches should be located in its institutional context. The institutional context is given by the formal and informal rules within which job searching takes place, including the laws, regulations, policies, ideas and taken-for-granted assumptions about how one 'normally' gets a job. Job searching is not a purely economic activity that occurs within a disembodied market but is 'embedded' in social networks that are themselves located in broader institutional contexts (Granovetter 1995). We have concentrated on looking at the role of social networks, but there are many ways to extend this area of research through a more developed institutional perspective that recognises factors such as the industrial relations system, employment policies and practices, and variations across occupations, industries and organisations. It is important to take seriously this context in the analysis of job-search processes.

References

Aguilera, Michael. 2008. 'Personal networks and the incomes of men and women in the United States: do personal networks provide higher returns for men or women?'. *Research in Social Stratification and Mobility* 26(3): 221–33.

Akerlof, George. 1970. 'The market for "lemons": quality uncertainty and the market mechanism'. *The Quarterly Journal of Economics* 84(3): 488–500.

Atkinson, John and Meager, Nigel. 1986. 'Is flexibility just a flash in the pan?'. *PersonnelManagement* (September): 26–9.

Australian Bureau of Statistics (ABS). 2007. *Job Search Experience*, Catalogue no. 6222.0. Canberra: Australian Bureau of Statistics.

Becker, Gary. 1993. *Human Capital: A theoretical and empirical analysis, with special reference to education*. Chicago and London: University of Chicago Press.

Bian, Yanjie. 1997. 'Bringing strong ties back in: indirect ties, network bridges, and job searches in China'. *American Sociological Review* 62(3): 266–85.

Bian, Yanjie. 2002. 'Institutional holes and job mobility process: guanxi mechanisms in China's emerging labor markets'. In *Social Connections in China: Institutions, culture, and the changing nature of guanxi*, eds Thomas Gold, Doug Guthrie and David Wank, pp. 117–36. Cambridge: Cambridge University Press.

Bian, Yanjie. 2004. 'The networking space in occupational mobility: a comparison of Hong Kong and inland cities of China'. *Hong Kong Journal of Sociology* 5: 103–17.

Bian, Yanjie and Soon, Ang. 1997. '*Guanxi* networks and job mobility in China and Singapore'. *Social Forces* 75(3): 981–1006.

Boxman, Ed A., De Graaf, Paul M. and Flap, Hendrik D. 1991. 'The impact of social and human capital on the income attainment of Dutch managers'. *Social Networks* 13(1): 51–73.

Bridges, William and Villemez, Wayne J. 1986. 'Informal hiring and income in the labor market'. *American Sociological Review* 51(3): 574–82.

Burt, Ronald S. 1992. *Structural Holes: The social structure of competition*. Cambridge, Mass.: Harvard University Press.

Burt, Ronald S. 1997. 'The contingent value of social capital'. *Administrative Science Quarterly* 42(1): 339–65.

Clarke, Simon. 1999. *The Formation of a Labour Market in Russia*. Cheltenham, UK: Edward Elgar.

Corcoran, Mary, Datcher, Linda and Duncan, Greg. 1980. 'Information and influence networks in labor markets'. In *Five Thousand American Families' Patterns of Economic Progress. Volume 8*, eds Greg J. Duncan and James N. Morgan, pp. 1–37. Ann Arbor, Mich.: Institute for Social Research.

De Graaf, Nan D. and Flap, Hendrik D. 1988. 'With a little help from my friends: social resources as an explanation of occupational status and income in West Germany, the Netherlands, and the United States'. *Social Forces* 67(1): 452–72.

Dockery, A. Michael. 1999. 'Evaluating the job network'. *Australian Journal of Labour Economics* 3(2): 131–58.

Drentea, Patricia. 1998. 'Consequences of women's formal and informal job search methods for employment in female-dominated jobs'. *Gender and Society* 12(3): 321–38.

Elliot, James R. 2000. 'Class, race, and job matching in contemporary urban labor markets'. *Social Science Quarterly* 81(4): 1036–51.

Falcón, Luis M. 1995. 'Social networks and employment for Latinos, blacks, and whites'. *New England Journal of Public Policy* 11: 17–28.

Fernandez, Roberto M. and Castilla, Emilio J. 2001. 'How much is that network worth? Social capital in employee referral networks'. In *Social Capital: Theory and research*, eds Nan Lin, Ronald S. Burt and Karen Cook, pp. 85–104. New York: Aldine de Gruyter.

Fernandez, Roberto M., Castilla, Emilio J. and Moore, Paul. 2000. 'Social capital at work: networks and employment at a phone center'. *American Journal of Sociology* 105(5): 1288–356.

Fernandez, Roberto M. and Fernandez-Mateo, Isabel. 2006. 'Networks, race, and hiring'. *American Sociological Review* 71(1): 42–71.

Flap, Henk and Boxman, Ed. 2001. 'Getting started: the influence of social capital on the start of the occupational career'. In *Social Capital: Theory and research*, eds Nan Lin, Ronald S. Burt and Karen Cook, pp. 159–81. New York: Aldine de Gruyter.

Franzen, Axel and Hangartner, Dominik. 2006. 'Social networks and labour market outcomes: the non-monetary benefits of social capital'. *European Sociological Review* 22(4): 353–68.

Granovetter, Mark. 1973. 'The strength of weak ties'. *American Journal of Sociology* 78(6): 1360–80.

Granovetter, Mark. 1974. *Getting a Job: A study of contacts and careers*. Cambridge, Mass.: Harvard University Press.

Granovetter, Mark. 1981. 'Toward a sociological theory of income differences'. In *Sociological Perspectives on Labour Markets*, ed. Ivar Berg, pp. 11–47. New York: Academic Press.

Granovetter, Mark. 1995. 'Afterword 1994: reconsiderations and a new agenda'. In *Getting a Job: A study of contacts and careers*, pp. 139–82. Chicago: University of Chicago Press.

Green, Gary P., Tigges, Leann M. and Browne, Irene. 1995. 'Social resources, job search, and poverty in Atlanta'. *Research in Community Sociology* 5: 161–82.

Green, Gary P., Tigges, Leann M. and Diaz, Daniel. 1999. 'Racial and ethnic differences in job-search strategies in Atlanta, Boston, and Los Angeles'. *Social Science Quarterly* 80(2): 263–78.

Hanson, Susan and Pratt, Geraldine. 1991. 'Job search and the occupational segregation of women'. *Annals of the Association of American Geographers* 81(2): 229–53.

Javanovic, Boyan. 1979. 'Job matching and the theory of turnover'. *The Journal of Political Economy* 87(5): 972–90.

Kirnan, Jean Powell, Farley, John A. and Geisinger, Kurt F. 1989. 'The relationship between recruiting source, applicant quality, and hire performance: an analysis by sex, ethnicity, and age'. *Personnel Psychology* 42(2): 293–308.

Lin, Nan. 2001. *Social Capital: A theory of social structure and action*. Cambridge: Cambridge University Press.

Lin, Nan, Ensel, Walter and Vaughn, John. 1981. 'Social resources and strength of ties: structural factors in occupational status attainment'. *American Sociological Review* 46(4): 393–405.

MacDonald, Glenn M. 1980. 'Person-specific information in the labor market'. *The Journal of Political Economy* 88(3): 578–97.

Manwaring, Tony. 1984. 'The extended internal labour market'. *Cambridge Journal of Economics* 8(2): 161–87.

Marsden, Peter V. 1987. 'Core discussion networks of Americans'. *American Sociological Review* 52(1): 122–31.

Marsden, Peter V. 1988. 'Homogeneity in confiding networks'. *Social Networks* 10(1): 57–76.

Marsden, Peter V. and Gorman, Elizabeth H. 2001. 'Social networks, job changes, and recruitment'. In *Sourcebook of Labor Markets: Evolving structures and processes*, eds Ivar Berg and Arne L. Kalleberg, pp. 467–502. New York: Kluwer Academic/Plenum Publishers.

Marsden, Peter V. and Hurlbert, Jeanne S. 1988. 'Social resources and mobility outcomes: a replication and extension'. *Social Forces* 66(4): 1038–59.

Marx, Jonathan and Leicht, Kevin T. 1992. 'Formality of recruitment to 229 jobs: variations by race, sex and job characteristics'. *Sociology and Social Research* 76: 190–6.

Meagher, Gabrielle and Wilson, Shaun. 2007. 'Are unions regaining popular legitimacy in Australia?'. In *Australian Social Attitudes 2*, eds David Denemark, Gabrielle Meagher, Shaun Wilson, Mark Western and Timothy Phillips, pp. 195–216. Sydney: UNSW Press.

Phillips, T., Mitchell, D., Tranter, B., Clark, J. and Reed, K. 2008. *The Australian Survey of Social Attitudes, 2007*. Canberra: Australian Social Science Data Archive, The Australian National University.

Rees, Albert. 1966. 'Information networks in labor markets'. *American Economic Review* 56(2): 559–66.

Rees, Albert and Shultz, George. 1970. *Workers and Wages in an Urban Labor Market*. Chicago: University of Chicago Press.

Schultz, Theodore W. 1960. 'Investment in human capital'. *American Economic Review* 51(1): 1–17.

Stigler, George J. 1961. 'The economics of information'. *The Journal of Political Economy* 60(3): 213–25.

Yakubovich, Valery and Kozina, Irina. 2000. 'The changing significance of ties: an explanation of the hiring channels in the Russian transitional labor market'. *International Sociology* 15(3): 479–500.

www.ingramcontent.com/pod-product-compliance
Lightning Source LLC
Chambersburg PA
CBHW060930170426
43192CB00031B/2886